Diane Eichenbaum

*Harness the Power of Your Sun Sign and
Become the Person You Were Meant to Be*

SOUL

SIGNS

A FIRESIDE BOOK
Published by Simon & Schuster

Soul Signs *is dedicated to*
the healing work of astrology
and to all the people who love and use it.

FIRESIDE
Rockefeller Center
1230 Avenue of the Americas
New York, NY 10020

FIRESIDE and colophon are registered trademarks
of Simon & Schuster Inc.

Manufactured in the United States of America

10   9   8   7   6   5   4

Library of Congress Cataloging-in-Publication Data
Eichenbaum, Diane.
Soul signs : harness the power of your sun sign and become
the person you were meant to be / Diane Eichenbaum.
p.   cm.
"A Fireside Book"
Includes bibliographical references.
1. Astrology.   I. Title.
BF1708.1.E34   1998
133.5—dc21   97-29815   CIP

ISBN 0-684-82366-7

Contents

6   **Contents**

Acknowledgments

I wish to express my gratitude to my daughters, Terry and Elizabeth, for supporting me in this great adventure of writing my first book, for listening every time I phoned to read a page and hear what they thought. Thanks for being there.

Soul Signs wouldn't have happened without the encouragement of Jan Miller, my literary agent and good friend, and the kindness and support of my editor, Sydny Miner.

This book is a miracle. It could only have come into being with the encouragement of wonderful friends, who spent hours reading and critiquing for me: my sister, Bobbye Butler, who knew I could do it; Jill Ungerman, for her generosity of spirit and her skill, giving me the equivalent of a college course in writing; and Hattie Wiener, who preceded me in writing her first book, *Retro-Age*, and helped me with the proposal.

Thanks to my friends who gave so much of their time and talent: to DeLois Faulkner, who let me write in her beautiful house in Santa Barbara. To Dawn Gaskill, Connie Simmons, Ann Satterfield, Colette McAlister,

Kay Lee, Martha Burton, M'Layne Murphy, Connie Hetzel, Arlene Johnson, Beverley Wilson, Linda Stasi, Jackie Eckles, Beverly Bledsoe, John and Beverly Sterry, Karen Gresham, Harl and Jimmy Asaff, and Bobbye Hall, who all lent me an ear and an eye and cheered me on.

Thanks to Denise DeBaun, who sat down and read the whole book cover to cover and gave me the compliment of saying: "Did you write this?" I also want to thank all of my clients through the years for allowing me to share their lives and see astrology at work.

Above all else, I owe so much to astrology for being such a fascinating subject that I have never been bored with it for one minute in over twenty-five years.

Introduction

Here we stand poised at the cusp of the twenty-first century, a time when technology and science have literally reached to the stars. Things that were once mysterious are now explainable. Even good old staring into space isn't what it once was. We actually know what's out there now. Or do we? We've just been informed by astronomers that there are billions more stars and constellations out there than we once thought. What next?

So where is the excitement? Where is the wonder? Have we lost something by losing the old ways to embrace the new? Have we traded "chatting" on the Internet after dinner for talking to each other in the town square? Have we traded the questions for the answers, and still come up short?

I believe that we're all seeking something—anything—that will give us meaningful information about ourselves and the universe we live in. We may know how to get to Mars, but we still don't know why it's there, and what it means to us.

We may be more educated about the world and the heavens than our ancestors, but trading technology for thought hasn't kept us from asking the same old questions. We still want to know how to make our lives more fulfilling in terms of love, success, happiness, and simple peace of mind.

Ironically enough, all the advances in technology have led us back to the same place as our ancient ancestors—the stars. We're feeling lost and we're striving to get back in touch with other humans, with ourselves, and most important, with our spiritual natures. During the twentieth century, many of us tried to do this by turning to psychiatrists, to metaphysics, even to drugs and alcohol. We've all been looking for the answers, not knowing the right questions.

I'm not exempt. I admit it. Before I started studying astrology in 1972, like many others, I thought astrology was a fun thing but not something that could be taken seriously, because it wasn't scientifically substantiated.

Then one day something changed my opinion. As I was talking to a woman at a party, I was amazed to see that she looked just like a lion, with a mane of hair and the broad nose that all members of the cat family have. I casually asked what sign she was and she replied Leo. Surprised, I wondered if astrology could actually have some validity. Is there some universal principle or law affecting us all that I had overlooked? The question sent me on a quest that has lasted for twenty-five years.

Astrology, as you know, isn't new. It isn't even *old*. It's ancient! Before the time of the Greeks, only royalty had access to the knowledge and wisdom of the heavens. Today, who doesn't know their astrological sign? Can you honestly say that you skip right by the horoscopes in your newspaper each day? Not many people can. We all want to know what the future holds.

When astrology is used solely as entertainment or just to foresee the future, its deeper significance as an integrated holistic system of thought is often overlooked.

Astrological information that's readily available in books and columns is sincere, but sometimes it has to be taken with a grain of salt. Humankind can't be divided neatly into twelve convenient groups, with completely identical personalities and destiny. We're not astrological Barbie dolls.

The Sun is the first thing an astrologer looks at when reading your chart.

As the Sun makes a complete circle through the constellations, it makes a mighty powerful impression on the people born in each Sun sign. Combined with the ascendant, which is found by using your time of birth and the Moon's position on your date of birth, it provides much of the essential data for an astrological interpretation.

Astrology is a simple way to grasp the nature of another human being. The strange behavior of somebody you're crazy about—whether it's a lover, a spouse, a child, a parent, or a friend—can often be explained by understanding a bit about the person's Sun sign. We all act through the invisible influences of our sign even if we don't realize it.

Believe me, you don't have to be an astrologer to understand aspects of your own character and the characters of those around you. For instance, a Gemini learns to be patient with her Aquarian husband's abstract mind. He is not interested in the small details that she loves so dearly. In a good relationship, they'll work it out, and—yes!—learn to compromise. Compatibility—physical, emotional, and astrological—is all wound together in a package. When you pull the string on one, the whole thing begins to unravel.

Human Becomings

Your Sun sign is not so much a matter of who you are as what you are becoming. As you evolve and develop in consciousness there is an opportunity to express your Sun sign's soul power.

Interestingly enough, the word *soul* comes from the word *sol*, or "sun." Power is the pure life force to which you are naturally entitled. *Soul power* indicates a divine source of authority and influence as well as mental and moral validity. Each Sun sign has a separate piece of this information.

The ancient message coded into the signs is God's promise of hope for meaningful direction in our lives. The unequivocal message of the stars is the freedom to embrace our soul power on an evolutionary path through eternity.

Combined with other methods of self-evaluation, the study of astrology has given me a totally different approach to solving problems in my life. I have come to realize that the power of my own Sun sign is uniquely mine—given to me at birth to harness for my own benefit and use in this lifetime; it cannot be taken away.

I didn't have to go outside of myself to find it. I already had it. As I learned to acknowledge and accept my power with confidence, I was able to better receive from my soul. This revelation has expanded my thinking and has allowed me to live a fuller life.

This message, revealed in meditation, was very simple: I was told by my inner voice to accept my life as an opportunity to grow in consciousness, meeting each day with expectancy and hope. (I have found that the messages from the soul are usually brief and very clear. Don't expect a big echo chamber and weird music when your soul is speaking to you. Life is not a 1940s movie.)

As I see it, one third of the people in the world are actively interested in their Sun signs, while another third couldn't care less. That leaves one last third potentially open, and looking for answers.

The Sun sign is the symbol for your personal identity in this lifetime. It's as individual as your fingerprint. In fact, think of it as the fingerprint of your soul.

Part I

The Evolution of Astrology

Ancient Stargazers

I often wonder if the rudimentary astrological systems practiced in ancient Egypt, Babylon, Sumeria, and China were based on childlike superstition or on an evolved system of information from an earlier unrecorded time lost to us today. There appears to be no answer. We *do* know that throughout antiquity astrology and astronomy were given equal scientific weight.

Some say that Thoth/Hermes, the ancient ibis-headed priest, brought astrology to Egypt from Atlantis. He was venerated as the messenger of the gods, and was said to have written forty-two books of sacred learning, four of which were on astrology. These books were destroyed in Alexandria twice, first by the Romans and then the Christians. No matter how it is presented, the Hermetic wisdom that has come down through the ages signifies mastery through the regeneration of the body, the illumination of the mind, and the transmutation of the emotions.

Astrology is one of our oldest and most treasured heritages. In ancient

Mesopotamia and Egypt, the written sign for God was a star. From the top of ziggurats Babylonian astrologer-priests observed the stars and recorded their findings on clay tablets. In Britain great astronomer-mathematicians constructed Stonehenge and other stone monuments to track celestial movements. The early Mayans, whose culture dominated the Yucatan Peninsula in Mexico from 3113 B.C. until the Spaniards came in the fifteenth century A.D., observed the heavenly bodies from their pyramids and developed a circular astrology chart with animal symbols.

One of the best-known references to astrology is recorded in the New Testament. The Book of Matthew tells of three magi (learned astrologer-priests) who followed a large star to find the newborn Jesus. Priests and astronomers in ancient times were educated in astrology and predicted events from the placement of the stars. Their religious practices were centered around solar and lunar movements, and most of their temples were built with this in mind. The word *magus* means "master." Astrologers today think the magi knew about the convergence of Jupiter, Saturn, and Venus on that night, easily seen by the naked eye and so close together that they looked like one huge star in the night sky. They interpreted its meaning as the reincarnation of a great soul and came with presents to honor the child.

Many people in the Western Hemisphere today are not familiar with the Eastern philosophy of reincarnation, the rebirth of the soul into a new body over many lifetimes. According to this belief, we are reborn by God's grace and given many opportunities to overcome the ignorance and confusion that tripped us up in other lifetimes. This is called self-mastery.

Certain beings, after living many lifetimes, attain an evolved state of consciousness and come back to earth to help others. In the sixth century, the Nicene Council in Constantinople banned the theory of reincarnation, so this ancient and meaningful tradition is overlooked in the West. There are many theories as to why it was deleted from the dogma of the church, but it is interesting to note that the concept of reincarnation was alive at the time of the early Christian disciples.

In Asia it is not unusual to hear of great beings—people advanced in spiritual studies—visiting a great soul at birth. There was a star at

Krishna's birth, and he was visited by the Great Ones. When the last Dalai Lama died, three Tibetan lamas, or monks, one of whom was an astrologer, followed particular portents and signs that ultimately revealed to them the identity of the newly reincarnated Dalai Lama.

The origins of astrology are lost in prehistory. It almost seems as though astrology came into the world fully formed. There are differences from culture to culture, but they are slight. Astrology may have come to us from an ancient age that the Egyptians call the First Time. This was when great beings or sages walked the earth and taught people how to live in their time realm, the eternal present. Perhaps astrology was a part of the teachings of these godlike beings. Astrology was brought to the West when Alexander the Great conquered Sumeria and Chaldea in 280 B.C. The astronomers of Alexandria discovered an enormous number of ancient clay tablets that we are still interpreting today. Alexander's military exploits gave birth to a civilization that was part Greek and part Asian. He always had Hindu yogis as part of his entourage and many were astrologers. The Hindu system of astrology is said to be at least five thousand years old.

The Chaldeans had been recording lunar and solar eclipses and the movement of the planets from ancient times—for "four hundred thousand years," according to their tradition. Their ability to track astral movements far exceeded their scientific understanding. It was the Greeks who fine-tuned the daily movements of the planets with their own expert calculations and added their mystical panorama of gods (which they had "borrowed" from the Egyptians) to create the charts we have today. Mythology is probably based on the lives of important people in prediluvian times. If our world were wiped out by some great catastrophe, would people living far in the future cast Madonna as Venus and Sylvester Stallone as Mars? We can only wonder.

The Chaldeans did charts only for the king or when important events occurred. The Greeks saw every reason to chart the birth of individuals (very democratic!). To this day, astrology is primarily lunar in the East and solar in the West. A lunar chart is based on the position of the Moon at birth, whereas a solar chart is derived from the position of the Sun. Again, this difference comes to us from the Greeks, who, perhaps influenced by Alexander and his sojourns into Egypt where the sun god was prominent, saw the individualistic and dynamic symbol of the Sun as the empowering body.

Baghdad, the largest seat of learning in the Middle Ages, linked astrologer-priests in India, China, Babylon, and Persia with the scholars of Spain, Italy, and Greece, preserving the teachings of the early Chaldeans and Greeks. This confluence of knowledge created a rich heritage of spiritual, philosophic, and intellectual truths we can still draw on today.

Many famous people have used astrology as a tool. In ancient Persia, Zoroaster, a priest who flourished 258 years before the conquest of Alexander the Great, became renowned for his practice of astrology. A reformer and prophet, he created a religion that influenced Judaism, Christianity, and Islam. In China, emperors were chosen because of their astrological knowledge. In Greece, astrology flourished at the highest period of its culture and power, a period that most influences our culture today.

Astrologers in ancient times were great mathematicians and astronomers. Most of them were also occultists or alchemists who had the benefit of manuscripts that have been destroyed or just dropped out of sight. Tragically, much of their knowledge was never recorded and has been forgotten.

Great thinkers such as Pythagoras, Plato, and Aristotle used astrological principles in their philosophies. Pythagoras created an intellectual tradition of mystical wisdom that deeply influenced the development of classical Greek philosophy and medieval European thought. He was particularly interested in the influence of astrology and numbers as they affected all human endeavors. Copernicus acknowledged Pythagorean concepts in his hypothesis that the earth and the other planets rotate in orbits around the sun.

The philosopher Plato, who lived in Greece around 360 B.C., saw the universe as a celestial sphere composed of a single substance, a composite of Sameness and Difference, mixed with Existence. Hippocrates, a contemporary of Plato and traditionally regarded as the father of medicine, declared that a doctor who did not use astrology to aid him in making a diagnosis and prescribing a remedy deserved to be called a fool! Aristotle, influenced by Plato, added cause and effect, a more rational approach to heavenly cycles. These ideas formed the basis for astrology until psychology took the reins in the twentieth century.

In medieval times, Arabic scientific texts and Greek manuscripts were translated into Latin; among these were astrology texts from ancient times. The Renaissance poet Dante, author of *The Divine Comedy*, credited his Sun sign, Gemini, for his eloquence. Two centuries later, Nostradamus, physician and astrologer to three French kings, wrote predictions for the future disguised in verses that are still being unraveled today. His projections were based on the movements of the planets and visions he saw emanating from a fiery pot. John Dee, astrologer to Queen Elizabeth I, picked the date for her coronation according to the alignment of the stars. Her powerful reign of forty-four years proved his expertise at selecting a propitious time.

Most astrologers in Europe were members of secret societies: the Masons, the Knights Templar, the Rosicrucians, and the Golden Dawn Society. The early American statesmen who wrote the Constitution and the Bill of Rights were also members of secret societies.

Powerful people have always sought help from the stars, though they often prefer not to make that information public. Royalty, heads of government, clergy, and presidents of the United States often have their own personal astrologers. Yet the profession of astrology is not without its disadvantages and the probability of falling from grace. An ancient clay tablet from Mesopotamia tells of an eminent astrologer to the king who failed to predict an eclipse and was banished to make bricks in the hot sun. Hitler had many astrologers. If he didn't like their predictions, he had them shot.

Napoleon's astrologer was a monk named LeClerc. One wonders if LeClerc told Napoleon the whole story. Perhaps Napoleon, being a Leo and overly positive, heard only what he wanted to—a typical Leo trait!

Although the Catholic church did much to discredit astrology, the popes had astrologers at their disposal, and the Vatican still has the most extensive collection of astrology books in the world.

After the Renaissance, astrology was not taken seriously until the late nineteenth and early twentieth centuries. Albert Einstein was interested in metaphysics. Carl Jung, a Swiss psychiatrist, based his theory of personality types on the knowledge he gained from the ancient metaphysical arts. He had an astrologer do charts of all his patients, which he used to get a preliminary take on their basic nature before beginning treatment. Even now, with our extraordinary breakthroughs in science, astrology is being acknowledged as an irreplaceable tool for self-knowledge and personal growth.

As we enter a new century, we are about to make a great transition into an Aquarian age. It is one of twelve successive 2,160-year periods, each of which corresponds to one of the signs of the zodiac. A complete cycle of 25,920 years is based on a phenomenon known as the *precession of the equinoxes*. Due to a very gradual wobble of the Earth around its own polar axis, the Sun gradually moves backward through the zodiac.

Great ages are dominated by the influences of their ruling sign in the same way in which individuals born with different Sun signs are influenced by the principals of each sign. During these great cosmic ages, the dominant constellation influences all processes of life on Earth, including the symbols of art and the ceremonies of religious expression. Each sign highlights specific functions, and as you read history with a sharp eye you can relate it to the consecutive ages.

The great age of Taurus colored all religions with the symbol of the bull. Then, circa 2000 B.C., the Taurean age was succeeded by the Arian, and the ram-headed god Amen-Ra became the perfect symbol for cosmic spirit. In the next age, starting in the first century A.D., the fish became the symbol for the now-ending Pisces age. As we enter this new century, we are about to make a transition into the influences of Aquarius. During the last Aquarian age, approximately twenty-six thousand years ago, the lost civilizations of Lemuria and Atlantis flourished. Edgar Cayce, the Sleeping Prophet, said in his trances that these ancient people had achieved a level of science much higher than we have today. These people were natural conservationists; the sexes were equal in opportunity and status; they used all their brain power; and until the end of their civilization they lived their spiritual beliefs daily. Perhaps the influences of the new age will bring the advances we need to attain such heights again.

A Man-Made System

Astrology is a combination of science and esoteric theory. The science of astronomy is used to set up a chart, but the interpretation is an art based on the wisdom of the interpreter. It is a man-made system designed to help us understand the complexities of life. The complete zodiac of twelve signs behaves as a single rational unit, and a well-trained astrologer can decode this creative intelligence.

Since astrology is a system, it can be used very simply or very abstractly. Compare astrology to playing the piano: you can play with one finger and pick out a simple tune or you can play with both hands and accompany an orchestra.

The Sun signs are based on the constellations, which are imaginative groupings of fixed stars that lie along an ecliptic belt encircling the Earth. The Sun goes through many constellations—Orion, Delphinus (the dolphin), and Cygnus (the swan)—that are not included in the present zodiac. The Babylonians listed eighteen constellations; as astrology evolved, this number was simplified to ten, then eleven, signs with varying degrees of power. Finally, in the second century A.D., the Greek astrologer Ptolemy gave us what we know today as a balanced zodiac with twelve houses. His theories of astrology were written in a book called the *Tetrabiblos*, and his knowledge greatly affected the growth of astrology.

The East continued to develop an astrology that was primarily fatalistic. We can thank the Greeks for adding the element of logic and the possibility of individualizing the Sun signs through personal participation with the chart.

The word *zodiac* means "animal circle." The zodiac circle that we use in the West is divided into twelve equal sections, called *houses*. All of the signs have animal rulers except the air signs Gemini, Libra, and Aquarius and the Earth sign Virgo. These four Sun signs are gifted in thinking and communicating, so a mute animal symbol wouldn't be appropriate.

A particular Sun sign rules each of the twelve houses and is named for the shape of the stars in that constellation. For example, the first sign is Aries; if you really use your imagination, you can see the shape of a ram in the stars that form the Aries constellation. Leo is the easiest to imagine: the body and tail are plainly drawn by the stars, and the head needs only a little conjecture.

Early astrological charts were called *horoscopes*, meaning "look at the hour." The circle of the chart is a map of the sky. The seven visible heavenly bodies—the Sun, the Moon, Mercury, Venus, Mars, Jupiter, and Saturn—and the four more recently discovered planets—Uranus, Neptune, Pluto, and Chiron—are included. This is called a *natal chart*. It shows the ascendant, or rising sign, position of the Moon, and the houses in which all the planets fell at the time of birth. It is with this information that an interpretation of a person's life is done.

Contemporary Astrology

Until the latter part of the eighteenth century, our solar system consisted of seven celestial bodies: the Sun, the Moon, and the five planets. Although the telescope was discovered in 1608, it took many years until the discovery of Uranus (1781), Neptune (1846), and Pluto (1930). Astrology continues to evolve. Chiron, the latest addition to the zodiac, was discovered in 1977, and astronomers are still not sure if it is a planetoid or a comet. Astrologers are observing it to assess its influences.

The discovery of these new bodies coincides with changes in world knowledge and advancement. As we have evolved scientifically and developed large enough telescopes to find more planets in our solar system, we are synchronistically ready to step forward into new states of consciousness. For example, in contemporary astrology, Uranus brings in new ideas and technical advances. When Uranus was discovered, the people living at that time awakened to the idea that they had the right to be free. New machines such as the cotton gin and the steam engine were invented in the late eighteenth century, and today many uses of electricity are ruled by Uranus. Sometimes called *the awakener*, this vibrant planet brings cultural changes, spiritual revelations, and political revolutions. The revolutions began first in America, then in France and Russia, and still continue today.

Uranus is still emanating freedom as it orbits the Sun every eighty-four years. It has not yet completed three cycles around the Sun since its discovery, but the world has changed appreciably in that time. We are encapsulated in the Uranian world of computers and information in the 1990s; we can only guess at what new inventions, revolutions, and revelations await. Whenever Uranus falls in a natal chart, there will be change and liberation.

Neptune is a planet of mystery, never visible to the naked eye. Neptune brought into human consciousness the existence of realms smaller than the eye can see. We live in a world of illusions and delusions. Neptune rules the subconscious, where our dreams are born and where we are free to create without the restrictions of earthbound reality. When Neptune was discovered in the middle of the nineteenth century it was a time of great suffering and idealism. In 1846 the Irish potato famine was underway; Karl Marx's *Communist Manifesto* was published in 1848; Harriet Beecher Stowe wrote *Uncle Tom's Cabin* in 1851; and in 1859, John Brown made his famous raid on Harpers Ferry.

With the founding of the Theosophical Society and Christian Science, spiritualism flourished in England and the United States. Important new products—ether used for painless surgery, plastics made from oil products, and the first color photo images—were developed. In a natal chart Neptune indicates idealism and fantasy.

Pluto is a tiny planet at the edge of our solar system. Scorpio is ruled by Pluto, which governs sex, other people's money, and death. With Pluto's discovery in 1930 came the Great Depression, the rise of the Nazis, and World War II, with its atomic devastation. The cyclotron was developed in 1931, followed by the positron in 1932 and nuclear fusion in 1938. The computer was discovered about this time. A new level of technology had been reached—powerful enough to destroy us.

Until that time the average person had little hope of transformation on a physical or emotional level. If you were sick, little could be done. Pluto's transformational power was made available through psychoanalysis and new medical techniques. Human beings could change right down to the cellular level. Pluto in the natal chart represents transformation and regeneration.

Chiron is the celestial body whose placement shows your life quest and soul purpose. It is considered to be an important indicator of your role in the new Aquarian age. The astrological logo for Chiron is the letter K over a small circle. It looks like a key and symbolizes Chiron's power to open doors to higher consciousness. Its orbit, between Saturn and Uranus, symbolizes a bridge between the personality, which involves the Sun, the Moon, and the five near planets, and the soul, which involves the outermost three planets, Uranus, Neptune, and Pluto.

A mythological being, Chiron was a centaur (half man, half horse). He was teacher to the gods, goddesses, and important mortals. Chiron is said to rule herbs and healing as well as astrology and other mystical disciplines. Through Chiron's influence, the study of metaphysical subjects has grown into a cultural movement. For example, when I started studying astrology in 1972, I had to order all my books through the mail; now I can buy them at any bookstore and even some drugstores.

Chiron's position between Saturn, which rules time, and Uranus, which rules transpersonal experiences, brings a new concept: the eternal now. We can gain from these timeless experiences by getting in touch with our soul and starting anew on a path of continued growth. With Chiron in our universal consciousness we can all seek out our part in healing a wounded world.

The Hologram

People often ask me why astrology works and how the planets in our solar system can affect us. This is an age-old mystery that has never been completely explained, but there are many theories. The most logical explanation to me is the holographic theory.

A hologram is a three-dimensional photograph shot with a laser beam.

The print of the photograph is illuminated by another laser beam and a realistic three-dimensional image of the original object appears. When the print is cut in two, each half holds the complete image. This process can be carried on as long as the print can be halved.

The universal holographic theory I speak of indicates an image of wholeness or completeness, much like the zodiac itself. You can take the zodiac apart sign by sign or planet by planet and derive separate meaning from individual parts, but each part still holds the basic wholeness of the complete zodiac.

According to this theory, a deeper level of reality, a more complex dimension beyond our own, a superhologram of the past, present, and future all exist simultaneously. This theory also suggests that time is an illusion, that given the proper tools, we can reach into this level of reality and perceive scenes from the past or the future.

I think astrology is one of these tools. The effects of the Sun signs and the planets are very real. Their subtle vibrations are felt by the emotional body. Each sign has its own special essence and message that stimulates different responses. As certain aspects in the heavens are formed, we become aware of uneasiness, anxiety, and fear; other aspects bring a sense of power and joy.

A counseling session with an astrologer often leads the way into a feeling of resolution and hope. You may find that an astrological reading confirms and validates what you are already feeling, and the information encourages your self-awareness as well as your emotional and spiritual growth.

The Present

The *Encyclopaedia Britannica* defines astrology as "a type of divination that consists of interpreting the influence of planets and stars on earthly affairs in order to predict the destinies of individuals, groups, or nations." Although astrology is an excellent vehicle for prognostication, I am not concerned with divination or the future at this time. I want to focus on our Sun signs in the present moment. The present is much more stimulating than the future or the past.

Many of my clients come in for future forecasts, but I feel we must be in the present moment to create the future. The forecasts I give support the time my clients are living in, right now. The present is a point of balance between past and future, and our lives are a constant process of evaluating the interplay between them. We can calculate the positions of the planets and the signs for any given moment, and decode their meanings, but as co-creators with God we have a choice in how we react in any given moment as we play out the events of our lives.

Scientific Thought

In the last twenty years the tendency to deny the connections between the heavens and human events has decreased.

We are increasingly aware of powerful magnetic fields that exist throughout the solar system. The Earth's atmosphere is constantly bombarded by a solar wind and a stream of subatomic particles from the Sun emanating from the big bang of universal creation. The argument that no scientific evidence can account for the influence the heavens have on human lives is less convincing all the time. Studies of fish, birds, and other life forms show that they have the ability to navigate by these fields, indicating that the nervous systems of living organisms are sensitive to electromagnetic forces. Also, theories of how the planets influence each other in subtle ways are little understood at this time.

Only as we enter the twenty-first century do we understand that physical distances are not so important as we thought. It doesn't matter whether subatomic particles such as electrons are five feet or five billion miles apart; they still communicate with each other.

In *The Case for Astrology*, John Anthony West covers all the pros and cons of astrology. He writes in summary: "Not only is the factual evidence supporting astrology commanding, but it is also now possible to develop a plausible theory for the manner in which astrological effects manifest themselves within the framework of the known physical world. Modern physics and astronomy both make it clear that the ancient concept of the *Harmony of the Spheres* is no longer a poetic metaphor but a legitimate analogy drawn upon a unified solar system in which each part affects every other part via the well understood phenomenon of resonance."

To me, one of the most reassuring illustrations of universal love or a loving God, however you see it, is that our Sun and Moon appear to be the same size from Earth. Although there is a tremendous difference in their mass, from our position in space, they are perfectly balanced. I find great meaning in that. Out of chaos comes perfect symmetry. No wonder the ancients were so taken with the heavens.

Celestial phenomena have great practical significance today as in ancient times. If Adam created astrology through God's direction, as ancient philosophers attest, he was wise in his choice of the stars as celestial messengers. Among the objects of nature, none is so appropriate as the stars to convey to all ages God's sacred message of inspiration, wholeness, and liberation.

Part II

The Sun Sign:
A Fingerprint of the Soul

In 1972 I decided to take an astrology class. It was a life-changing experience for me. I'll never forget my first astrological reading. It was done by my astrology teacher Elbert Wade in Dallas, Texas. Little did I know how much that reading would influence my life. Of course, all of this new direction showed in my chart: Pluto, the planet of transformation, exactly trined (a very favorable aspect) my Moon in Aquarius, the sign of astrology.

Astrology has guided me down many paths. I am never bored with astrology; it is as fascinating now as it was in 1972. The study of symbols leads in many directions, and the symbolism in astrology has made my life an evolving and poetic experience. It whets my appetite for more knowledge. Astrology has been the basis for a personal search to understand myself and others. It has furthered my education in untold ways, taking me to many new philosophies and ideas that have enriched my life and led me to a serious practice of meditation yoga. Through my readings I am able to offer my clients not only the benefit of my extended study of astrology, history, and religion but also guidance based on the many things I have learned in pursuit of my psychological growth and spiritual path.

The zodiac gives an important overview of our strengths and weaknesses. In fact, astrology provides important information that normally takes a long time to find out. It is an art, a way of symbolically bringing subjective material into your objective reality. Your Sun sign best describes your basic nature and the way you express your ego. In the world today, as in ancient times, people want to know their own Sun sign and the signs of the people they are involved with. Sun signs help us to see the patterns in our lives we couldn't see otherwise. Each sign gives us a sense of sacredness and the right to express our soul.

Each Sun sign has a soul trait that is positively yours to use. I call this your *soul power*. On the other hand, through the inherent patterns of your Sun sign you can create behavior that will sabotage you in your daily life. You see the world your way and your diseased ego takes over. I call this *ego blockage*.

Freud developed the threefold concept of the psyche: the superego, which is the higher self; the id, which is the basic self; and the ego, which resides in the reasoning area of the mind as an objective point of reference. The ego is our sense of identity in the world.

These three parts describe the dynamics of the human mind. I am using them because they are common words in our society. Since the ego works constantly to integrate your inner feelings with your thoughts of the outside world, protective defenses are formed, particularly in early life. These defense mechanisms are based on your fears, either real or imagined. Fear and confusion in early life cause you to suppress your real feelings and form ego blockages that plague you through life. These blockages create scripts that you constantly play out until you wake up to the truth of the soul.

The ego blockages of all twelve signs are based on the fear of loss of control. Each Sun sign has a natural, preordained preference of needs and wants. When these are denied, blockages are formed in the personality that remain until there is awareness and healing.

What is your Sun sign's soul power, and how do your ego blockages prevent you from achieving full self-realization? This knowledge alone can help you improve your life. The ego blockages exist to aid you in making better choices. It helps, however, to begin by being more positive in your outlook.

Each of us has a specific lifetime lesson to learn that is innate to our sign. I call this the *transforming path*. These life lessons seem to recur again and again, even when we try to stop them. For example, Cancers' transforming path is family relationships. Family matters are their major concern. But despite their soul power of nurturing, it's impossible for them to parent all the people they know. Still, when they operate out of their ego blockage of manipulation, they impulsively try to please everybody; instead, they end up drained and depressed and no one is pleased. Sadly, people pleasers are often unaware of the manipulation behind their actions.

Cancers are sitting ducks for possessive parents and demanding children. By feeling they're the ones who can make everything right, Cancers lose themselves. A fear of being unloved or abandoned is the motivating force that creates the dysfunction. By resisting the urge to be the perfect parent or child, they can improve their relationships with family members and work out their own life lessons.

One thing you can count on: no matter what Sun sign you are, your transforming path will show up in your life in some way. The transforming path is neither good nor bad; it is neutral. The lesson lies in how you perceive it and how you make peace with it.

Emotional Attachment

According to *Webster's*, emotions are "a psychic and physical reaction such as anger and fear, subjectively experienced as strong feeling and physiologically involving changes that prepare the body for action."

In daily life, you are in continual emotional reaction to your environment. Your personal relationships are constantly stimulating a myriad of emotional responses, and life would be dull without them. But living your life under the extreme pressure of emotional highs and lows is physically very draining.

As the world is bombarded with information, especially at this time in history, it adds to the emotional conflict in your life. Astrology works because when properly used it frees you from attachments to your emotions. It helps you get "unstuck." This is not to say that your emotions are negative. It is your *attachment* to emotional dramas, without the benefit of objective mental process, that keeps you from right action.

The mind and ego are good friends, but it's easy to get stranded in the mind and negate your feelings when the ego is blocked by past conditioning. To know yourself well, you must feel your emotions without overreacting, make positive mental assessments, then act on your decision.

Emotions such as love and empathy are essential to our spiritual and emotional health, but anger and fear seem closer to the surface in our world today. So often in daily life your sense of well-being is diminished by fearful and reactive responses to the environment. Just reading the newspaper or hearing the news every day is enough to set off a negative emotional experience. However, it is possible to become free of the tyranny of your emotionalism. Let your feelings guide you to your ego blockage and understand what your responses and actions mean. These battles are not won easily, but awareness is more than half of the struggle.

It is gratifying to realize that when you define your problems, you have a fighting chance of solving them. By combining my spiritual studies with the practice of astrology, I learned that each Sun sign is endowed with the inherent authority to transform negative behavior into positive action.

The energy of dysfunction is exactly equal to the energy of creation. There is a law of balance in the universe; at every moment there is a completely positive world and a completely negative world available to each of us. Whatever we focus our minds on, be it positive or negative, pulls our energy in that direction.

All that is necessary to move into positive action is a shift in perspective and an intense desire to change. Astrology, a system of symbols, has the eye-opening information needed to effect this life-changing transformation.

You must change the way you look at the world, be more detached, more objective, and less reactive. Have a loving heart; be kind to yourself. There are more tremendous rewards when you learn to be more patient and take the time that is needed to connect to your soul. You become centered, fears automatically disappear, and the door to immense power is opened.

Quantum Leap

It is possible that in the future we will learn to deal with our emotions in a more mature way. When this happens, astrology may become obsolete and ultimately not work as a guide and learning tool. We teeter on a new age as we go into the twenty-first century. Humankind's consciousness is about to make a quantum leap. It will feel as if we are all waking up together. When we reach this glorious evolutionary point of mental and emotional balance, there will be no more war on Earth.

But according to Hindu beliefs, until we reach this pinnacle, we are living in a time of great peril, the *Kali Yuga*, a time when people are ruled by their heads, not their hearts. If your mind isn't open to the higher intelligence of the heart, then the emotions are repressed and unresolved. Everywhere on earth fear is promoted to maintain worldly power, and people are frightened of anything spiritual. It seems safer to take refuge in the analytical mind, separated from your emotional and spiritual needs.

If you are ready to enlarge your consciousness at this time, astrology can be an important part of that process. To use astrology you must want questions answered. When the right questions come, the right answers are assured. Good old skepticism doesn't hurt at all. In fact, when I first started reading charts my attitude was totally skeptical. It took me five years of disbelief to be convinced that I was dealing with something divinely tuned and of great service to all who were blessed to use it.

A Tool of Aspiration

Looking around local bookstores, I discovered that although the self-help field is flooded with excellent books, little has been written for the public correlating astrology with hope, aspiration, and personal growth. I felt it was time for people to use astrology as a tool for growth and change, not just as pigeonholes for personality traits.

My goal in writing this book is to take Sun sign astrology and make it a hands-on tool for emotional and spiritual transformation. This method will point the way to your natural ability as shown by your Sun sign, ascendant, and Moon position. As you discover your soul power, it is also important to look at what keeps you from this natural gift. It would be a good thing to read all the Sun signs, as all of the signs rule some area of your life in your natal chart.

To open up to personal happiness, you must acknowledge emotional blocks that inhibit your power. What are our weaknesses but arrows pointing the way to our true power? The quality of the relationship you have with yourself is up to you. This book is written to help you in this self-discovery, the first step in any healing process.

Emotional healing comes through self-examination; you return to a healthy state of wholeness when you face the fears, anger, and denial that hurt you emotionally in the first place. Healing is wholeness, and when you know who you are, the healing is complete.

Huston Smith, a teacher of the world's great religions, said:

> If life told us the answer
> it would take our
> freedom
> away from us.

It would be great if astrology had all the answers. It does not. But it is an enjoyable tool with an endless wealth of information that continues to reveal itself through observation and study.

Your Soul Power and Your Ego Blockage

It's difficult to comprehend that the stars somehow exert an influence over us. There is no logical way to explain it.

We know that the Moon affects our bodies' fluids and the Earth's oceans. Scientists say that electromagnetic forces have a real influence on our nervous systems, and I have found that people look and act like their Sun signs, but that isn't proof.

You can calculate and interpret astrology endlessly, but to truly benefit from it you must make a leap of faith. You must go outside your normal knowledge base into the world of symbols.

Astrological symbols are some of the most ancient in the world. They have been found all over the world in some form or other, and there seems to be an overlap between the symbols in every system, East or West, suggesting an earlier connection.

Symbols are pictorial devices designed to evoke an idea or concept in its entirety. They are a means of bypassing the intellect and talking straight to the heart, the center of understanding. I didn't know why astrology works, but I can experience the symbols in a chart, know their meaning, and share it with others. That's what I do.

By surrendering to these transcendent symbols and allowing their inner meanings to come into your consciousness, you, too, can partake in their mystery. It is an empowering thing to do.

As an astrologer, I have noticed that most people either don't know about, or somehow refuse to engage, the power of their own sign. It seems to be far easier to see your shortcomings and faults and to deny the soul powers that are offered as your natural birthright.

Thankfully, these powers bide their time, waiting for your awakening. They do not go away. When the day comes that you feel worthy and ready for an expanded experience of power, you need only reach out to what is rightly yours.

Astrology separates the circle of life into twelve Sun signs and distinguishes each part. Your sign is a powerhouse all by itself. Your soul power is at your fingertips. If you aspire to it, it enhances, strengthens, and develops your consciousness. This is where you need that leap of faith. Do not worry about astrology's validity, but realize that astrology symbolically gives you the information you need to be balanced mentally, physically, and spiritually.

Many people are afraid of their own power. I imagine the hesitation comes from the fear that we will misuse it or get trapped in it. Power is a hot potato! It means having control, authority, influence over others. It's very dynamic. Power walks with heavy feet. It carries a lot of responsibility with it. It's easy to see how fear of power could confuse people who are stuck in their ego blockages.

But it isn't power that corrupts—it's your ego's fear of losing it that distresses you. The ego always wants control. It wants the power and it tries to keep you from the pure soul power that is rightly yours. The first step in removing your ego blockages is to acknowledge them. This is where astrology helps.

I have a vivid imagination, so I'm a magician at worrying. Steven Spielberg's *Raiders of the Lost Ark* is nothing compared to the dramas I spin with my fertile brain. I have spent many nights with brain fever—thoughts whirling in my head about something that I cannot change or should have done, back and forth, back and forth, to no avail. Worry comes from trying to be in control of the past and the future, when the present is the only time we have to be productive. As a Capricorn, my ego blockage is over-achievement. It has taken me years to learn how to let go of the outcome (the future) and just enjoy the act of creating without worrying about the result. To allow my soul power of contribution to work in my life, I had to learn to surrender to the here and now. It is my ego blockage of overachiev-ing that sets it off anyway. When I stay in the action of the goal, each moment is full of excitement and creativity and I accomplish much more.

The Healthy Ego

Being secure within yourself is a serious issue. You must learn to see life events from a level of confidence. You must know who you are. Being grounded in that knowledge allows you to make better choices. Like everyone else, you want to be more alive, to be noticed and remembered for yourself. Desiring to enhance every moment you live, you take on a vitality that makes everyone you meet happy to know you. You have zest for life. You are powerful!

To attain this confident state, you must evaluate yourself and under-stand your ego. This requires self-observation; you must look at yourself with laser vision. Then, when you know who you are, your development as a "human becoming" is set in motion.

Transactional analysis transcribes Freud's three categories of human consciousness—id, ego, and superego—into the *child*, the *adult*, and the *par-ent*. I use three corresponding classifications to describe the personality: the basic self, the mind, and the soul.

The ego I'm discussing here is twofold. The healthy ego combines all three parts of consciousness. It is powerful because it is connected to your soul, which is a wiser part of you that gives you the detachment necessary to handle your emotions and express yourself in a positive way.

The other, unhealthy ego is a dysfunctional combination of id (the child) and ego. It is the part of you that is emotionally immature and reactive, born of fear that sets up self-imposed limitations. The unhealthy ego gives rise to ego blockage.

If you are a Leo and your ego blockage is excessive optimism, it's hard to stop yourself from taking a risk even when you know that the chances are against you. You love to win against all odds, to push the envelope. Your soul power instinctively knows you don't need another failure and patiently sends you thoughts of delaying gratification. The resolution comes when the healthy ego, the adult, is convinced of its ability to be happy without such extreme stimulus.

I caution you not to view the ego as evil. The ego is necessary as your personal point of reference; it differentiates between and integrates your outer and inner worlds. The healthy ego is your true sense of self; it evaluates situations and makes decisions. As a seeker of truth, you must see yourself as powerful before you can be emotionally healthy. Attitude is everything!

Learning how to delay gratification introduces high standards and ethics into your personality. As you mature, your soul (sometimes called your conscience) steps in and socializes you to understand others, as well as to handle the stress of conflicts. This is sometimes experienced as a wise voice in your mind—not to be confused with the critical mind, which can be overbearing and negative. Always listen for the still, small voice that never criticizes but calmly suggests a realistic and loving approach to a problem or confrontation.

There is a stage of maturity that starts around adolescence where the ego has the capacity for rational understanding, introspective thinking, deductive reasoning, and socially acceptable behavior. In this stage you start separating your own ego from your parents' authority and involvement. Although this step is a necessary part of your learned knowledge, it is not easy. That is why the teenage years are so hard, like having flu of the personality. A teenager's immature ego feels the need to break free from family, so there is usually rebellion against authority at this time.

The next stage is the highest level of personal development, with a more integrated form of thinking, including the ability to consolidate concepts, connect ideas, and relate truths to one another. This stage is full maturity, but frankly, not many people ever reach this point in their development. In fact, your ego blockages come from your early childhood experiences and the unresolved emotional reactions of your adolescence. This continuing anxiety doesn't allow the maturation cycle to click in.

The ego blockages shown by your Sun sign are formed by the destructive defense mechanisms that developed early in life and are based on the natural propensity of each sign to certain behaviors. Your unproductive and self-defeating behavior is caused by an immature adolescent ego that is damaged and seeking to control and manipulate.

However, all is not lost. You are capable of maturing throughout your whole life. Evolving is what your life is about. Actually, little has been said about the pure joy of maturity. When I was very immature, not so long ago, I thought that the quote "The reward of patience is patience" was redundant. Now I can see the wisdom there. With calm endurance and tolerant understanding, the ego and soul make peace with each other and together bring the greatest happiness you will ever have. You don't need anything to improve it. Like a fine old wine, life grows better with age.

The heart is the mediator between the ego and the soul. Only the heart can achieve balance. Within your own heart is the wisdom to achieve this wonderful act of equilibrium. The more conscious you are of your personal rights as a human being, the better your chances of connecting your ego needs with your soul needs.

It is important to stop and think that if the immature ego (the basic self) is to make a sacrifice and give up its old ways, it must be offered something in return. It must be compensated with something superior to its old selfish desires, such as peace of mind, a sense of safety, and more comfort in day-to-day life. This means you have to wake up, communicate directly with reality, and, most important, change your values. This is not easy, but it is rich in rewards.

You have to acknowledge that the answers are inside, not outside on some unreachable star. You are asked to discard the irrelevant in your life and acknowledge with simplicity of heart that you are a *human becoming*. You are free to undertake your quest for reality with the open heart of a child, yet from a mature viewpoint.

The Soul and the Basic Self

People of all signs operate on two separate levels of consciousness. The highest level, the soul, is totally wise and loving, spiritually evolved, and materialistically unattached. The soul is who you really are at your deepest level. Some say our soul stays with us until our reincarnation cycle is finished and we become pure spirit. We cannot see it, but to be truly happy we must form a connection to it. Ovid, a Roman poet born in 43 B.C., said, "Those things that nature denied to human sight, she revealed to the soul." The soul is in every pore of your body, and you can connect with the information that is constantly coming in by looking within yourself. Meditation gives you a way to access the information.

Here again you must take a leap of faith. Most people say that you communicate with your soul through a heartfelt experience that illuminates your consciousness. Also, you can't live in fear and confusion and at the same time experience the soul. Your heart shuts down and breaks communication. It is possible to know about the soul in your mind and still be shut off from the heart. It is a lifetime lesson to keep the heart open to the soul. It's quite a trick, kind of like patting your head and rubbing your stomach.

Your mind must be clear of negative thoughts and emotions to have a soul experience; if you are not connected to the soul, your blockages are controlling you. It is through your soul that the power of your sign manifests itself, although the soul is really independent of the personality. The personality is the soul's vehicle in this life, but it's not attached to it. Your soul comes into the earth plane with lessons that are necessary for your evolution. Meditation and contemplation are perfect methods to clear the negative head talk of the mind and to accommodate this rich source. Your soul desires to liberate you from the endless lifetimes of reincarnation on earth and send you on your way to new worlds of experience.

By the way, there are all kinds of meditation: you don't necessarily have to sit around all of the time in an uncomfortable pose. Walking is a great way to go into the meditative state, and chants or soft, peaceful music can guide your mind to a peaceful place.

Many spiritual sources speak of contacting ethereal guides. The Bible is full of mystical contacts with God—for instance, the burning bush that spoke to Moses. All the prophets in the Old Testament heard voices from on high, some with visions, some without.

Other levels of consciousness are inhabited by higher beings, who are there to guide and inspire us. Some of these beings are angels who never incarnate, and others are great teachers who are not incarnated at this time. They are sources of unlimited knowledge and wisdom and live in higher dimensions that we are only vaguely aware of. These great beings are fully awake to what Plato called the world of ideas—the conceptual thoughts and pictures that record the past and compose the future—and occasionally they give us a message. Native Americans have animal spirit guides, and many people in the world say they are guided by deceased Indian shamans.

We don't know if these wonderful beings are autonomous or simply beautiful manifestations of our own souls. The American prophet Edgar Cayce said that his guide never showed himself, but seemed to be a wiser and universally connected part of Cayce himself. Through his guide, Cayce had access to a whole energy field of information that he called the Akashic records. Cayce maintained that everything that has ever happened in time and space is recorded in that realm, and that this level of consciousness is open to everyone with the right keys. I believe him, but we must evolve to a certain spiritual level to tune into this wealth of information.

In my readings I feel that I tune in to this information and it gives me guidance as I interpret the symbols of astrology. My soul and the soul of my client connect, and the correct information comes through my mind. I explain it to my client as clearly as I can. There is a lot of power for healing in that connection, and when the reading is finished, we both feel refreshed.

Carl Jung believed that there is a repeating story in everyone's life that is related to ancient myths or archetypes. Each myth has its own special significance that helps us find meaning in our lives. Jung felt that we enter the collective unconscious—the realm of the soul—in our sleep, that through our dreams we can discover our own myth, which helps us with self-discovery. Once we discover our personal myth, we have the information we need for healing our emotional wounds.

I was thrilled when I found out that our souls are connected to all the other souls on earth and all the great beings in the universe. Religion, psychology, and metaphysics all agree that there is a higher level of consciousness that we contact in meditation and prayer. Through our souls we have communication with higher levels of consciousness throughout the universe. It is comforting to know that these great sources are available to us for information and loving support. In this state of higher consciousness we have a sense of unity with all things. From this source we draw power and inspiration.

When you are in your soul power, it is both individual and universal: you do not lose your identity. When you are soul-connected, there is a part of yourself that is detached, that is listening and watching all the events in your life. This is where the power lies. In order to have your full soul power, you must be both observer and participant at the same time. You must observe yourself as you observe others, hear yourself as you hear others. You must be able to see yourself as others see you and understand.

When you develop these skills you become more and more powerful in soul consciousness. However, it is easy to fall out of unity with your soul power. When you become too wrapped up in the emotion of an event, you are operating out of your blockage, and your power is lost.

The other level of consciousness—the basic self, the id, or the child—is just the opposite of soul power. It is where your ego blockages take hold and you act self-involved, nonreasoning, and materialistic. Because the basic self does not think or reason, it responds totally out of feelings. Much of its motivation is to be happy by seeking sensual comfort and safety. To feel safe and content, the primitive self acts out in immature ways, craving one thing after another without proper thought.

Your ego blockages are formed by the defense mechanisms the basic self sets up in early life. Amazingly, the positive powers that are waiting to be

↑ ku soul

Soul Signs

realized lie deep in the subconscious right beside these blockages, and it is the basic self that controls both of them. You must make peace with your basic self in order to overcome your blockages and expand into your potential.

It is comforting to know that your soul watches over the basic self, always giving reliable support and unconditional love. You can depend on this wonderful gift of protection always being there for you. Few people understand this; instead they remain suspended in dread, fear, and anger, expecting the worst of themselves.

To add to the confusion, both levels of consciousness speak to you through the mind. But which voice should you listen to? The mind is like the ocean, never still. As you mature, you develop the discernment needed to balance these opposite facets of your personality. The basic self seems to have the loudest voice, wanting to take charge and rebel against the soul, like a mischievous child.

The resolution comes when the basic self, suffering from an ego blockage, welcomes the soul power's guidance through trust and surrender. At the same time, a healing occurs in the transforming path as the mind integrates the ego's need with the soulful solution. This is a liberating experience and life becomes much easier.

You can get in touch with this guidance by stilling the mind and listening to your heart. It's the voice that always tells the truth.

The Mind

→ Lono soul

Patience and discipline are the prerequisites for watching the mind, like a parent watching over a child. Your mind is a wonderful computerlike entity that is limited by its own nature. It is the mind's job to categorize past information and pull the possibilities of the future together.

If you stay in the mind and avoid your feelings, as you are prone to do, you are never really alive. It is through the feelings and the emotions that you live vibrantly in the moment. To be identified with something is to be united with it. If you are totally identified with the mind alone, your life is devoid of feeling and life events are only recorded, not truly experienced.

The mind seems to work in dualities, or comparisons and contrasts. There are always two sides to everything. When you are in mental and emotional conflict, weighing thoughts back and forth, it is easy to be depressed. This duality keeps you continually juggling ideas and situations—past and future, right and wrong—hindering you from being content in the moment you are living right now.

This feeling of unrest is abated when you realize the true seat of the mind is in your heart; if you listen well you will hear wise counsel from your own soul. You must identify with your own soul power. At this level of consciousness your transforming path is transcended. Love and intelligence are integrated, and your life flows with peace of mind to any problem that arises.

Consciousness

What is consciousness? You start developing your personal consciousness the day you are born and you enter your physical body. However, it appears that the brain itself—and perhaps the whole body—was developed in order to receive and understand aspects of universal consciousness. This contact is necessary to perform your duties. It is astounding yet energizing to think that you are a part of an immense holographic system and your body is your antenna.

This act of being conscious entails the awakening of the mind to critical awareness and at the same time being mindful of strong inner feelings. Your consciousness is much larger than the brain and seems to be able to go anywhere in the universe it desires.

As a child I wondered why people never discussed their inner life, an infinitely richer and more natural state of consciousness than the ordinary outer one. I was 8 or 9 when it really hit me that no one talked about the real things in life. I assumed that my family and everyone I knew had another hidden life. I thought it was the best part, but since it was not discussed I figured it was forbidden and didn't mention it to anyone.

I was an imaginative child, very visual, so the richness of my subconscious was one of my joys. In my life this rich subjective state was channeled into drawing, reading, and observing nature until I was able to gain enough control over my life to express myself outwardly, to become more consciously aware of how to balance my inner and outer world. In Latin, the word *illusion* means "inner." I think most of us have to learn our own way to integrate the polarities of the mundane world and the illusory inner world as we mature into adults.

Love Is a Power

The highest level of love is realized on the soul level, sometimes called the "higher self." This level is an essence, a vibration that is totally unconditional love and acceptance. As you develop your Sun sign's soul power, a feeling of comfort and unconditional love begins to permeate your body and mind. You are then able to be who you really are. When you find peace of mind, your heart naturally opens and you will want to share with others. Your ego blockage is no longer running the show. When you have this joy in your heart, life problems don't seem so tragic. No matter what happens you can maintain your serenity.

The truth is, love can only be shared. It is not an item to be given—that isn't its true nature. Love is a universal power that is integrating and balancing. You must realize that you are worthy of this highest love, so be open to it. It is there all the time, waiting for you to receive it.

I find that people like to give to others, but because they are not taught how to receive, they feel uncomfortable with compliments, presents, or even a kind word. Sadly, the sense of power that comes from giving to others seems to disappear as we move into a receptive position.

The price of giving is receiving. When people give from their hearts, it is not a power play. A wise person acquires the watchfulness and trust necessary to receive what is good, which in turn allows others the power of giving. By following God's generous example, the gift of giving and receiving is yours to enjoy. Attachments disappear, and the longing for something outside of yourself is gone.

You are living in a very exciting time. You have a chance to understand your higher consciousness and its creative potential. More and more people are seeking out paths that develop the spiritual or cosmic aspects of the mind. You have a chance to become more conscious and more loving, to laugh more. A sure sign of an advanced being is a sense of humor. Your soul path is a lighter perspective and a lighter step—a chance to be free.

Your
Transforming
Path

We are each born with specific lessons in our life cycle. In India this dilemma is called *karma*. And along with the lessons you are fated to learn, you are also born with your own genetic program, environment, generational issues, and family dynamics—all beyond your control.

It's a real juggling act!

Your Sun sign's transforming path explains why certain conditions are prevalent in your life and why these patterns seem to occur over and over again. Your transforming path is the fate you must face in your life. It is a system of thought that you have in common with all the other subjects of your Sun sign.

Fate

When you consult an astrologer and have your life pattern explained, you become aware of your fated aspects, good and bad. To me it makes sense that these traits reflect the unfolding of natural processes from other life-times as well as hereditary patterns and family programs in this lifetime.

Your fate is continually created in how you think and what you do. It isn't necessarily negative, although we seem to want to think of it that way. Every action we take (karma means "action" in Sanskrit) causes an equalizing reaction; good produces a reward and bad produces an effect that needs correction, yet we are free at any moment to change everything. We have the right as souls to overcome any error we have seeded in a past or present life. Your transforming path gives you a clue on how to balance the scales of fate.

Liz Greene, a world-renowned astrologer, says in her book *The Astrology of Fate*, "Understanding our fate is understanding our relationship to the natural laws of the universe." The healing of fate can only be done after there is a recognition of a higher power. After this breakthrough in consciousness, our free will and our sacred freedom of choice help us overcome the ignorance brought over from past lives.

Our ego blockage, our soul power, and our transforming path are all fated. Aeschylus, one of Athens' great tragic dramatists, says in his play *Prometheus Bound*, "Even Zeus the King of the Gods cannot escape the thing decreed." You choose to come to the earthly plane on your birthday at exactly the right time for your soul lesson. Just like your blood type and bone structure, your birth time and all that it entails cannot be changed. You can, however, function at your Sun sign's soul power, evolving past the doubts and fears of the ego blockage. Your response to your fate then changes, and unrealistic expectations disappear. When you make a decision to roll with the punches, your pursuit of happiness is greatly improved.

As the German philosopher Nietzsche said, "The fate of man prepares happy moments, not happy times."

Fate versus Free Will

When I'm discussing astrology with a group of people who know nothing about the subject, the topic of fate always comes up. Is our life totally fated? Do we have any choices in our life? What control do we have? What can we do to change our fate, or is it even possible? The answer could be a book in itself. This is what I see as an astrologer and a student of life: Astrology is based on a law of natural order wherein there are basic tenets that support growth and maturity.

Each separate Sun sign has in its very nature enough innate wisdom to be totally powerful in the world, creating everything you need in life. One thought or one word can change your life if you operate from enough power. This is done through contact with the brilliant and innately powerful part of yourself, your soul. This wise, all-knowing part of you gives you the good judgment needed to learn from your life experiences. The subtleties are easier to see. Instead of confusion you can just *know* when to advance or retreat. You can experience a higher quality of life, and self-doubt disappears.

It has been written. This is the meaning of fate, and since the planets go through the constellations in a predictable fashion, our fate is written in the stars. An important spiritual saying I've heard many times is, "Everything is where it is supposed to be." I take this to mean that we are born at the perfect time and die at the right time to fulfill our destiny and fate. You can't come into the earthly plane at the wrong time or leave at the wrong time.

I also believe there is a positive connection between human conduct and the ordered law of nature. I don't feel you are meant to be punished, although when you look at the world it seems there are many people who are. There is no way you can see the total picture from your individual viewpoint. You cannot possibly know the beginning and you don't know the end.

The ego blockage is attached to outcomes. When you are attached emotionally to controlling a situation, you lose your higher state of consciousness and fall into greater entanglement. You must stay in the moment and surrender your will to a higher will to get past your ignorance and confusion. Surrendering to the best part of yourself is a great strength.

I believe in reincarnation. This gives me a different perspective about the things I don't know or understand in this lifetime. At this time in history, being so egocentric and living with a sense of powerlessness, we want to control everything. We cannot. Wanting to be in control is the primary goal of our ego blockage.

In the past, particularly until the eighteenth century, human lives were dominated by monarchs, priests, and the military and controlled by rigid religious ceremonies and social rituals. There was very little individual freedom or self-will. The leaders were caught in the model of the government they had created, just as much as the peasants. But today with all our freedom (particularly in the West) we are shortsighted and confused, blind to the consequences of our actions, creating toxic conditions year after year. We have lost touch with nature and natural law. As we enter this new age of Aquarius, I hope that we may create an evolved and integrated way of looking at our fate with more responsibility for our actions and the effect they will have in the future.

Why Me?

The hardest lessons to learn are the ones that seem to be unfair. Where did this come from? Why did this have to happen to me? I hear these questions every day. The sign you are born into can give you invaluable information on how to deal with difficult and painful situations.

For example, a Libran client came in for a consultation. She was in her early thirties; attractive, as Librans often are; and her career was going great. The problem was, her love life was nonexistent, but she felt that it was time to get married and have a family.

Although she had dated a lot, and had even become engaged at one time, marriage terrified her. Whenever it was time to move forward in a relationship, she balked. By asking questions I found she was very much attached to her family. This gave me the clue I needed to help her.

Libra is the sign that rules the East. In the Eastern Hemisphere ancestors are revered, and often the whole family lives together. The ego of each person is not as individualized; there is a family group consciousness in the East that is not as prevalent in the West.

Librans born in the West are often attracted to Eastern philosophy and sometimes take on Asian characteristics. Knowing that she was a Libran gave me the insight into her dilemma. Libra's power is conscientiousness, the ability to see everything from a point of empathy and always consider others' needs. This is a wonderful power, but her blockage of absolute perfection was stopping her from finding happiness with a man and creating a family for herself.

As I thought about her problems, this occurred to me:

1. She was trying to marry to please her family and to find the perfect man for them, not herself.
2. Her image of herself was based on what other people thought of her.
3. She was one of those people who present a picture of assurance, but deep inside she was in conflict between her thoughts and feelings.

During the reading I learned my client felt an urgent need to please everyone and to be perfect. Although extremely efficient and decisive in her work, in her love life she didn't know she had the right to have what she wanted. She actually didn't know what she needed from a man to be happy in a relationship. When we are shut off from our common sense and become absolutely ignorant about simple things, our transforming path is at work. Haven't you noticed other intelligent people doing the dumbest things? It's obvious to everyone but them that their thought processes are off. You can be sure they are in the throes of their transforming path.

After explaining to my client that her transforming path in this lifetime was personal relationships, I suggested that she could learn a lot by dating men who were attractive to *her*. I suggested that she get to know them as friends, and not be so focused on the outcome of a relationship from the first date. Seeing every man as a potential husband who must be accepted by her family hooked her into the fear of rejection that always accompanies perfectionism.

Perfectionism was keeping my client focused on outside mental issues.

Her goals were based on I *should*, I *ought to*, and I *have to*, and she didn't know how to turn to her own heart feelings. As my client learned to recognize her patterns she began to make better choices. I suggested further that she could talk to friends who are happily married and get information on how to date with marriage in mind from books or workshops. I also thought she should see a counselor of her choice.

I believe in going through therapy when you have a problem making productive decisions. Astrology *is* an awareness therapy, but if the problem is deep-seated a person needs to talk it through with a qualified therapist.

Choices

Many times you are confronted with situations you cannot control, like being fired, the total surprise of an illness, or rejection by a loved one. You also go through predictable times such as adolescence and middle age, which can turn your life upside down.

Every day you are presented with choices that could affect you for a long time. You are basically a *decider*. Some decisions are made quickly without much thought, and others hang you up for a long time.

Dealing with choice is part of your cycle of maturation. It helps to remember that making choices is one of the greatest gifts you have as a human being. Making correct and considerate decisions is easier when you

1. Have the fortitude to endure the tension and delay action
2. Think through all the possibilities and consequences
3. Calm down, remember your soul power, and listen to your heart before you take action

No matter what their Sun sign, my clients most frequently ask me, "How do I know what is right for me? How can I decide what to do?" I feel it is never difficult to know what is right. Most of the time you know in your heart when you are making a bad choice, even if you deny it. If there seems to be a conflict between two directions and both feel right, take it as a message that you are not in tune with yourself. Delay your decision for a while. I have a Cancer friend who wisely says, "When in doubt, don't." When you are more relaxed your natural precision takes over. You might also say, like Siddha master Gurumayi Chidvilasananda: "When in doubt, be kind!" Another guide is, "When in doubt, serve." Get out of your own way and look at the big picture. It's easier to see what's best for all concerned.

When you see yourself as limitless and being a co-creator with your soul, life becomes the adventure it is meant to be. You can always feel what's right and trust yourself. The power for change and rectification is not in the past or the future; it is in the moment you are living right now. If you make a mistake, you can almost always succeed the next time. If you don't, try again.

When destiny brings a life-changing moment, you are really being given an opportunity to take action in a creative way. We are responsible for all of our actions. We are responsible for the consequences, but nothing is so fated that it cannot be changed. The power of choice is one of your greatest assets.

Your transforming path is really neutral. It's all in how you look at it. You have the choice to see things as positive or negative in every second.

When your transforming path is activated by life frustrations, a feeling of ignorance controls your mind and it is difficult to make the smallest decision. Frozen in fear, afraid of making a mistake, you go into the extreme black-and-white belief of right or wrong, win or lose. The answer is to give up the outcome. You can't control it anyway. Keep your goal; without the constant fear of making a wrong decision, your soul power will lovingly give you the answers if you listen.

Participation in the Energy Flow

Your life has many cycles that can be observed as streams of energy throughout your lifetime. To observe the energy flow you must look at life from a point outside your regular consciousness. Some people call this objective viewpoint The Witness. From this soulful position we have the clarity to make better choices.

In my mind's eye I have a mental picture of this stream of psychic energy. It is like a river, reflecting every color in the rainbow, yet emanating a beautiful translucent blue.

When I traveled in Egypt it was very apparent where the Nile River was used for irrigation. The vibrant green of the cotton crops and other vegetation ran right up to the desert, as if someone had taken a ruler and drawn a line to where the moisture stopped. Directly at that point was the desert. There was no intermediary condition—it was either green vegetation or yellow desert. When the flow stopped, it was dry and barren.

The Nile is abundantly alive and has a luminous look; it is a very purposeful river. The water runs so fast that it seems like threads that are woven together, like a rope that is being pulled to the sea. This is how I visualize the flow of psychic energy—beautiful, full of colors, refreshing, life-giving, and welcoming. Wherever it flows, life is renewed.

How many times have you had a chance to move with ease, to go with the flow, but picked the desert of hopelessness instead?

If your goal is to stay in the flow, here are some things I have observed in my life and the lives of my clients that may help you.

1. Your soul operates through the power of love, and being watchful gives you the understanding you need to overcome past conditioning.

2. As much as you would like to, you can't make anyone happy; you can only share your happiness and contentment with others.

3. The catalyst for healing old wounds comes through forgiveness; the past is released, putting you back in the flow of appreciating life.

4. As you lovingly observe your life, you reach a point where you have the opportunity to notice that everything happens for the best.

5. When you know that everything that happens is in "divine

order," you can learn to trust your present judgment in achieving your destiny.

6. When you are in the flow and difficulty arises, it is understood that complaining is a waste of time.

7. Loss and frustration are a part of life and come at the proper time. These events are our teachers; this is how we learn.

8. Instead of asking, "Why is this happening to me?" ask, "What can I learn from this?" "How will it strengthen me?" "How can it make me more aware?"

9. The good times are made even better by the strengthening you gain from the hard times.

10. In situations of great despair and stress, when your prospects seem the weakest, you have a chance for your greatest transformations through surrender to higher power.

"Going with the flow" means being able to establish a relationship with the process of life as a whole. Ralph Blum, author of *The Book of Runes*, described the Scandinavian rune called *Flow* this way: "When in deep water, be a diver."

Don't be afraid to dive in! Life processes are cyclical, and what seem like punishments are necessary and important opportunities for purification and growth. They clear the way for rebirth into your soul power and wash away the yearnings of this lifetime and the last that keep you in the continuing cycle of reincarnation.

The Value of Confusion

How many times are we faced with the dilemma of sorting out the reality of a situation? "Should I go or not?" "Is this the right person for me?" "What job or school should I choose?" Remember, truth is always relative to your own personal viewpoint—it is illusory. We are pulled apart by the two sides of our personality, the human condition, made up of our mind and feelings, versus our inner spiritual nature. In this confusion there is no means of escape from doubt and indecision except through *a pure and simple act of faith*. When you practice this god-given gift of free will, there is no one to give you the answer but your own soul.

There is a universal law of chaos or confusion that the Hindus call *maya*, "the great illusion." There is always a veil of illusion in everything that comes into our path, and every moment gives us a chance to break out of this delusion. The question is, do we really want to lose our illusions? Can we face the truth? Our ego blockages certainly relish illusion, and denial is rampant in most people's lives. Every situation we encounter gives us a chance to see ourself: Other people reflect us. We see what we want to see.

Now that we live in the information age it seems as if we are overwhelmed by facts and *disinformation*, all aspects of *maya*. With the information comes the necessity of sorting through facts that may be true, false, or misleading from the media, the politicians, and even from the most trusted sources: our parents, teachers, mates, and indeed, our spiritual teachers. But it is illusions that allow the individual to act by free will. Without the law of chaos or maya we would be trapped in rituals and rules, blind to reality without hope of change, hopelessly confused. I have found that confusion always precedes a decision. It is in this very dilemma of "Is it fact or fiction? Real or unreal? What do I want from this?" that we are stimulated to reach forward and make the soulful decisions that liberate us from the ignorance and confusion left over from past lives. It's like cleaning out your closet: When everything is out on the floor, it's a big mess, but after you sort things out and reassemble them, you have a wonderful feeling of accomplishment.

It seems that the world is a playground for souls who seek to enjoy life separately from the Supreme Being. As souls born into the material world we seek more and more autonomy, more material reality, and more personal power. We become deeply enmeshed in individuality, overdeveloping the ego and extending the reincarnation cycle. Since it is virtually impossible to be happy outside of God-consciousness, our souls have a deep longing to return to the supreme bliss of our heavenly home. It is the soul's longing that seeks to lead us back to God, but this must be done without losing the soul's free will, a delicate balance. Great teachers are sent to help us understand, but through maya, many teachers are misunderstood and rejected. Thankfully, if you want higher knowledge, through universal mercy there is always adequate evidence to distinguish truth from illusion. You can be liberated from your reincarnation cycle, and higher power supports your growth.

In our world today, with our bent for left-brain logic and tendency to ignore the intuition of our right brain, we are sitting ducks for maya. To wake up from our left-brained sleep, we must open our minds to subtler planes and slowly feel our way back into the flow of reality. This flow continues into other realms or spheres of consciousness, and as we evolve we are more attuned to this higher knowledge and God's truth.

Have you ever asked yourself what characteristics you have developed in this life that you would like to take with you throughout eternity? What trait have you developed that you would carry with you, that you would perpetuate in your eternal life? And what memories and yearnings, what unfulfilled desires and emotional attachments, keep you returning to the earthly plane?

This is where the transforming path comes in. If you have attachments, fears, and varying opinions about money, for instance, you could come back as a Taurus with the transforming path of Values. As long as we have earthly desires and confusion (maya), we come back to the scene of the crime. Every moment counts. You become what you think. You create what you fear. I've had many times in my life when I've wished for just five minutes off, but it doesn't work that way. The universe records every thought and every deed perfectly.

You become very sensible when you realize that by participating in the energy flow, the ups and downs in life provide you with the only satisfaction there is—an interesting and varied life with much to figure out.

Evangeline Adams, a great astrologer who practiced in New York City in the 1920s, said: "Knowledge is power, and astrology is the master key to the lock of the truth." Your Sun sign and your chart give you the guidance to arbitrate your fate through the use of vision, self-direction, self-control, and willingness to be connected to your soul power.

Part III

What Your Sun Sign Reveals

A Language of Symbols

Astrology is a remarkable symbolic language that enables us to have an objective perspective of ourselves. It deals with the world of potentials and possibilities, a step beyond our three-dimensional world. Primarily it gives us a prospect of heightened consciousness, an elevated method of self-judgment.

Most people judge themselves too harshly. Have you ever asked what someone's problems are without getting a lengthy response? Just knowing the power and blockage of your sign gives you the clarity to make positive assessments and decisions. It's good to know what's positive about ourselves as well as what's negative.

As a young woman, I wasn't happy with the traits I was supposed to have as a Capricorn—being responsible, practical, methodical, and disciplined. I wasn't too keen on my worst traits either—being inhibited and prone to overachieving—since I knew they were true. What turned me off was that there was no mention of love and fun, which was foremost in my mind at that time. I didn't like my sign.

It took me years of maturing to see how valuable these Capricorn traits are in my life, but I still say that I would like to read just one horoscope column that talks about Capricorn's love life instead of about business.

Through my practice I discovered that I was not alone; few people know how to use the positive aspects of their own Sun sign. Difficulties begin when we deny the power and intelligence that is our natural legacy by holding to the view that we are merely a limited consciousness in a physical body.

No one is ordinary; we are all *multidimensional beings in human form*, on an evolutionary path. Some of this self-doubt can be avoided simply by knowing your Sun sign's special quality, your own powerful gift. You also benefit from the powers of your ascendant, the placement of the Moon, and even your opposite Sun sign.

In my twenty-five years as a professional astrologer I have continually used astrology as a tool for my own psychological and spiritual growth. It takes a lot of courage to look at your own chart and see the cold hard facts about yourself, but there must be a surrender to truth and a real desire to change before the chart tells you as much about yourself as it does about others.

The astrologer benefits personally from astrology, for understanding one's own chart leads to self-knowledge, and this heightened awareness opens the door to the soul. What I learned from my own chart not only helped me understand myself better; it enhanced my readings for my clients. I was able to be more accurate in my interpretations, seeing not only large events but tiny details as well, making the sessions very personal and ultimately uplifting.

By reading thousands of charts, I've learned how to interpret not only your Sun sign personality, but also how key people fit into your life. Just by knowing their birthdays I have enough information to correlate your compatibility with them. Compatibility charts can even be done for you and your dog or cat.

I have had wonderful feedback from my clients over the years. Astrology works! And it is especially helpful in filling in the gaps in your self-understanding. Your relationships with family and in fact everyone in your life show in your chart and also how you relate to them *daily*.

As your blockages or hang-ups are revealed in the readings, you are encouraged to take the action that will offset destructive behavior. One client recently said to me, "Not only does your reading tell me about myself and my future, it inspires me to fulfill my true destiny."

As the astrology charts revealed more and more to me, I began to see how Sun signs pointed to very specific, powerful characteristics that naturally draw people into their higher nature. Over the years I watched the lives of my clients radically evolve with astrological guidance. Astrology is reality therapy. It gives you a chance to see what your strengths and weaknesses are. Rather than being a victim of life operating out of a poor self-image, you can emerge as a powerful human being.

Your Sun sign is a body of consciousness that you could call your "family" sign. Your ascendant, which is determined by your time of birth, describes your looks and your personality. Usually people act more like their ascendant than their Sun sign. (My teacher told me many years ago not to guess people's Sun sign for this reason.) The Moon, which changes signs every two and a half days, determines how you react emotionally to life events. Your Moon position gives you an idea of how you were brought up. It is the sign of family, and particularly the mother. These three together give guidance on how to create a satisfying life. Just knowing these three things about yourself is enough to keep you busy in your search for your soul.

How to Use This Book

Sun sign astrology is based on your birthday. This is the system I have used in this book. With this method it is not necessary to set up a chart, but it's good to know your ascendant, which is determined by the exact time you were born, and the position of your Moon, found by getting a copy of your natal chart.

By simply knowing your date of birth, you can learn a great deal about yourself. You share your Sun sign with people from all over the world. Wherever you go, you can discover a Sun sign buddy. Select your own Sun sign or those of your family and friends. Be aware of the attributes of your loved ones as well as your own.

The next twelve chapters are written about each Sun sign. I have endeavored to give you an understanding of the qualities of each sign, with special emphasis on the ego blockages and the soul power. The complete circle of the zodiac is a cycle of experience. The zodiac is a blueprint of the universe; the signs have a natural sequence and give every type of experience that is needed to induce soul growth. Each sign is a distinct and separate piece of the soul. I suggest you read all the Sun signs, as each sign rules an area of your life—money, home, relationships, career, and so on. With a copy of your chart you can follow each house from your ascendant on and learn a lot about yourself.

Astrology charts are easily available at this time. There are many reputable astrology computer services that will send you a chart for a few dollars, but the best way is to have your chart read by an astrologer and ask for a copy of it.

Because we are so affected by our moods it is good to read your Sun signs more than once. What seems heavy one day could be a source of information that helps you another day. You are not doomed to your ego blockages. If you acknowledge and accept your soul power, you are on the way to a better relationship with yourself.

Each Sun sign is magnetically linked with its opposite, so look up your opposite sign. You can find more on this in Part 4 of this book.

As you look to astrology for new avenues of information and self-help, good luck. I have never been disappointed with astrology, and I welcome you to its wonder and practical efficiency. May *Soul Signs* provide you with a deeper knowledge that will enrich each moment of your stay on Earth.

Aries

March 21–April 20

Fire Sign Ruled by Mars

SOUL POWER: *Courage, Instigation*

EGO BLOCKAGE: *Self-Gratification*

TRANSFORMING PATH: *Consideration*

Aries is the first sign of the zodiac. It may seem curious to you to begin the year on March 21 rather than January 1, but in astrology the energy of springtime, the vernal equinox, when new plant and animal life emerges, is nature's new year. When the precessional age of Aries commenced around 2000 B.C., leaving behind the great age of Taurus, there was a shift from matriarchal societies to male dominance. The Old Testament records that the worship of the bull (Ba'al) ended and the ram was used in sacrificial ceremonies. In Egypt, the house of Amen-Ra began, starting a period of monotheistic worship. This was the beginning of the patriarchal age. Interestingly, in both the Hebrew and Egyptian cultures the leaders were called the Great Shepherd and carried a staff. The Arian soul power of instigation spurred them on for two thousand years to create the male-dominated societies that have held on until the present time in the age of Pisces.

The first moment of any action comes in a fiery flash full of potential. If you notice this precious moment and take advantage of the possibilities it offers, you are assured a successful enterprise. In the zodiac, Aries is considered to be this fiery instigating action, making you a self-starter who risks all to accomplish your goals.

You are fearless. It seems the natural thing for you to initiate, probe, or pioneer. Aries is ruled by Mars, a war god, and symbolized by the ram, which rules the head. Many Arians look like rams with the curls on the sides of their head waiting for horns to appear. You are warriors the day you are born; you like to win, you like to be number one!

Courage is Aries' soul power, and when you desire to accomplish a goal you have what it takes to head right into action. Your power is the start-up energy that begins the cycle of the Sun's path through the twelve constellations. Since the soul power of courage is your lifetime endowment, it is easier for you to overcome your blockages than other signs.

Courage comes from the French word *coeur*, which means "heart." It implies firmness of mind and will in the face of danger or extreme difficulty. Arians have the temperament to hold their own against opposition, interference, or temptation. The power of courage also helps to bear up in periods of your life that are not conducive to adventure or risk. There are many times that you must persevere, let go of The Winner persona, and just hold the fort. When Aries focuses on the importance of the moment and wants to help, solving problems is your specialty.

I don't want to ignore the introverted Aries, who never speak out or try to get attention. You are quietly running the world with your courage and mental astuteness. An Aries client of mine said recently that she would put some of the positive information from the reading I did for her on her List of Boasts. I loved the idea and have such a list going for myself right now in my desk drawer.

A fourth-grade teacher in California asked the class to write on "Hope for the World." Here are excerpts from one little girl's answer. I don't know what sign she is, but she has an Arian spirit.

I am the moon.
I am the sky.
I am someone that no one else has been.
I am the person that gets everything they want.
I am the one and only princess in the world.
I am an astronaut that always goes to Pluto.
I am bigger than anything.
I am a big rule.
I am the world.
I am as nobody could be.
I am a ballerina that never falls when she is dancing.
I am a flower that never dies.
I am a glass that never breaks.
I am books books and more books.
I am someone big.

Gloria Steinem, an Aries, is an example of staying in for the long haul in the women's liberation movement. It's been interesting to see how she has grown personally as the movement has progressed for twenty years. Her youthful looks and ideas are still fresh and appropriate for the younger women of the 1990s.

Aries are fighters for freedom of expression. They are noble warriors in life, full of stubborn persistence, and will not acknowledge defeat. Two Aries men who courageously pioneered new ideas for the world were Thomas Jefferson and Joseph Campbell. Jefferson bravely helped to create the United States by challenging and committing treason against the crown of England. He believed in the rights of the colonies and confidently did something about it. He was the principal author of the Declaration of Independence, yet he had a lively personal life in France, which was very controversial. Arians are always on the cutting edge, and Jefferson was a true Renaissance man, talented in multiple ways. His lovely house in Virginia, Monticello, which he designed, is full of his inventions, and his gardens still delight visitors. He had a noble head with a florid complexion and red hair—truly Arian.

Joseph Campbell's famous statement, "Follow your bliss," is certainly an Arian sentiment. Campbell is known primarily for his work with the mythical Hero, which is a Sun symbol. Campbell's original approach to mythology was needed in a time when joy had been removed from the mystical experience by a too-literal society.

It is perfect that Arian Joseph Campbell writes about the Hero. From childhood, we all have been fascinated and moved by stories of people who are like us in some respects, who seem to accomplish more than we do. These heroes are not all mythical beings, like King Arthur and Lancelot; today many are modern sports figures, astronauts, and even cartoon characters such as Superman. All heroes are seekers of something greater than themselves, and they face enormous odds to accomplish their goal. Aries fits this category perfectly, and since we all have Aries in our natal charts somewhere, you and I are all seekers and consequently the heroes of our own lives. In classical stories, the hero or the king often dies at the end. Perhaps this indicates that the ego is evolving as we conquer each battle in life, and we must die to the old form to begin the new.

Aries—and the Aries in us all—have times in their lives when they are intensely bound to start over again and more or less forced to use their soul power of instigation. After I quit the job I had had for a long time and started working for myself, I dreamt that I was at the bottom of a swimming pool with all the parts of my body separated and drifting. I remember that I was horrified and woke up instantly. I didn't get much relief from my anxiety about the meaning of the dream until I read in Jung about the falling apart, or death of the ego, phase of personal growth. Jung talks about the inflation and deflation of the ego as we go through life passages. My dream of falling apart certainly was a deflation of how I wanted to see myself. The dream meant that my life had gone as far as it could go in the direction I was going. After a peak experience of some sort, whether it is positive or negative, there is a tendency for life to fall apart and be carefully reassembled, in a way to go to new heights. Then, the same process starts over again. This made a lot of sense in my life at the time, so with much relief, I let go of the past, sorted out new goals for myself, and, feeling renewed, went on with my new life.

When your desire to win the prize is fulfilled, then you start over. After every triumph there is a deflation. You are reborn and move on to new ideals; so goes life. Arians are always ready for a challenge. You seldom stay down for any length of time; you are the fighters of the zodiac. You can't stay dejected too long. You'd be too bored.

Perhaps the planet Mars was selected to be the ruler of Aries because physically Mars is a red planet. Red is the color of desire and passion—certainly very descriptive of the Aries approach to life. Most Arians love red.

The symbol for Mars is also the symbol for male energy: a circle with a projected arrow on its side. The circle symbolizes love or completeness, and the arrow indicates moving into action.

I have never met an Aries who didn't have strong ideas about everything. Aries is the energy of "Let's go for it at all cost." A fire sign of great faith, this Sun sign does not ask why but jumps in to enjoy the event for action's sake and learns from the experience itself.

Aries, you are a winner in anything you do; you go for the golden ring. The word *lose* is not in your vocabulary. You seek out careers where there is a lot of action, such as sports, the military, and entrepreneurial businesses. Arians like to work independent of others. They generally don't like authority figures and have the soul power of courage to face the unknown.

Aries rules both England and Germany, and people that are born in these countries are exceptionally individualistic. It's ironic that the hard-headed, independent people of England queue up like lambs without a complaint. It is also interesting to note that the royal family of England has German roots.

The appearance of Aries is dynamic: strong body, long face and neck, and ruddy complexion. There is a reddish shine to your hair, and many Aries dye their hair red or auburn. You Arians are always on the move, your eyes fiery and directly focused on the goal.

You like a lot of action, and Aries male actors are attracted to a challenge. Think about action personalities like Eddie Murphy, Steven Seagal, Andy Garcia, and David Letterman, who never sit down. Aries women, who include Paulina Porizkova, Reba McIntire, Ellen Barkin, and Diana Ross, are stunning in their dramatic demeanor.

Arians are very expressive. You are *feelers* who like to experience physically. You can be naively fearless, often acting without taking the time to be aware of the dangers or implications of your actions. This leads us to the blockage that all you Arians have in accepting your power and accomplishing your goals: self-gratification.

Okay, Aries, get out your boxing gloves. I'll be telling you all the contradictory things about yourself. Take heart. On your plus side, you are the first to take it on the chin then wholeheartedly move forward with inspiration and enthusiasm. You are unstoppable!

The blockage of self-gratification keeps you moving and shaking, stimulating the desire to experience everything you can physically, but mental processing is not your thing. With Arians' tendency toward self-absorption, you have a great deal to learn about relating to others. This attitude of "Me first at all cost," really costs you the happiness of the intimacy a relationship can bring. If you always have to be first, you are by yourself. How can people be close to you if you are always on the move, even if your goals are purposeful? Aries must watch out for egocentric behavior.

The transforming path of Aries is consideration. The word *consideration* means to have careful thought, with patience and sympathetic regard for others. To be a true success, you should slow down long enough to consider other people's needs as well as your own. Self-gratification is the antithesis of consideration. You can deny your egocentric behavior by thinking you are considerate of others, when that couldn't be further from the truth. Take the time to do an inventory of what is really happening in your relationships, and take the time to confirm your conclusions with others. Aries can get off track when they fuse their feelings and attitudes onto other people. This leads to totally wrong assumptions.

When a baby is born, the first (very Aries) action it takes is to cry, screaming for acknowledgment and testing out how it feels to be a separate human being. As an Aries, your early need to be acknowledged follows you throughout life, giving momentum to your desires. Like a baby, you will keep protesting until you get your way.

One of the most profound aspects of Aries energy is the desire to win every battle or conquer any difficulty that arises. Aries likes to be first, resisting any attempt to be stopped or controlled. This attitude throws you head-on into one power struggle after another. Whether the action is good or bad is irrelevant. Discernment flies out the window when the thrill of excitement is the goal.

Your urgent desire to persevere under any condition without accurately assessing the facts keeps getting you into trouble until finally an event occurs that spurs an awakening. Then you have to become more conscious of the total picture in spite of yourself.

The popular television series *Star Trek* is a wonderful example of this bold Arian risk taking. The spaceship *Enterprise* under the commands of Captain Kirk and Captain Picard travels through the galaxies for years, experiencing one adventure after another, barely recovering from one trauma before another crisis arises. This highly successful show has been running for more than twenty years but never once has there been any report on the results of their mission. Their goal seemed to be adventure for adventure's sake. As a grounded earth sign I would have loved to see just *one* show where they carried through with a project and gave the results. Appropriately, William Shatner is an Aries, as are many other actors who worked on *Star Trek.*

Another major blockage of Aries is their obsession with love and sex. One such romance addict was the famous Arian Casanova, born in Italy in 1725. History called him an adventurer, but his lady friends called him a philanderer, not an unfair judgment considering the "take-it-when-you-can" quality of the Aries. But don't think it's only Aries men who are sex-obsessed; there are female Casanovas, too. Out of neediness, both sexes choose impossible objects of affection with no hope of receiving any real love or nurturing in return. As long as your goals are for conquering your lovers, the outcome is assured: disaster and heartbreak.

Often Aries men and women find themselves in relationships with a person who plays hard to get. It really whets your appetite to be the aggressor. Arians often confuse desire for love. Many young Arians come into my office confused about their love life. I teasingly ask them to show me their belt with all the notches, one for each person they've chased and conquered. Then, there's the secret list—the ones who got away.

Aries, you must realize that *winning* love is not the goal of a relationship. You may capture someone's attention for a while, but you can't make anyone love you. If you're lucky or skilled enough to win their love, it puts them into a losing position even though they might not be aware of it at first. Instead of real love, it's "I win—you lose." Then you lose interest and move on to the next acquisition.

Aries feels that love is a challenge. As long as there is a chase and bounty to win, you are excited. When the chase is over and the loved one has succumbed, boredom sets in and the Aries love addict is off to new challenges. This love of the chase used to be considered a male trait, but many of my female Aries clients come for a reading wanting to find out when their next love object will appear. A reassessment of their approach to dating is necessary. A compatible relationship with attraction on both sides may not be as exciting as the chase, but it is much better in the long run. There are always people who like to be pursued. They need extreme attention to build up their ego, but as Aries soon tires of baby-sitting, they are off to new hunting grounds.

It isn't surprising to learn that many people addicted to cocaine and speed are Aries. Your planet Mars rules adrenaline, and getting high can be very exciting to you. I have seen many Aries sick from burned-out adrenal glands from either pushing themselves too hard, drinking too much caffeine, or, worse yet, speeding on drugs. One time I was reading an Aries client, describing the general characteristics of Aries by saying, "You are a speeder," when my client jumped up and said in shock, "How did you know?" I was as surprised by her reaction as she was at what I had said. Seeing her chart and all her ungrounded Arian energy, I was not surprised that she was so burned out she took amphetamines. Addictions can lead you on a merry chase through meaningless jobs, problematic relationships, and other confrontational life situations that are never resolved. Confusion and depression lead you down a self-destructive path. All of this wasted energy wouldn't be necessary if you thought about the consequences of your actions, substituting patience and perseverance for immediate gratification.

What Can Be Done

Now that I've painted a dreary picture of your pitfalls, I will flip over to what you can do to correct them. Since you are endowed with considerable courage, the cure is within your reach once you decide to pursue it. And the strength of your recovery is exactly equal to the strength of your blockage.

Three Steps for Healing Your Blockage

1. As soon as you are aware of the need for self-gratification, know that it is your ego blockage surfacing. It is part of your lower self, heading you into a downward spiral. When a blockage surfaces, you become overwhelmed with anxiety. The first feeling is of ignorance: "How do I handle this without making a fool out of myself?" The second feeling is usually fear. Then come the defense mechanisms.
2. Slow down and use your soul power of courage to transcend your self-negating thoughts and actions. This requires a leap of faith and a commitment to a spiritual path. Courage takes risks, and you have plenty of that ability.
3. Understanding your transforming path of consideration helps to free you from the self-destructive behavior of self-gratification.

This can guide you to your spiritual path. Although Arians are independent, their fate is to be put into life situations where other people's needs seem paramount. Careful consideration must be given to everyone's needs—yours, too—to resolve the issue at hand.

Let me take you through the process. Your blockage is self-gratification and your power is courage. You mustn't worry about having to give up your life of adventure. There's nothing wrong with gratification. It's your lack of consideration that needs healing. You must learn to temper your impetuous nature with forethought and patience and use your transforming path of consideration for others as well as for yourself.

The next step involves the readiness to detach from blindly jumping into self-destructive behavior even though it appears to give you immediate gratification. By using your innate soul power of courage, you can face the challenge of releasing your urgency. You must give yourself time to better evaluate the situation.

Let's imagine a typical Aries scenario. You have a great job in a company you like, but the pay isn't what you want. One day you hear of a job in another company that intrigues you; you would make much more money and have a longer vacation. You make up your mind then and there that the job must be yours. As it happens, the job is not right for your career plan. It pulls you off course. Does this stop you from going after it? No way! It makes you want it even more. After you hear about it, you don't sleep a wink until you have applied for the new job. That's your blockage of immediate gratification kicking in.

How to Apply the Three Steps in This Situation

Let's visualize the scenario again, and this time show you stepping on the brakes and using your head instead of speeding ahead to get your self-gratification fix.

There you are at your great job having just heard of a tempting new position. You find yourself obsessed with winning it at all costs. That "I have to have it" feeling, even though you know in your heart of hearts that it's wrong for you, is the signal that you are on the downward spiral of self-gratification. When you are in conflict, it is important to slow down and ask the soul for help in making your decision.

This time, instead of taking irresponsible action and applying for the job, you recommend a friend who's perfectly suited for it, or you simply decide to wait until you find the job on your career path with more money and a longer vacation that's right for your future.

Congratulations! You've just achieved a terrific breakthrough. You worked through an important lesson by being aware of your power of courage, moving past your blockage of self-gratification, and succeeding in moving forward on your transforming path of consideration.

This compulsive feeling of "I have to have it" could apply to anything: a romantic attachment, a house, a job, a diamond ring—you get the idea. If you find yourself feeling you have to hurry to get something, it's best to slow down and give it some thought.

Aries need to practice *due process*, a legal term meaning research of cause and effect. For instance, you wouldn't go out and buy a company without checking its balance sheet. There is a logical agenda of things to do before you know what you are getting into. When you are able to rise above your need to get your quick adrenaline fix, and take the time necessary to check things out, you are not as likely to end up feeling hopelessly deflated.

I have an Aries daughter who changed jobs every two years until she realized that all that change kept her from growing in the job and forming good personal relationships with her officemates. She was always looking for something new and different, thinking there was something better ahead of her and not knowing how to settle down. Now, she's in a job where she has multiple duties that keep her from being bored, and *she* interviews people for jobs. (Finally, all those interviews paid off!)

It's not necessary to start out all over again with nothing to show for the work you've done. Life is an adventure, and the ups and downs are all just a part of the process. You do have the ability to make better choices. If you think over the possibilities and take the time needed for the right answer, you are, in the words of the little Arian-spirited fourth-grader, "bigger than anything, a big rule, the world."

Dynamic Aries, when you decide to build something lasting, your natural soul powers of courage and instigation are available for your enjoyment. The antidote to overreaching and incessant striving lies in taking the time to stay in touch with your feelings. Your soul power lies in your heart. The true mind is balanced in the heart, and if you are not present in your body, you will not know what your heart feels. Norman Vincent Peale, a great theologian, said, "Throw your heart on what you are doing and then follow it."

Fire symbolizes spirit, and as a fire sign you are a vibrant spiritual being. Let me assure you, Aries, my adventurous spirit, of one thing you can truly count on in life: spiritual growth is the most satisfying fix of all, and the ability to understand your spiritual nature is what Aries is all about!

Taurus

April 21–May 20

Earth Sign Ruled by Venus

SOUL POWER: *Manifestation*

EGO BLOCKAGE: *Self-Indulgence*

TRANSFORMING PATH: *Values*

Taurus, the second sign in the zodiac, is where the creative force of the universe makes a dramatic change, becoming feminine and irresistibly magnetic. When Taureans operate out of the power of the soul, they picture themselves worthy of all that is good on earth. This fundamental sense of deserving creates an ambiance of satisfaction, sensuality, and unlimited ownership. Through their God-given worthiness, Taureans radiate with the soul power of manifestation.

If you Taurean earthlings are mindful of what you need in order to feel safe and content, it is your nature to attract it into your space. Your innate power of manifestation is the ability to visualize what you want and then attract it into your life. As an earth sign your nature is magnetic. You have an extraordinary ability to charm, to induce, and to actually make your requirements materialize.

As Taureans, operating out of your soul power, you are always comfortable on earth, and as you mature you have the ability to accumulate wealth. What you have to watch out for is getting stuck in a "not a penny more, not a penny less" syndrome: making just enough money to cover the bills each month, and if a windfall comes in it pays to put on a new roof. The key to your financial success and security is knowing your highest value. When you see yourself as intrinsically valuable and desirable, your ability to magnetize expands and comes into fruition. Then you manifest all you need and more.

The idea of personal ownership is very important in developing the true values that are a Taurean's transforming path. To have soulful values, there must be careful consideration of other people's needs and a true perspective of what is best for all. Evaluating the intrinsic worth of anything substantial takes careful appraisal and study. Beauty or worth is in the eyes of the beholder. How you value your life and what's in it is up to you. The transforming path is neutral; either you see your world from the standpoint of the soul or you judge everything from the helpless, impoverished viewpoint of the diseased ego. The choices that make up the quality of your life are up to you.

You are born with the divine right to have your own physical and psychic space, and to pursue happiness in the way you see fit, as long as it doesn't hurt anyone else. The sign of Taurus is very powerful. Taurus has a primordial, youthful energy, yet it is perfectly balanced with a wise, old soul essence. Your Taurean key to personal happiness comes from acknowledging that your soul power of manifestation will always support you in the things you want. This brings considerable peace of mind and attracts more abundance.

Taurus is an earth sign, and you love all the things that the earth plane has to offer. When your soul incarnates in a Taurus body, you are required to evaluate everything from a very physical perspective. Being so close to the earth, Taureans are extremely sensitive to Moon phases and Earth vibrations. These subtle vibrations act on the Taurean emotional body, causing unfounded fears to surface. By reacting to your fears, you indulge your deepest sense of helplessness, which is loss of control, and you needlessly give up valuable energy by worrying about the consequences.

When your identity is soul-based, Taurean values stabilize and the focus you put on physical things changes to an appreciation of intangible riches, such as love, trust, and peace of mind. Removing yourself from negative surroundings is imperative for happiness, yet you are often attracted to the very thing that upsets you, such as difficult relationships with heart-wrenching power struggles. After you decide to change from ego-based gratification to soulful consideration of others, you are receptive to what is true and good. Taurean strength is receiving, and as you learn gratitude, the desire to acquire is tempered. You learn the joy of giving to others. Giving freely opens a space for more sources of abundance.

There is solace for Taurean worriers in these universal laws:

1. What is yours will come to you.
2. No one can take away what is yours.

Carl Jung's theory of synchronicity is helpful in understanding how these laws work. Jung said that whatever is born or done at any particular time has the quality of that moment of time. To apply the law to your daily life, you have the power to manifest what you need, and it is yours as long as it resonates with you. *We are what we think.* The quality of your values, your attitude, and your thoughts affects what you draw to yourself. Your very beingness attracts the possibilities of your future. Then *you* have the choice.

Laws that encourage trusting the universe are good for contemplation. It is a good thing to sit in a meditative position, clear your mind, and invoke your higher power to help you with the problems you need to solve. As you release yourself from the blockage of self-indulgence, you can trust the law of grace to work in your life. Whatever you need to feel whole and complete will come to you. You must be careful, as there is another law, one we've all heard before: "Be careful of what you ask for, because you just might get it!" On the other hand, if something was taken away from you before you were ready, it was no longer yours to have.

Taureans are born with an innate desire to be physically satisfied; sensuality is your foremost gift. The first thing a newborn baby does of its own volition is put something into its mouth. The next thing is to hold on to it for as long as possible. Taureans have a deep desire for oral satisfaction or basically any kind of physical enjoyment. You enjoy anything that looks, feels, and tastes good.

Taureans are the artisans of the zodiac. You love to design and are master crafters, whether in the art studio or the kitchen. Your art is often organically based, as in the crafts of making pottery or flower arranging, and there is always a sensual undertone to your painting and sculpting.

Taureans love good food; you like to eat and you are a culinary artist. The secret to your success is your heightened sense of taste. You have an affinity for putting simple, wholesome dishes together, perfectly seasoned.

Taurus is the sign that rules the throat. As well as being gourmands, you are the musicians of the zodiac and often have beautiful singing voices. You can make your living with music. Many of the great singers have a Taurus Sun sign, ascendant, or Moon. Think about Barbra Streisand, Cher, Janet Jackson, Willie Nelson, and Perry Como. Mick Jagger and Elvis Presley stunned the public with their sensual movements; both have a Taurus rising sign.

Some of the most beautiful actresses on the screen are Taurus. Audrey Hepburn, Candace Bergen, Jessica Lange, and Ann-Margret are examples of the lush good looks of the sign. Not only do you Taureans have the natural beauty of luscious skin and hair, but your dramatic flair sets you off in your choice of clothing and environment.

Taurus men and women have beautiful skin, and a penchant for taking good care of it. Look at the bottles of skin care, perfume, bubble bath, and hand-cream products in your bathrooms. Most Taureans are very body-conscious, working out to create a beautiful body. Many of you seek out plastic surgery to look as attractive as possible.

The planet Venus is the ruler of Taurus. Venus worship manifests itself daily in our culture today, and Taureans especially desire to be young and beautiful. The symbol for Venus is a circle (of love) over a cross (life on earth); it is also used as the glyph for woman. If you look closely at the symbol, you can see that it looks like a hand mirror. We have been told that life is a mirror. Perhaps the glyph for Venus reflects this truth. If you look at yourself honestly, you can see more than your physical being; you can see deep within your soul. An honest inventory of your deepest reflection gives you an idea of what you attract, what you will manifest. Will it be from your power or your blockage?

Taurus is the banker of the zodiac, with a consuming interest in real estate and the stock market. The best organizers in the business world are Taureans and you often end up owning the whole bundle. Your success isn't so much your ability to take chances as it is your ability to hold on to tangible things of value, such as real estate, art, or jewelry.

The words that best describe this earthy sign are *lush, lavish,* and *extravagant.* It is hard for you to do anything in a small way. You make wonderful consumers, always looking for beautiful things to buy. Having a good perspective on the true value of products is your forte, and you seem to be able to manifest what you want for a very low price. Many Taurus people are excellent merchants.

Taurus has a strong survival instinct. Although a Taurus values a stable, secure environment, when pressed by life-threatening situations, you lose your judgment and doggedly push on to your own detriment—the Taurus block of self-indulgence. Look at Hitler, a Taurean. He launched a disastrous attack on Russia when it was logical to continue his invasion of England.

The same thing happened as Saddam Hussein, another Taurus, stubbornly controlled his country with propaganda in the Gulf War. His lack of trust in his own soldiers and the assassination of his most important generals left him in a losing position.

With Venus as the ruler of Taurus, it is a bit surprising that there is so much drama and suspense in store for you. Although the Venusian energy of Taurus is tender and sweet, on a bad day it can turn for the worst. As you examine the characteristics of the bull, you find a much more complex personality than might be expected. The picture that comes to mind as you think of a Taurean domain is that of a peaceful kingdom where everything is organically in its place, an idealistic landscape where the lion lies down with the lamb. This pastoral picture is spoiled right away if the bull sees someone intrude into his territory. Interestingly enough, the countries that are ruled by Taurus are Ireland and Israel, beautiful places where political differences create territorial unrest, inevitably producing a toxic environment.

Although Taurus enjoys a peaceful and calm ambiance, if you become threatened this atmosphere can change quickly into a very turbulent scene. God help the person trespassing on your property. As a Taurean, you claim not only your own space; you have even been known to bullishly claim other's space as well. (Think again of Hitler and Hussein.) Your blockage of self-indulgence is really an exaggerated approach to what is the Me and Mine syndrome, or the Precious Child complex. A blocked Taurus has a selfish approach: your money is my money, your land is my land, or simply, anything I can get my hands on is mine. Banking and finance are ruled by Taurus, so it's not surprising when corporate greed runs rampant and the money systems in the world fall into manipulation and usury. Taurus's soul power of manifestation must benefit both parties equally or the outcome is tainted and leads to devastation.

Self-indulgence is a deep-seated emotional need to control your environment and the people in it. Demanding that *your* needs be met is foremost in your mind. When you doggedly bite off more than you can chew, an urgent feeling of scarcity and deficiency prevails. Imagining yourself deprived, you act like the most mistreated person in the whole world, ignoring your fabulous power of manifestation and compulsively creating your own downfall. I call this the "Nobody loves me, everybody hates me, I'm going to go out to the garden and eat some worms" drama. You purposefully dig a hole and hopelessly roll around in the mud bemoaning your misfortune, like a child waiting to be rescued. Being so accustomed to chaos and disaster, your depression keeps you stuck in disappointment. You Taureans were probably the first people to take Prozac.

A Taurean's tendency to overreact is based on your tendency to fearfully take everything at face value. When difficulties arise in your domain a fight-or-flight reaction keeps you compulsively running into oblivion. In a turbulent, fast-paced, and troubled world ruled by urgency, it is easy to lose sight of true values. After years of fearfully creating a downward spiral of unrelenting pressure, you can become physically and emotionally ill.

A lot of my Taurus clients are diagnosed with Epstein-Barr or chronic fatigue syndrome. Living life in the fast lane with the constant stress of survival is very depleting for the mind-body connection. Other, more staid Taureans are just as hard on themselves, hiding out and worrying about things they can't control until they are mentally and emotionally worn out.

I jokingly call Taurus the Princess and the Pea sign. Hans Christian Andersen wrote a lovely fairy tale about a beautiful princess who could not sleep a wink all night long because there was a tiny pea underneath her mattress. The discomfort of a tiny bump was very apparent to her because of her precious royal blood. Often our precious Taurus friends react to slight disruptions and have been called princes or princesses behind their back.

I'm afraid not many of us want to confront testy Taurus.

Taureans must face their blockage of self-indulgence before it leads to loneliness and despair. In a Taurean's life lessons there will always be situations that force evaluation of self-worth and worthiness. I don't know why so many Taurus people think poorly of themselves. In your negative egotism you act like you have the most important inferiority complex of all. Perhaps it is your urgent need to feel safe and secure in an unsafe world. Neither money, nor sex, nor unlimited power is the answer, although a Taurus might think so.

Being kind to yourself, identifying with your own fundamental goodness and a renewed sense of deserving what is perfect for you, transforms your values. Simply delaying gratification opens up unlimited avenues for attaining the heights of your desires.

It is not wrong to care for your own needs, but it is necessary to heal feelings of inner impoverishment. As you learn to respect yourself, you will experience a feeling of well-being that is an essential part of attracting what you want and what is truly yours.

One of the greatest beings who ever walked the earth was the Buddha. He was born under the sign of Taurus. His teachings, as well as all the other mystical paths of the world, make it clear that there is an enormous reservoir of power within you. If you can learn to use it properly, it can transform you and the world around you.

What Can Be Done

Taureans are always wanting something. However, if you are asked what it is you want, it is hard for you to narrow it down.

If you want to change and face your blockage you must know what your needs and wants are, more so than any other sign. It's important to remember that the strength of your power is exactly equal to the strength of the blockage. Trusting your soul power of manifestation is the key to healing the self-indulgent tendencies that are undermining your pursuit of happiness. There is no lack in the universe.

Three Steps for Healing Your Blockage

1. Recognize your blockage of self-indulgence as soon as it surfaces. It is a part of your lower self and will cause you a lot of unhappiness.
2. Trust your soul power of manifestation to transcend your fear of want. In order to surpass your self-indulgence, learn to have confidence in your ability to manifest everything you need.
3. To free yourself from self-indulgent behavior and open to your spiritual path, you must change your values. This is your transforming path. As your values improve and you surrender your defensive ways, the world opens up to you.

Okay, Taurus, you deserve all good things, but enough is enough. Your blockage is self-indulgence and your power is manifestation. Your emotionally indulgent ways creep up on you when you least expect it—for instance, when you're shopping for stockings and you buy a fur coat! Or when your boss asks you in an angry voice to rewrite a letter for the third time and you quit on the spot even though you will have to take a lower-paying job in this market! Your transforming path of values makes it necessary for you to appraise the situation with more mature eyes. If you don't, you will create the same undermining situations over and over again.

The word *value* means "to rate or appraise." It also means to estimate and appreciate. By being objective and not so enmeshed with your fear of rejection, you can sort out what is best for all concerned.

Your indulgences aren't fun for long. There is always a reckoning day when the bills have to be paid. The power of manifestation is working at all times to supply you with everything you need to have a happy and fulfilled life! There is no need for urgent indulgences.

Here is a Taurus story I have heard many times. You have broken up with a man who is not right for you. He wasn't there for you when you needed him and he constantly rejected you by flirting with others. But you want him back! Saying, "I want him at any cost," you give in to the indulgent part of your personality and set up a no-win situation for yourself. The denial sets in as you indulge your fantasies of how sweet he was on your birthday when he gave you flowers. You totally ignore the fact that he didn't ask you to his office New Year's party. One indulgence sets off another, and it isn't too long before you've gained ten pounds and hate yourself more every day.

How to Apply the Three Steps in This Situation

This isn't simple, of course. Deep-seated fears about your self-worth are at play here. With a history of abuse (and overly sensitive people always feel abused), whether it is emotional or physical, there is a lot of guilt and self-hatred to work out. In this case I would suggest a therapist to alleviate the damage of the past. It is time for a total evaluation of your goals and time for a hard look at your self-undermining tendencies.

Taurus is the sign of love, and a relationship is very important for personal happiness. You deserve the love you want. By delaying external gratification and internalizing love for yourself and others, you can begin to heal this dilemma.

As you learn to value yourself more, the patience to process your problems is self-evident. Trusting your soul power is the beginning. You deserve love and have the ability to manifest what is good and true in your life. There is no need for you to hold on to what hurts you and grab at crumbs of happiness. These simple steps of inquiry will set up a plateau for you to attract a purposeful and satisfying love life.

1. Just say no to negative situations at the beginning or as soon as you are aware of them.
2. Bring positive people and surroundings into your life. This is an absolute necessity for the support you need and will build your self-esteem.
3. Ask yourself this question: "Is this person, place, or thing loving to me?" If not, walk away and don't look back.
4. You are love. Accept this and be willing to receive everything you need.
5. Emotional reactions must not supersede the facts of the actual situation. Be practical. Don't indulge yourself!

A *good thing* is something that conforms to the moral order of the universe. *Good* is another word for *God*. Believing in your own worth ensures you can operate out of your incredible power of manifestation, bringing all that is good and true into your life.

As you learn to operate out of soul consciousness, attachments disappear and the world is yours.

Gemini

May 21—June 20

Air Sign Ruled by Mercury

SOUL POWER: *Inspiration*

EGO BLOCKAGE: *Scattered, Easily Influenced*

TRANSFORMING PATH: *Authentic Communication*

Without a doubt, the most charming of all the Sun signs is Gemini. When you invite a Gemini into your life, your social life perks up, you laugh more, and life is just more fun. Gemini is a dualistic sign symbolized by the twins and the roman numeral II. The Gemini personality is youthful, with a lively mental curiosity about life. Gemini's planetary ruler is Mercury, the planet closest to the Sun with the fastest orbit in our solar system, a planet that the ancient astrologers perceived to govern the mind.

Mercury was the messenger of the gods in Greek mythology. Often called capricious, he was curious, inquisitive, and somewhat amoral in nature. Mercury wore a winged cap and winged shoes, symbols of swiftness. The winged cap is very powerful, derived from an ancient bird symbol representing the agility and expeditiousness of the mind that has been handed down through the ages, similar to the ibis-headed god Thoth of Egyptian mythology.

Mercury has magical powers as the guide and messenger between the three worlds: Olympus (the higher world), Earth (the middle world), and Hades (the lower world). His messages were mostly love notes to the many gods and goddesses on Mount Olympus, and his exploitation of the gods themselves gave him his dubious reputation. This accounts for Gemini's love of news and gossip.

Mercury's attributes of cleverness and imagination manifest in the Gemini personality in multiple ways, creating a many-faceted personality that enjoys variety and diversification. Gemini is always curious about what is going on in the immediate environment and concerned about the close relationships of brothers, sisters, aunts, and uncles. Even neighbors or neighborhoods are considered to be very important in your life.

The mercurial Gemini nature has the ability to casually adapt to life's ever-changing circumstances, gathering all kinds of varied impressions and thriving on change. It has been said that you are always looking for your twin; this accounts for the wanderlust you can fall into as you long for your lost or unobtainable sibling.

The power of Gemini is inspiration. Geminis are gifted speakers and do very well in any business where you make a living doing spontaneous, unrehearsed speaking. They are physically and mentally agile, and they can turn on a dime if it is needed to correct an uncomfortable situation. I have a Gemini lawyer who has helped me through many difficult decisions. When I tell her the terrible problem, she is unfazed. She cocks her head for one minute as her mind whirls with possibilities and then cheerfully says, "Okay, here's what we will do." I'm always impressed by her inspired solutions. Geminis always have an answer for every question, an idea for every problem; without getting emotionally involved, they are incredibly quick-minded. Their computer minds never come up short on the information needed to solve a problem.

With your Gemini cleverness you have tremendous potential for success in any area you choose. You are talented in so many ways with mind and body, it is very difficult for you to decide which talent you will develop. The careers you could choose are endless. Gemini rules the hands; consequently you are talented in anything you can do with the fingers, any kind of artistry—cooking, writing, and painting. But what you do best is talk.

My mother had a Gemini moon. She loved to write long letters full of minutiae about her daily life at home in Arkansas, and I looked forward to reading in perfect detail what she and my father did daily, down to the exact description of the food she prepared. When I was living in another city in my early twenties, her words helped heal my longing for home.

To understand Gemini you must understand how the intellect works. Because of the mind's complexity, it is necessary to define its characteristics. The mind is conscious mental activity that perceives, thinks, wills, and, most important, reasons. The mind cannot feel; it only records. It can record feelings, but the more subjective parts of the mind are very complex, and few people understand how they work. This is not to say the subconscious is not a part of the mind; but much in it is not remembered at will.

The mind alone, separated from subconscious understanding of the heart and soul, leads us to dual conclusions of either right or wrong, positive or negative, past or future. The twins are the perfect symbol for Gemini's dualistic nature, which keeps you in a constant state of restlessness. The mind must be stilled to be in the present; therein lies the truth.

The transforming path of authentic communication encourages Gemini to be more discerning. *Webster's* definition of truth is "a transcendent, fundamental, or spiritual reality." To speak the truth requires serious consideration of the facts, knowing what is the right action and what is destructive. Truth is the highest goal of communication, and Gemini must learn to define it accurately to attain the positive aspects of your transforming path. Sometimes, trying to please everyone, Gemini misconstrues the truth.

Keeping close to the facts without emotional avoidance avoids distortion or misrepresentation. When you are disconnected from truth you are in danger of leaving a trail strewn with half-truths and confusion. Being present in the truth of the moment and knowing your personal responsibility to it is a great power. On the other hand, this ability to distort the truth can be very amusing. Gemini are great storytellers, and many are hysterically funny. Comedians like Joan Rivers, Bob Hope, and Stan Laurel have a take on life situations that is biting, yet entertaining.

The Gemini dilemma comes from fantasizing about the future because Geminis think the present moment is boring. It is easy to be pulled in other directions when you rationalize that what is ahead offers greater possibilities. This creates a lot of havoc for you and for others as you incessantly jump from one thing to another. Like your opposite sign, Sagittarius, you think that the grass is greener on the other side, and you can't resist a look.

It's important to understand that the past and the future are fragmented. It is impossible to remember every minute detail of a prior event, even if it happened the day before. The future is always flexible and must be, for us to use our free will. Even what we see with our eyes is not an absolutely true or total picture. Our brain records the important visual elements of each scene and logically fills in the rest of the picture, based on personal experience and beliefs, much the way an astrologer correlates the symbols in a chart. Ask any detective who's interviewed witnesses at a crime scene.

Gemini's tragic flaw is self-sabotage. You see what you want to see and hear what you want to hear. Your wonderful editing ability can work against you. Your agile mind will circle around endlessly, giving you new information until you are exhausted. When you learn this about yourself, you can be inspired to have more patience with the facts at hand. To give each idea more time you must stop the mind whirl and enter the powerful present time. Take the time needed to correctly gather the best information possible. Remember, you have all the time you need when you are centered in the moment. You can stretch time instead of speeding through it.

Gemini's openness to scattering forces and being easily swayed keeps your life in chaos. When you are in a hurry and make hasty choices, you soon find out that quick decisions have long-term consequences. Gemini's favorite question is "What's happening?"—but don't get your feelings hurt if your answer is ignored. Geminis always have the story all figured out, and they interrupt with some delicious bit of news that is so fascinating that you let your own boring story go by the wayside.

It is very appealing, this habit of hurry, hurry and what's happening. Many cultures thrive on it, particularly Americans. The United States has a Gemini ascendant. Italy and Greece are two other very gregarious countries that are ruled by Gemini, where community and communication are their major interests.

Remember, we all have Gemini in our chart somewhere. It's what gossip columnists base their businesses on. The media and the world of information are ruled by Gemini—those notorious tabloids sold at the grocery stores and newsstands, which tantalize impulse buyers, couldn't be published without this cultural addiction to information. Magazines, newspapers, television, even the telephone company are Gemini, thus Mercury-ruled. The telephone company uses Mercury as a symbol of its services. The press is included in Gemini rulership; that is why it's almost impossible to confront the media: They've already moved ahead to the next story.

The winged cap that Mercury wears endows Gemini with the power of invisibility. Although this power implies going into higher realms for superior information, on the contrary, you may use the magic of Mercury to disappear when it's time to face the havoc that you are responsible for. Confronting any Gemini group or person operating out of their blockage of scattering forces is next to impossible. You're gone, en route to the next event; the past is done, that's old news—"Hey, what's happening?"

The Gemini world is mobile and transitory, thus travel is an important part of a Gemini's life. Airplanes, trains, and cars are ruled by Gemini. You love to travel and seem to attract it as a part of your work as well as your personal life. Gemini's expertise is to observe facts and link them together. Traveling helps to broaden your experience. Geminis have an almost uncanny way of picking up on things not spoken. If thoughts are in the air, as we've been told, Gemini is likely to hear them.

Geminis are rarely stuck in the past; you are more likely to be living in the future. The antidote to scattering your energy is to be totally aware, grounded in the present moment, and use your concrete intelligence. When you analyze the situation honestly, your communication is inspirational, but this can only come when you are ready to change yourself. It is ironic that you seem to have eyes in the back of your head as far as others are concerned, but when it come to self-observation you draw a blank. Your intentions are good, but you are just in such a hurry that introspection is put back somewhere with sewing buttons on your raincoat, putting pictures in photo albums, and other impossible-to-cope-with details that you never get around to.

Change and variety are the mottoes of this versatile sign, but Gemini's friends better watch out! Change can mean that you are eating alone after your Gemini buddy calls and cancels again. Old-time astrologers used to say, "Never trust a Gemini!" This is an unfair accusation of the balanced type, but scattered Gemini is just like a butterfly (one of its symbols) flitting after this week's most appealing flower in the vicinity, and it may not be you.

There is a thrill in scattering the mind into the future or in reviewing the past (although Gemini is a future sign). You like to move on. When you are unfocused, responding to all the stimulation available in our modern world and being easily swayed by others, it is like being on a dry drunk. Life becomes a merry-go-round, a ride that never ends until the broken promises, lost opportunities, and half truths build a wall that is a prison to the soul.

Gemini energy is many-faceted; you seem to have many personalities, not unlike the character in *The Three Faces of Eve*. This kind of neurotic behavior creates mental confusion so intense that logical decision making is impossible. With so many choices and so little time, Gemini is pulled apart and becomes hopelessly scattered and ineffective. Staying focused on one thing is almost impossible for you if you don't understand your soul-based power of inspiration.

We live in a time when the concrete mind is venerated and we are encouraged to be linear in our thoughts and neglect the nonlinear, more creative right brain. The mind works better when both sides are balanced, but few people are able to consciously integrate right- and left-brain thinking at this time in our evolution. Our left-brained world has been taught to always look ahead to the future; this outlook is like chasing rainbows, it is exciting but at the same time discouraging. There is a sense of futility in seeking what is out of reach; when you do accomplish your goal you look for something else even more exciting. This search for something more or better keeps you separated from the soul, the source of your creativity and your soul power of inspiration.

Geminis are great at coming up with ideas, but not at following through on those ideas. The only way to stop the endless scattering is by finishing each project as it comes up instead of leaping forward into another one just to keep the excitement level high. Gemini likes to speed through life just like Aries. I always tell my Gemini clients that you can manage two careers and one hobby—then you have to draw the line.

Fear is often hidden behind your excessive activity, and you may be sad behind your cheerful face and debonair demeanor. The twins have an underlying fear of being trapped in a boring position with no way out. It is this paranoia that makes you choose difficult situations instead of making the wise choices you are capable of. There is always the enchantment of a new job, a new relationship, a new home. When you are off track, it is very hard on your friends and family, as they can see you, a delightfully irresistible person, on a road to self-destruction.

It isn't easy to confront you charming, changeable, and capricious beings. In the first place, you aren't easy to stop; you are in a hurry to do something that is extremely important, and you're late, so it's hard to find the right time; and secondly you won't listen anyway. Your mind is somewhere else, in a less boring place than here.

The search for excitement makes you a sitting duck for drug addiction. Many Geminis are attracted to drinking and drugs, speeding up your lives to impossible limits and making the merry-go-round go even faster. One of the most exciting, sexy, and funny stars of the twentieth century was Gemini Marilyn Monroe, before alcoholism and drug addiction took her life. Monroe had the ability to transform right in front of your eyes, from an average pretty girl (maybe a little plump) into a glowing beauty. This amazing transformation seemed to come at will, especially when there was a camera around.

Geminis like John Kennedy and Donald Trump seem to attract duality, especially with women. Many Geminis have hidden agendas and find it hard to be faithful in a relationship. Another interesting tidbit: Geminis usually have dual letters in their name. Marilyn Monroe, for instance, has two Ms, two Ns, and two Rs.

Not only are Geminis charming and attractive; they are often very beautiful. Gemini tens are Nicole Kidman, Annette Bening, and superb Naomi Campbell. Gemini Clint Eastwood is in an act by himself—gorgeous.

You Geminis love to gather data; but by asking so many people for advice you end up more confused than you were before, swinging back and forth as you receive different input. This exacerbates the issue and makes it twice as hard to sort out. In your duplicity you like to have two of everything—two doctors, two therapists, and even two astrologers for advice. Sometimes there are even more than two, as Gemini rules multiplicity in general. In fact, there are so many varied opinions from so many people that it is impossible to sort through all the information, so what's the use of your inquiry; you go your own way and do whatever you want to anyway.

What Can Be Done

Gemini has one of the brightest minds in the zodiac. Their soul power of inspiration is the answer to healing the compulsive need to want more information than is necessary. The answers are already inside. It's important to remember that the strength of your power is exactly equal to the blockage. Trusting the power of inspiration, your natural gift opens up a self-satisfaction so deep that there is no need to scatter your potential or be swayed by others.

You are inspirational right now in every way. There is much metaphysical knowledge and guidance waiting for your attention. Get the facts but let your heart and soul be your guide.

Three Steps for Healing Your Blockage

1. As soon as you observe yourself feeling scattered and changing direction, recognize your ego blockage surfacing. It is part of your lower self and is heading you into a downward spiral. Fear of being bored or trapped sets off a chemical reaction that triggers urgency.

2. Harness your soul power of inspiration to transcend your negative thoughts and actions. Gemini is never at a loss for an idea. Scan your creative mind and slow down. Take time for reflection. Allow your soul power of inspiration to help you transcend your negative thoughts and actions.

3. Be honest with yourself; then when you want to be heard, you will have a ring of truth in your voice. Your transforming path of authentic communication is neutral. You are not being punished by having to make so many choices. These are opportunities that life sets up for you to have inner and outer resolution. Gemini is ruled by the planet Mercury, who rules the mind. He is also called the ruler of the crossroads. With a Gemini there seems to be one crossroad after another. To free yourself from scattering your energies, you must take an inventory of what you want to accomplish. You must stop rushing through life by the seat of your pants or no one will listen or take you seriously.

Now let me take you through the process of growth and change. Your blockage is scattering forces and your power is inspiration. Geminis want to be aware on all levels but drop the ball by taking on more than they can do. The information boom we are going through in the 1990s is a magnet to Gemini. What good is all that information without a commitment to yourself? More data is not what you need. Instead, learn how to narrow things down and create a life that is emotionally sound and grounded in reality.

The Gemini saga of checkered work patterns and fractured relationships is repeated with every twin until you come to the conclusion that time is relative. There is always plenty of time to meet your goals. Everything you need is within your reach, and all you have to do is to see yourself as worthy of the time needed.

I have a Gemini client who is a wonderful man. He is a psychotherapist and has a large clientele. His dilemma is how to marry again. He doesn't have time. He was orphaned at an early age and his major fear is abandonment. Although he knows the basic reason for his fear, he plays all sorts of games of denial with himself so he won't have another failed marriage or broken relationship. He's still the little boy who was left by his parents. Although he has been a devoted father, he fills his life with so many home and family-related activities, he doesn't have time for his own emotional life. When he finds someone he likes, he comes on strong, then drops the ball. "I'll see you when I have more time," or "I'd love to get together but my son is going off to college, and we have so much to do." The outcome is depletion and loneliness. When he met a women who was perfect for him, he acted out his blockage of scattering forces and there was not enough time to see her. Of course, he was running scared!

How to Apply the Three Steps in This Situation

Hidden in the inspirational soul power of Gemini is the motivation that can transcend scarcity or rejection. Gemini, you have the power to take action and get the answers for yourself with your active mind and body. The energy needed to have your own emotional needs met is available to you if you release the past hurts and calmly plan what you want to do. Helping others is a wonderful thing for self-healing. It opens your soul power of inspiration. But living in a space of deprivation and continually wanting more eventually dries up the power needed to heal others.

The Gemini therapist eventually will get burned out. Not only is he personally scattered, but his profession is one that tends to overwork. He seems more interested in delving into others' problems than facing the anxiety that pushes him over the top. Being so easily influenced by other people's needs keeps him from confronting his own problems. Searching for more time, more friends, more money is a never-ending task, leading to certain burnout until life pulls the plug.

The following are helpful guidelines for your transforming path.

1. The answer is inside your own soul, not in the endless pursuit of solutions outside of yourself.
2. This moment is the most powerful asset you have to accomplish your goals. Now is the most positive time.
3. Face your feelings. They are there to help you weigh your choices.
4. Your feelings are not necessarily true for others, but they are true for you in your own experience. Use them to guide you.
5. Put love first in your life. Work and other mind-expanding pursuits can wait.

The word *inspire* means the intake of air or breath. Being inspirational is your thing; it follows that you could benefit from deep-breathing exercises, particularly since the sign of Gemini rules the lungs. Breathing deeply centers your consciousness in your body, creating a clear mind that makes decision making easier. Yoga is a great discipline for you Geminis.

Another point to consider is that there is always plenty of time. When we work through our soul power of inspiration, there is exactly enough time to accomplish your goals. So breathe easy.

Beware! Your friends get tired of trying to give you advice, for even if you ask for it you seldom take it! What you really need is a sounding board; then you can figure out the answer. This is greatly aided when you open your heart. A certain time set aside every day for silent contemplation of subjects that give you joy is a must for Geminis. Reading books on spiritual subjects (One at a time, please!) heals your indecision and helps you find hope and blessed discrimination.

Remember, you are inspirational when you calmly set out to share the wonderful ideas and words that spring like a fountain from your heart.

Cancer

June 21–July 22

Water Sign Ruled by the Moon

SOUL POWER: *Nurturing*

EGO BLOCKAGE: *Oversensitivity, Manipulation*

TRANSFORMING PATH: *Family Relationships*

Cancer, the Moon Sign, rests at the base of the zodiac, forming a foundation that supports all the other Sun signs. Enigmatic and understated, you Cancerians give the impression of being passive or easily manipulated. But no matter how much you restrain yourself, this clearly is not the case. Sensitive, yes! But sensitivity can be a great asset in life. It takes a Cancer a long time to open up, but underneath that cool exterior lies a passionate and very empathetic human being. Remember, beneath your hard crab shell, you are very tender, yet when you find a comfortable place to station yourself, your perseverance can move mountains.

Cancerians are water signs. Water symbolically rules the emotions, putting Cancers in touch with their deeper feelings at all times. The element of water is very adaptable yet durable, and Cancer has tremendous tenacity that can stand the test of time. It was water that carved the Grand Canyon; it took eons, but that made it even more spectacular. We really live in a water world; our bodies are 90 percent water, and most of the world is covered in oceans, seas, or lakes. It's your world, Cancer, bank on it.

Cancer has the capacity to feel, care, and build emotional bonds with others. This is where your soul power of nurturing comes in. With Cancer's grounded position in the chart, it seems to be your destiny to nurture and support others. To manifest your soul power there has to be profound awareness of the well-being of others and a desire to contribute to their progress and development. Cancers have this ability naturally. Your gift is a compassionate nature that supports others with equity and consideration.

You take it upon yourself to be very thoughtful when it comes to making any situation better. You have a well-developed protective streak and are emotionally attached to the welfare of your loved ones.

The Cancerian look is full-bodied, with large eyes. There seem to be two types of Cancers. One type looks like the full moon with a round face, and the other a long face that looks very much like the man in the moon. I have found more Cancerians with the long face: Jerry Hall, Sylvester Stallone, Princess Diana, and Anjelica Huston. Round-faced Cancerians include Robin Williams, Pamela Anderson, and Kim Alexis. Then there are the mixes: Tom Hanks, Betty Buckley, and Chris O'Donnell, all very good-looking folks.

The first four Sun signs—Aries, Taurus, Gemini, and Cancer—are called *primal*. Human development starts at Aries with physical awareness, Taurus with physical possessions, and Gemini's desire to analyze and speak. Cancer consciousness possesses a deep inner awareness called *emotion*. Cancerian people have unseen antennae that reach out and absorb the vibrations in their surroundings. Spongelike, you unknowingly absorb from your environment and are overloaded with emotional impressions. Often you can't distinguish your own emotional input from that of the people around you. Some people live in a fish bowl; you Cancers live your lives in a soup bowl. You are extremely sensitive to your surroundings, drawing unseen fluctuations into your consciousness like psychic experiences.

When I took my family on a sightseeing trip to the Alamo in San Antonio, Texas, my younger daughter (who has a Cancer ascendant) ran up to me with a sorrowful expression and said, "Mom, I can feel the poor people who died in this building." I was feeling the same way, with chills on my arms, but I was shocked to find that she understood what she was feeling. She was only 10 years old. I realized then how much she was being affected in ways I couldn't control.

You must take into consideration that you are affected by everything that is going on in your environment, and that processing this information takes time and thought. Cancer is forced to identify each emotion as it arises to know what to make of it. Out of this deep responsive caring, personal feelings of duty, responsibility, and devotion are developed. On the other hand, when you are emotionally engulfed by others' feelings as well as your own, quick and easy solutions are hard to come by. It's like dealing with a flood.

Cancerians naturally attract whatever is necessary to arrange a safe haven; you are nesters. Your apples don't fall too far from the tree, if you have your way about it. Cancers are very attached to the past and there is a deep-seated desire to honor tradition. The desire to hold on to what is familiar makes you very cautious, and changes are discouraged. Regard for your elders creates a traditional approach where experience is respected and the ability to recall what happened in the past is revered.

History is a favorite subject of Cancerians. You like to celebrate holidays in an old-fashioned way, without changing what your parents did. You want to raise your children just as you were raised. Family rituals are very meaningful to you. If you opened your packages on Christmas eve, it had great meaning and can't be changed to Christmas morning. This may be well and good, but problems arise if you are still emotionally bound up in doing what pleases your loved ones or living in the past without considering your own needs of the moment.

The tribal peoples of the world are ruled by Cancer. There are many tribes that are still intact all over the world, trying to hold on to a way of life that is endangered by modern technical advances, which push them further away from their native soil. Peoples in Brazil, Thailand, and Central America face this dilemma, while in our own country, Native Americans have been pushed aside and discredited for centuries.

In tribal consciousness there is a fervor to honor heroes of the past. Shamans perform elaborate ceremonies to invoke the spirits of the dead and take participants into the unseen realms of other worlds. Veneration of deceased loved ones slowly developed over time into ancestral worship, particularly in Asia. The United States is also a Cancerian country where history is venerated and the family is honored. The United States, in true Cancerian fashion, provides good homes for more people than any other country in the world.

Cancer's deepest desire is to set down roots. You have an urgent need to have a protective space where you can relax and feel protected from the elements, a safe place where children can be conceived and nurtured. The Sun sign Cancer rules the socialization stage of establishing a home, where immediate family and close friends are accepted and protected. In the early ages of human development, as long as people lived in environmentally enclosed family units, they considered all others on the outside to be enemies. They could destroy their enemies, even their neighbors, and sometimes their alienated kin, without remorse.

The world today, still operating out of Cancerian tribal consciousness, seems to have dropped back into primitive times. The adolescent gangs in the United States operate on this principle. It seems that thousands of years of advancement in values and ethics can fall away in the blink of an eye. If you are not of the same political persuasion, ethnic group, or religious faith you can destroy your own countrypeople without remorse. This isn't to say that Cancerians are murderers, but it illustrates that Cancer is an emotionally *reactive* sign, with an underlying tendency to want control, which can breed ruthlessness and manipulation. You can be so emotionally bonded with family that in extreme cases all others are considered enemies.

Cancers are very adept at manifestation, especially when it comes to attracting a good home. Your talents don't stop there. Like Taurus, you are very magnetic and seem to attract whatever you need. This is particularly true if you can come to accept your natural ability to pull in what you want. You are gifted in buying property, with a sixth sense that helps you with timing and selection. You often make money in real estate; your precognition facilitates selling at the right time.

Although Cancer rules home and family, there are other more complex meanings. Old astrology books say that the fourth house rules beginnings and endings; it is the house where the soul enters and leaves the chart. Since Cancer rules the mother, it is easy to see the correlation with beginnings, the birth of the soul. However, the endings take some thought. Perhaps when we die it is like another birth into a new dimension. Doctors are finding that many people who are incurably ill prefer a home setting for the most important task of leaving earth, instead of remaining in a very expensive but emotionally cold hospital atmosphere.

Traditionally, Cancers are intuitive people who love family and children and are always focused on home. This homey image of Cancer as a sign ruled by the moon and a universal symbol for mothers has changed since World War II, when women were forced to join the workforce. After the war they didn't want to give up the freedom that jobs outside the home provided for them. In most families today both husband and wife are needed to support the family. As we see more and more women look for sustenance outside of their homes, many are becoming very successful.

In the competitive work world today, career goals take up so much time that marriage and children are put off. The next thing you Cancerian women know, you are in a rat race, with your biological clock ticking and time running out.

Many of my clients in New York wait until they are in their mid to late thirties to marry, and one of their constant questions is, "Can I have children?" I have read charts for several Cancerian women in their late thirties who have twins and triplets; one even had quadruplets. I don't know whether the cause is the mother's age, fertility drugs, or heredity. All of them have important careers and are still working.

The sign Cancer rules motherhood, but you are also the housekeepers, holding the keys to house and cupboard. You are the executives of the home. You have a strong need to provide food and protection with this energy. You are gourmets and first-class cooks. You enjoy working with food. Many Cancerians own restaurants, particularly family-owned ones. Cancerian men are very enterprising and often own their own businesses. If you walk into an office and see a woman in charge, she might very well be a Cancerian. Instead of being an executive in the home, Cancerian women are now executives in major corporations. Cancer as a cardinal sign is shrewd in spotting potential, and this gives them a sound business sense. Cancers are very ambitious for themselves as well as for their families.

A good example of a Cancer woman who had broken through a stereotype and stood up for herself was Princess Diana. She had outgrown her nickname, "Shy Di." Although she had been considered a lightweight by the British royal family, she passionately claimed her power by declaring her strength to the whole world on national television in an effective political move. Her own lack of confidence as a young woman had helped her develop a talent for working with the downtrodden. In a quiet and gentle way, her Cancerian personality charmed the world. Although she was very traditional in her desire to be a good mother, she felt that her talents allowed her to be a goodwill ambassador to her own country and others. She was a good example of a late-blooming Cancer who found herself as she neared her fortieth year. The world misses her sweet and gentle Cancerian ways.

Cancer's lunar vision is exceptionally good for speculation in real estate and the financial market. Very successful entrepreneurs are often Cancerian. Ross Perot is a triple Cancer, with Sun, Moon, and ascendant in the Moon sign. John D. Rockefeller was also a Cancer. He started an empire based on the oil business, and now the Rockefeller Foundation in New York (a Cancer city) owns some of the United States's most valuable property. It is said that there are more self-made millionaires in the sign of Cancer than any other. Many of you successful Cancerians are in the second half of life before you accomplish your goal. I have a client, a man now in his eighties, who became very successful late in life. At the end of his seventies his fund-raising business finally took off, much to his delight. Cancer's success potential is open-ended and continues throughout life.

Cancerians are seriously affected by the Moon. The Moon phases that control the ocean tides affect our physical bodies as well. Lunar cycles empower mood swings, and sometimes deep depression sets in for a few days until the Moon changes. The constant and unstable fluctuations from new Moon to full Moon set the scene for your ego blockage of oversensitivity. Your life can be a roller coaster of emotional highs and lows until you learn to observe your feelings objectively and think them through. This takes time and effort.

Symbolically, water in its boundless form represents the emotional immersion into the experience of living without having to evaluate or understand any of its effects. As a water sign, you find it refreshing and cleansing to just allow life to flow through you. Cancerians don't understand differentiation. This ability to merge without due process of the mind is a deep longing for Cancer but can create difficulties, particularly if the personality has been deprived of nurturing in early childhood.

We must remember that Cancerians really want safety and nourishment, not money, but in our world today money and achievement are the greatest symbols of security. The stakes for everyone are high in big business today. Living in an excessive and goal-oriented society, our young people are affected by false values and are being motivated for the wrong reasons. Cancerian youngsters are deeply affected by this dilemma until they are grounded in good values.

Sadly, some Cancer men have a hard time accepting the feminine side of themselves, the side that is intuitive and creative. It isn't easy for a man to be ruled by the Moon. You become moody and withdrawn, not understanding that your sensitivity is an opportunity to let your loved ones be closer to you. Withholding builds up defensive behavior, and unexpressed feelings make you moody and hard to live with. If Cancerian men are emotionally suppressed, they stay very close to their mothers and choose ultra-feminine women for wives. You want the women in your life to do all the emoting. In middle age, you often wake up to find your life is dry and uncreative. It is wise to see an astrologer or counselor at that time. You can be given a new lease on life, learning how to process your own emotions and express them to others. A man who has integrated with his female side is a joy to behold, as is a women who has learned to mentally process her emotions and feeling.

As a Cancer man you have all the tools to be warm, sympathetic, and affectionate when you give up your fear of losing your masculinity because of your sensitivity. Tom Hanks, Harrison Ford, and Bill Cosby are a few celebrities who seem to have integrated their lunar side into their personalities, making them good husbands and fathers.

Acquiring things is one of Cancer's favorite things to do, and most Cancerians have a house full of collections. They love antiques and objects of nostalgia. The desire to surround themselves with things reminiscent of the past seems to be a lifelong pursuit. Of course, this deep need to find *things* and to hold on to them is often a cover-up for unfulfilled emotions. A wise man once said that all the possessions you need are what you can carry with you. This is a little extreme for the average person. Perhaps a more realistic rule of thumb for Cancer would be to discard or pass on anything that is no longer of service in your life or to retain only that which contributes to the nourishment of your body and soul.

Too often you Cancerians become enmeshed in your personal relationships and can't separate your emotional needs from those of others. You are *born old*, seeming very mature for your years compared to other children, and extremely responsible in your behavior. You are never really childlike. This precocious behavior covers up an insecurity brought on by competing with adults as a child. You do get younger with age, like your opposite sign Capricorn, but there is always a serious side to your personality that doesn't go away. As a child you feel you should agree with adults, or at least please them, and this creates a great deal of stress. The overly responsible Cancer child even tries to take on the role of parent, often to the parent's dismay. Without the maturity necessary to handle the complexities of adult emotional and physical responsibilities, the burden weighs down the developing ego, creating helplessness and an underlying sense of doom.

Sooner or later the frustration of feeling incompetent moves into anger, which Cancer abhors and struggles to suppress; then your tendency is to implode, holding in the emotion. There will be a reckoning day. This suppression of your true emotions and attempt to please people in positions of authority can dog you for the rest of your life. It isn't good for your health. You tend to have psychosomatic illnesses, particularly in your stomach. Women often have problems with their reproductive organs. These are the areas of the body that Cancer rules.

Hypersensitive Cancerians obsessively feel the need to control your environment. Being so nurturing, you continually want to take care of everyone that comes into your sight, at the same time wanting to secure your position in your relationships. This is where your ego blockage of manipulation steps in.

Privacy is very important to you, and necessary to process so much emotion and feeling, but in extreme cases you develop a tendency to isolate yourself. Being overly sensitive, you feel a need to withdraw into a safe environment where you can regenerate yourself. But there is no such thing as a safe place on earth. It's only through your soul connection to a higher power that you find peace. Deep-seated fears of abandonment and anxieties around facing the world on your own create an urgent need to get in control. It might surprise you that Cancerians, generally so sweet, are also very critical and skeptical. As much as you like to please, you're not pleased easily. You vacillate between being coolly critical and severe and turning into a marshmallow, letting others manipulate you.

The transforming path of Cancer is family relationships. You Cancerians are very attached to your kin, particularly your mothers. Ask Cancers about their mother and you will hear an extreme response of either all praise or total criticism. In adolescence, when a break from parents is paramount, you Cancerians bypass this important transition. Thinking you are responsible for the happiness of others, you find it hard to break out of the enmeshment of childhood.

Cancer has trouble setting emotional boundaries. One of my Cancer clients went to his grandmother's house every Sunday for years and years, giving up his one free day of the week because he couldn't refuse her. Since most families have been in past lives together, your emotional relationships are highly charged. This is a real test for the individuals involved. Cancer wants everything to run smoothly and harmoniously. You invest a lot of emotional energy making things perfect for everyone (whether they want it or not) and you do expect a return on the investment. Your unrealistic assumptions must be checked out with the other person or you may make decisions with unhappy results.

As an overly sensitive Cancer you assume you know what's best for your family and friends, seldom bothering to get verification. Instead, you give away your power. You find your goal impossible to achieve no matter how you struggle, manipulate, or plead to continually please your loved ones.

Since mothers are ruled by Cancer, the institution of motherhood has the Cancerian ego blockages of oversensitivity and manipulation. I heard my mother say many times, "Just do it because I'm your mother." I swore I would never say that to my children, but I probably did. I'm not a believer in mother bashing because I'm a mother myself and I feel that it is necessary to mature and individuate into responsible adults who no longer need a mother per se. Then we can free her to be a good friend.

Cancerian lives improve appreciably after age 40. Maturing slowly, you can finally see that living in the past and being socially perfect is not the answer. If you are observant, every moment offers you an opportunity to move forward into a positive and creative attitude. Cancers must release their ego defense mechanisms of fear, guilt, feelings of inadequacy, and stringent self-judgment. Free yourself from the prison of walking on egg shells brought on by caretaking and realize that *by pleasing yourself you please others*. You can start a healthy communication with family and create a life in which you receive as well as give love and nourishment.

What Can Be Done

Cancer is one of the most sincere signs in the zodiac. Your bona fide characteristic of nurturing is the answer to correcting your blockages. You must look for safety inside yourself. Honor and think well of yourself; you deserve it. With all your caring for others, surely you can take a little for yourself. The ego blockages you have derive from fear of rejection and loss of control. Do an inventory of your life and see what, if anything, you really have to fear.

Three Steps for Healing Your Blockage

1. Realize that your ego blockage of oversensitivity is constantly at work, causing moodiness and depression. Your sensitivity is one of the best things about you; it's the excess that we are targeting.
2. Your soul power of nurturing consists of emotional caring, giving attention and affection where it is needed. Be sure you include yourself in this group. It is easier to take care of others if you can take care of yourself.
3. Cancer's transforming path is family relationships. Working through family dynamics affects us all, but it is your life lesson. All the Sun sign transforming paths are neutral; you are just more sensitive to family needs than other signs. You place such importance on your responsibility to kith and kin that you overdo it. Then you're in bondage, tied down emotionally and physically.

Remember, we don't belong to anyone and no one belongs to us. We share our lives with our family because the potential for closeness is self-evident. If we can't get along with our family, how can we relate to the world outside the home? This is a big problem in the world at this time, not just a Cancerian dilemma.

When Cancer becomes sensitized to a family situation, the ego kicks in, wanting to get in control. This can happen in an office as well because Cancerians are often in family businesses or set up their offices like a family. A Cancer starts to control by caretaking, often not consciously aware of the manipulation involved. It is important to ask family members if they need your help or advice. On the other hand, many times Cancer reacts to sensitive situations by simply withdrawing. This can be misread by your loved ones. It is necessary to express your reasons then and there for being upset. If you are too upset, make plans to discuss it later when you can get clear emotionally, and talk it over together after regrouping. Of course, this isn't easy stuff to do, but to be truly happy in your relationships you must work at it.

Here is a typical Cancer story. It's Christmas and the whole family is getting together; grandparents, parents, brothers, and sisters, with all their families—the works. Your husband has won tickets for a trip to Hawaii with you and the children, but you are actually afraid to call your mother and say you can't be there for the holiday. Of course, your husband is a Leo and believes in doing what he *wants* to do, not what he *should* do, putting you right in the middle. Your oversensitivity blockage collides with your transforming path of family relationships, and your emotional quotient goes over the top in anxiety. The decision is made; of course, you want to go, and you will tell your mother, but she will be terribly hurt. Or will she? It's not that you are doing anything wrong, so why do you feel so bad?

How to Apply the Three Steps in This Situation

A Cancer with her overdeveloped sensitivity is prone to projecting her own feelings onto others, and in this case projects her feelings onto her mother. We do not see things as they are; we see things as *we* are. Before you confront your family, confront yourself. Recognize that you are upset and emotional, then accept responsibility for that emotion. Here are some of the emotions that are being set off.

1. The fear you are experiencing must be sorted out. Whether it is real or imagined, it exists.
2. You are indulging in concerns over past situations in order to avoid taking action. This feeling is guilt.

3. The rejection you feel is based on earlier childhood attempts to gain approval.
4. The worry and anxiety is very wearing, incapacitating your ability to make a decision and prepare for the situation.

Typically, your response to these emotions is to rationalize them in order to avoid dealing with your feelings. Telling your mother that you are going out of town at Christmas isn't the bitter end—it just seems like it. Behind every emotion is a belief. Do you honestly think your mother will quit loving you? Ask yourself, "What am I getting from these emotions?" Remember, the drama is all in your head. We have a 100 percent chance every moment to be positive or negative, so *choose to be positive*. It is important to be objective so that you can change your response to the problem.

Cancer's transforming path of family relationships is nonpartisan; it's up to you to be discriminating and not use them for your emotional and physical stability. After taking this inventory and deciding to desensitize yourself over family situations, see your mom and tell her how excited you are about this wonderful opportunity. Change your attitude. Let her share in your good luck. You could also make plans to come home for Thanksgiving or New Year's eve. Another good idea is to request that they video parts of Christmas so that you can share too. If your mother is upset, it is her problem to solve, not yours. But if you are positive and emotionally clear no matter what her response is, it provides her with an opportunity to grow also.

Your soul power of nurturing is a great gift and must be honored. However, new boundaries that maintain your dignity while respecting the other person are mandatory. Your emotional well-being is your concern, no matter what your loved ones think.

Leo

July 23—August 22

Fire Sign Ruled by the Sun

SOUL POWER: *Generosity of Spirit, Love*

EGO BLOCKAGE: *Self-Absorption, Excessive Optimism*

TRANSFORMING PATH: *Power Games*

Leo is the most dramatic and flamboyant of all the signs in the zodiac, and rightly so. You are ruled by the Sun—a star. In an astrological chart the Sun sign signifies who you really are. As a Leo, you have a radiant, extravagant personality with the high standards necessary to create an environment of magnificence and splendor. You are the shining stars and Sun gods of the zodiac. Leo's soul power is generosity of spirit, and you easily move into leadership positions, looking over your kingdom with elan and magnanimity.

Leos are the kings and queens of the zodiac. One of the terrific things about you is that you are blessed with *noblesse oblige*. You feel it is your obligation to be honorable, generous, and responsible in all your endeavors, and it is your duty to inspire goodwill by helping others—or simply by entertaining them.

Leo is the sign of love. It rules the heart and it is your profound good luck to have what everyone on earth is seeking, love, as your own soul power. Being heart people you are born with the propensity to express your feelings from a secure foundation of being loved by all. Love and happiness come forth spontaneously from inside of you unless there is real damage to your ego in early life or your life lessons create a negative self-image.

Some Eastern religions say there are seven chakras, or psychic centers, in the subtle body starting from the base of the spine and going to the top of the head. The heart is at the center. The fourth chakra, the heart center, is called the *anahata*. It is the balancing point between the basic self (the lower three chakras) and the soul (the higher three chakras). Leos are blessed with a natural connection to the fourth chakra, the dwelling place of the individual soul. Great teachers say that your soul is symbolized by a flame in your heart that burns constantly, unaffected by worldly activity, a part of you that understands the power of love.

Leo, the fifth house of the zodiac, rules love and child. Who more than our children teach us unconditional love? It has been said that like a child we enter the kingdom of heaven. Your childlike enthusiasm takes you into each day with the hope of achieving your goals.

With your soul power of generosity of spirit, you are born knowing that everything you need is abundantly within your own reach. You generously share yourself with the world; there is no hiding for Leo. You are sure that everyone is glad to know you, just as you are pleased to know them. You have a giving nature. You intuitively understand how the universal law of abundance works; that which is given with heartfelt generosity will be returned tenfold. You enjoy giving expensive presents and shower your loved ones with costly items. Leos think that if they are going to give a present, give something that stands out. You know instinctively that the more you give, the more you get back.

In many ancient cultures the Sun was worshiped as a deity. Perhaps it was the light of the Sun, like the solar fire of creation and the brilliance of heavenly beings in divine encounters, that was venerated, not the Sun itself. As the Sun reflects God's image of light, you Leos seem to glow with good health and vitality, with a sincere and noble look. In India—a Leo country, shaped like a heart—the people believe that there is a point between the eyes called the *ajna*, or Sun center. There is a Hindu belief that if you meditate on this center, you grow adept until you achieve enlightenment. This may take many lifetimes. Enlightened ones enjoy a high position in the afterlife, with the Shining Ones.

King Arthur was a solar hero who created an ideal community called Camelot. His Knights of the Round Table represented a new vision of equality quite unknown at that time. We are still enchanted by his concepts, and every few years there is a new version of the Camelot myth played out on the big screen.

Alexander the Great was definitely a Leo type. He was educated by Aristotle as a boy. After being told by the Oracle at Delphi that he was invincible, he went on to conquer the known world by the age of 36. He didn't seem to be fazed by the Oracle's other prediction—that he would die young. He did so after naming seventy cities in the world Alexandria. Leos only hear the good news and discount the bad news. You Apollonians—Sun gods of the 1990s—can be found in every field as long as it is entertaining, in the spotlight, and first-class all the way.

Human beings have long perceived that the Sun moves forward every day in a very deliberate fashion. It is both reliable and warming. It is very reassuring to see the Sun rise each morning, bringing the hope of a new day. Perhaps this is why the Sun has been venerated as a god symbol since the earliest times.

With the Sun as your ruler, you are constant and reliable in your quest to move through life with aplomb, to be in the limelight, to seek adulation, to shine in the world. You are tireless in your efforts to entertain the people around you—that is how you have fun. It's a party when Leo gets there. Better still, when you have a party, it's bound to be big. You enjoy life, and want to live in the best way possible with the best of everything.

Leo activities are synonymous with glory, magnanimity, and magnificence. In fact Leo is the sign of royalty and takes on a sub-rulership of all monarchies no matter what Sun sign rules them. The grandeur that once was Rome, a Leo city, has resounded for thousands of years. France and Italy still have magnificent remnants of their royal past. England's nobility, a subject that we all seem to be enchanted by, are constantly in the news with their royal exploits. It's hard to find words that are large enough to describe the royal jewels on display in London today. California, where the movie stars live, is a Leo state. New York City has a Leo Moon and attracts the best talent into the most powerful city in the world.

Perhaps the oldest Leo symbol on earth is the Sphinx. Egyptologists say the Sphinx of Egypt, a lion with a human head, was built to commemorate the pharaoh Chephren. There are also those who think it was built to commemorate the age of Leo (approximately twelve thousand years ago), which preceded historic Egypt (which began in the Taurean age, around 2500 B.C.). Whoever it was that built the Sphinx, probably the most fascinating edifice on earth, produced a magnificent Leo creation that still inspires awe in all who see it. In astrological symbolism the Sphinx is a combination of Leo and Aquarius: a symbol of conquering the animal instinct (Leo) by adding the mind of man (Aquarius), who is made in God's image.

Ruling the fifth house of the zodiac, the house of children and creativity, Leos blaze their way through life with an abundance of affection, wit, and adventure. Naturally inventive, you create children of the mind as well as of the body. You always have the very best ideas, and your ability to create is limitless, whether it is planning a schedule, a political campaign, or just a party. Leos are winners, and enjoyment is your goal. No wonder your sign is often called the fun sign.

Leo governs romance, games, and speculation—anything that stirs the feelings. Lions are like big kids, very playful. You like to joke around and love being the center of attention. Leonine behavior is very like that of your namesake, the lion. A pride of lions will group together, lounging in the sun like one family—mother, father, aunts, uncles, as well as brothers, sisters, and cousins. Female lions share their milk with any young lion from the same pride that shows up. They enjoy true communal living. I asked a Leo recently what his favorite movie was and he said "The Lion King." His favorite song is (can't you guess?) "Hakuna Matada." It was brought to my attention by a Leo that The Lion King was a thinly disguised version of Hamlet, the son avenging his father's murder by the evil uncle. However, there is also a similar, much older myth from ancient Egypt, of Horus avenging his father Osiris's murder by his evil uncle Seth.

Fiery Leo is known for warmth and tremendous energy; you are the eternal children of the zodiac. With such youthful appeal, it's no wonder you are able to capture other people's imagination. Leo's appeal is straightforward and frank, coming from the heart rather than the brain. You are gifted with generosity of spirit. In matters of love you are lion-hearted, chivalrous, and romantic—and actually very conventional: you want to fall in love, get married, and have a family. To be surrounded by loved ones is your heart's desire. You are lovers and feel miserable if you are not in a significant relationship.

Leo's charismatic nature and creative style make you great entertainers. Lions are actors by nature and desire to be the center of attention. You attract stardom, just as the Sun in our solar system is a star with planets circling it. Destined for center stage with a lot of applause are standout lions Steve Martin and Magic Johnson, alongside golden guy Robert Redford and platinum-all-the-way Madonna. Rarely do we see you as shy, but some of you are not as extroverted as others. There is a quiet, even reserved, Leo, like Jacqueline Kennedy, but you quiet types are goal-oriented and want to be acknowledged just as much as your outgoing cousins. Some extroverted beauties who like the limelight and the beat are Whitney Houston, Mick Jagger, and Patrick Swayze.

Of all the Sun signs you are the easiest to spot. You love attention and stand out in any crowd with your dramatic good looks, usually sporting a great mane of hair. Your face is square with a high forehead, your nose is well-formed but a little wide, like a cat's. You are very elegant and carry yourself well with a pronounced leonine expression in your general physique. Leos have broad shoulders and slender hips. You look great in clothes.

As a Capricorn, I admire the ability of Leo to be very present and at ease in each moment and to effortlessly choose the 100 percent positive direction in life. Leo has a great "deserve" level. When I am tired from the constant pressure of being a Capricorn, I decide to draw on the Leo traits in my own chart and set out to enjoy myself as much as possible. Usually, this entails some lounging around for a while, then doing something glamorous for myself, like shopping at Bergdorf's or planning a trip to Bali.

Leos love to win and they are often drawn to political situations to test their prowess and showmanship. Bill Clinton, the president of the United States, is a Leo. Campaigning to win the election against all odds seems to energize him to heroic proportions. Clinton's strong will to win seemed to spur him on in an unrelenting campaign to victory even though he had extremely difficult aspects in his natal chart on the very day of the election. Most astrologers predicted his defeat, underestimating Leo's determination to achieve. Liking to win, you rarely give up without a tremendous effort. Odd as it seems, Leos are not hard-core competitors. You just like to win and enjoy the adulation and acclaim. After winning the goal, your enthusiasm for the race drops off appreciably, and there is little followthrough on the promises that got you there in the first place.

A Leo does have staying power, and you are not likely to give up your space. You don't want anyone else to have what you have claimed as yours. You are members of the cat family, and you don't like to be moved around. You have marked your territory, so after a little lounging around you can get back on track if the incentive is there.

Jung, a Leo, categorized people into four psychological types: the Thinker (mental), the Feeler (expressive), the Sensor (pragmatic), and the Intuitor (psychic). All of the signs of the zodiac fall under one of these types. Leos are definitely feeler types—high-spirited, spontaneous, uninhibited, and totally wrapped up in their feelings. It is very easy for Lions to be overdeveloped in the feeling department, and overreact to life situations with fiery enthusiasm, especially when they are criticized.

Leo's ego blockage is self-absorption; you can become so involved with yourself that you can't see beyond your own wants and needs. Behind your suave demeanor is more insecurity than you want to admit; you are actors and you know it. You are emotionally connected to your image, and how others see you affects your confidence. An egocentric Leo can put on a good front, seeming to be self-assured, but at the first hint of criticism or failure, you overreact emotionally. This behavior can be confusing to your friends, who can't imagine why you fell apart.

You go through many stages of development before reaching a secure and mature identity. The Leo stage is connected to the child part of the personality. You might say that Leo rules the ego and its development. The preceding sign, Cancer, tends to think of the family as a unit. Leo brings independence into the consciousness. Leos make a strong personal presentation and think in possessive terms: *my* wife, *my* home, *my* children, *my* job. Being self-willed isn't a bad thing; if you don't know who you are, how can you find your place in the world?

As a Leo, born with a strong sense of worth, you innately know you are divinely loved. This veneer is surprisingly easy to break when the lion has not matured past the adolescent stage of ego development, as is often the case. A mature viewpoint is more enjoyable than you might think, and it might surprise you to find that the soul is ever young.

The ability to risk is one of Leo's best traits; it is part of your soul power of generosity. There has to be risk to be successful in any endeavor. Leos feel they are divinely ordained; from this confident position there is a tendency to risk without enough forethought. All Sun signs are divinely worthy of success, but Leo is born knowing it and capitalizing on it. Sometimes the capitalizing part comes early in life, sometimes later. Look at Martha Stewart, a Leo, who took what she liked to do and created an empire in her forties. She obviously loves success and likes to be in the limelight. She puts herself on the cover of her magazine every month in true Leo fashion.

Your ability to take risks encourages excellence in extroverted activities such as acting, sports, politics, and just enjoying life every minute. You feel you have been personally invited to the "party of life" and you want to live it up and enjoy it. This strong desire to be the center of attention is a behavior that is natural to all children and all Leos. Your personal ego is developed in early childhood. This almost naive viewpoint creates a sense of entitlement that is firmly impressed until life situations slowly beat you down and you realize you are not infallible. Leo doesn't give up this entitlement easily; your world centers around you, and you want to keep it that way. This is charming in a child, but when it continues into adulthood it can be very irritating, and many a Leo loses relationships without knowing why. Consideration and empathy need to be developed in the Leo personality. You do have the capacity to develop these much-needed traits. Life is a two-way street and eventually you learn that.

You tell the truth as you see it. Lions place great faith in others, perhaps wrongly so. Easily deceived and slow to take revenge, you project your own values on others. It is often your downfall. The pride of the Leo makes you think deception is impossible. Many a Leo comes into my office heartbroken and confused because they were betrayed by their mate or business partner. Perhaps it's hard to live with royalty all the time. With all her beauty and poise, Jackie Kennedy was betrayed by both of her husbands. This would be an ego basher for anyone, and particularly for one so famous for her looks and charm.

Napoleon, a Leo, was betrayed by his wife Josephine at a time when he was the toast of France. He could conquer the world but his love life left something to be desired. As a Leo, your fate seems destined to let go of an ego identity that is no longer valid. This usually occurs in the area of life that is the most important to you: your love life. Just because you are divinely blessed in so many ways with your looks, personality, and vitality, doesn't mean you are free from relationship problems. Relationships are always somewhat difficult and you must learn both to *give* and to *receive* love.

Joseph Campbell writes that there is always a loss of power or even the death of the Hero, a Leo symbol, at the end of the myth. Leos always have a lesson with power games, their transforming path. It might help you to know that power comes from the soul, *not* the ego. Leos suffer a lot in the world because of their egocentric entitlement and total denial of anything wrong or negative in their life. The overdeveloped ego of the Leo must be surrendered eventually. Leos have to find out that there is power simply in being at peace with their own extraordinary qualities and trusting in their worthiness to all that is good.

Leo is considered to be a masculine sign in the zodiac. Female lions have masculine characteristics even though they are striking and many times exceedingly beautiful—like Whitney Houston, Arlene Dahl, and Lesley Ann Warren, for example. They often take on the traits of the male lion. In the pride (aptly named) the male lion shamelessly lounges around while the female makes the kill, and he feels entitled to the first feed even before the children. The male lion gets the fancy hairdo and the free lunch while the ever-resourceful female does all the work. Watching the habits of animals can be a great lesson. Many ancient civilizations used animal symbols to exemplify the attributes of their godhead, and astrology used them consistently in the different formats of astrology all over the world.

This brings up the subject of parenting. Leo females are good mothers in that you are affectionate and loving human beings, but your tendency to see everything through your own needs puts your children in second place and causes damage. Blending your children into your own ego identity may mean you give your offspring the best opportunities possible, but it stifles their own identity. You only want the best for the people you love, but the child's own ego needs mustn't be ignored and denied.

I remember a client whose Leo mother kept trying to get him to play sports as a child when he wanted to take dancing instead. He dreaded going home because she always waylaid him with a baseball and mitt and the dreaded words, "Let's play ball." In her eyes it was best for him. He turned out to be a great dancer on Broadway and won her approval anyway, but it took a lot of will not to be beaten down. The problem is, your sign is childlike and you want to be your own child. You don't ignore your children; quite the contrary. It's just that your own needs are more important. This egocentrism places your children's happiness in jeopardy, possibly with disastrous results.

The same is true of the Leo father. It's a lot of fun when Dad's around, but it is always on his terms. Many children of Leos feel they need to please their fathers. As a Leo, your error lies in being too liberal. It's no fun to reprimand children and much more fun to overlook their faults and give them whatever they want. You must realize the kids know they're being paid off, and they see it as a rejection.

Leo's other ego blockage is excessive optimism. Your proclivity to deny the obvious is unsurpassed by any Sun sign; when you're standing knee-deep in toxic waste, it's just plain stupid to say "Everything's fine." Amelia Earhart was a Leo. We can't help but think that if she hadn't been overly positive in dire circumstances she might have lived longer. Your total denial of the facts makes others worry about your sense of reality, yet it does seem that you can turn negative situations around just by your will. The energy it takes is enormous and Leos can suffer from physical heart problems as a result of overwork. Also, when your emotional heart has been broken, your physical heart is in jeopardy.

Leo's transforming path is power games. You are attracted to power situations and power people. We've all heard how power corrupts and have read many stories in history that illustrate the fact. But it's not power per se that corrupts, it's your fear of losing it. The diseased ego abuses power, wanting more and more, trying to fill a bottomless void. Your very nature is positive, however, and it doesn't take long for you to let go of negative control methods. It's definitely not your nature to have a low profile. You naturally draw the limelight, so scrupulous care must be given to ethics and values. When success comes from your soul power of love, it can't be corrupted.

What Can Be Done

The leonine proclivity to dominate is a serious blockage. You must face the fear and denial that keep you self-absorbed. It's important to remember that the strength of your soul power of love and generosity of spirit is exactly equal to the strength of your ego blockage of self-absorption.

Your blockage comes from the basic self, a part of your personality that does not reason and that has built up defense mechanisms in early life.

Look past your childish ways and face the things you don't want to see. Trying to be perfect is a waste of time.

There is nothing perfect in our ordinary world. When anything arrives at true perfection it immediately transcends into a state beyond our ordinary physical understanding. This is called a transcendent state. Your wounded ego must be healed to align with your soul power of love. By knowing yourself as a spiritual being, you express divine will, which is your greatest gift as a Leo.

When you realize your transforming path of power games requires letting go of the inflated ego, you can go through the changes without typical Leo fear of losing control. Then you're on the right track to a liberated state of consciousness and an exceptional life. Accepting your attraction to power is your key to change. You have it within you to change. You mustn't be frightened. To surrender is not losing—it's gaining higher understanding.

Three Steps for Healing Your Blockage

1. Now that you are aware of your ego blockages of self-absorption and excessive optimism, notice them as soon as they surface. A Leo learns very quickly how to be self-aware from a confident position.
2. Love has always been the key to personal happiness. Learn about all the kinds of love in the world; it is your essence, your soul power. Know that your soul power of generosity of spirit lies within your being—the eternal part of you that is really you.
3. Your transforming path of power games is your game in life. You attract power. You have the power to change.

I have a Leo client who is a writer; his dream is to write a screenplay for a movie or television series. He had been unsuccessfully trying to get published for ten years. Although he was turned down over and over again, operating out of his ego blockages, he wouldn't give up. This would be all well and good if he were on his own, but he is married and has two small children. His wife's inheritance was used up and she valiantly went to work to support them. (Sounds like the male lion syndrome to me.) Finally he was forced by the facts of life (rising costs, health insurance, his children's education) to see the needs of his family, and got a job as a teacher in a college. The outcome: He loves his work, and guess what? One of his manuscripts sold! After he gave up his doggedly egocentric approach, the situation changed. When Leo lets go of being in control, something better comes in its place. His will wasn't the answer in this case; it was his willingness to see his family's needs.

How to Apply the Three Steps in This Situation

The writer's ego blockage of self-absorption is easy to see. Instead of the "me" game, it's fairly simple to ask others what they think and need. Wake up and see the world through another's eyes for a while. Your soul power of generosity of spirit doesn't work until you are able to let go of selfishly wanting control at all times, of wanting the power for yourself. Your other ego blockage of being overly optimistic is a cinch to change. Face the facts!

Leo takes on responsibility very well when you feel it is your domain. Your egocentric behavior isn't malicious, it's just that you forget to empathize and communicate. The Leo writer could have considered his family much sooner, and I expect he will from now on. When he let go of his stubbornness and self-absorption, he won the prize. He didn't have to let go of his ambition, but being doggedly stubborn about his goals and indulging his excessive optimism was creating a downward spiral. When the facts are in front of you, you can't be excused. The world doesn't revolve around you—it flows with you and everyone else!

Leo, you need to remember these things:

1. Consideration of others is paramount to your growth. This is enhanced by asking your loved ones what their needs are.

2. The ego resides in the reasoning part of the mind and is an objective point of reference that balances the basic self and the soul.
3. You are not your ego.
4. True power comes from the soul, not the opinions of others.
5. You are able to draw on an unlimited source of power when you respect yourself just as you are.
6. Love is the greatest power there is, and it's yours.

Thinking positive is a great thing, but there are limits that must be faced. As Scott Peck says in his best-selling book *The Road Less Traveled*, "Life is difficult." He goes on to say that when you realize this and get over your resentment of this fact, life gets much better. Maybe that is why you Leos get hit with such rejection and betrayal. It takes a big blow to break down the egocentric will and let your soul powers of love and generosity work in your life. Wake up, Leo! Although life is difficult, therein lies the challenge and the riches. You are the star!

Virgo

August 23–September 22

Earth Sign Ruled by Mercury

SOUL POWER: *Productivity, Discrimination,* Orderliness

EGO BLOCKAGE: *Negativity*

TRANSFORMING PATH: *Service,* Nature

Virgos, you are the sharpest thinkers in the zodiac. Working with meticulous precision and attention to detail, you have the ability to get things done. Workable ideas are your forte, and you're never at a loss when it comes to solving logistical problems. Your mental orderliness comes from the fact that Virgo is a practical earth sign that is supported by the mental agility of the planet Mercury, its ruler. You are masters in the application of practical, useful, and concrete techniques, particularly in the work environment. You believe if it's worth doing at all, it's worth doing well.

Leo developed creativity, and Virgo discovered how to use it. Leo represents the perfect man, Virgo the perfect woman. It is well known that in most cultures of the world, even in the United States, women are the producers. Not to say that men are not productive, but it is their feminine side that holds them to a project until it is finished. As Rob Becker says in his delightful play, *Defending the Caveman,* "Men are hunters and women are gatherers." The cohesive qualities of Virgo are an important part of your effectiveness.

Productivity and discrimination are your soul powers, and as a Virgo you are happiest when you are of service to a tangible idea. It does your heart good to take on a project, analyze it, divide it up, do each part with precision, and, when it is finished, hand it over to someone tied with a bow. A job well done; how wonderful! You love to be of service any way you can.

It has been said in old astrology books that there is another planet in our solar system called Vulcan that will be recognized as Virgo's rightful ruler when it is discovered. Vulcan was the royal son of Hera and Zeus. Zeus threw him out of heaven because of his lameness. Vulcanalia, the chief festival of the lame god, was held in Rome on August 23, at the time the Sun moves into Virgo. Old-time astrologers say that Virgo must overcome some physical handicap in life. I have found that many Virgoans have hearing difficulties. It's interesting to note that Mr. Spock of *Star Trek* was a Vulcan and his ears were noticeably larger than Earthlings; he shares this trait with the fleet-footed god Mercury.

The god Vulcan was a blacksmith and the patron of all artisans; Virgo is the ruler of all workers. As new planets in other solar systems are being discovered today, perhaps there is a little planet in our solar system beyond Mercury and hidden in the brightness of the Sun. Until Vulcan is discovered, Virgo must share the planet Mercury's rulership with Gemini, which seems to work well enough for both.

If each Sun sign manifests an important aspect of God, the universe, the force, or whatever you want to call the higher power, Virgo represents the orderliness of nature, God's mind as shown through nature and the ability to organize and coordinate all of earth's inhabitants, or simply, nature's mind. As a Virgo, your sign rules ecology and biology, the earth's filing system for all the small plants and animals and minerals that enrich the earth. Virgo is a sign of purification and refinement, and Virgoans are inordinately concerned about their health and the toxic conditions on earth.

One of the most important changes in human history was when humans learned to cultivate grain. The symbol for Virgo honors this unknown ancient horticulturist by showing a beautiful woman holding a sheaf of grain in her hands. The Virgoan time of the year coincides with the time when the bounty of the fields is ready for harvest. The woman represents the ancient fertility goddesses Inanna, Hathor, and Demeter, and the sheaf of grain is a symbol of fertility. Among the ancient Egyptians this sign was symbolized by the virgin goddess Isis, who holds her child Horus, son of Osiris, instead of the sheaf of grain. In all ancient cultures she has a beautiful face and a gentle, nurturing attitude in her pose. She is honored for her fruitfulness, nurturing, and above all, purity.

I call Virgoans starched mothers, in that you are the mothers, nurses, and teachers who see to the child's health and education more than his or her emotional needs. Virgo parents need to learn to enjoy their children more. You mustn't live as if you are being graded on your efficiency as a parent; it makes your children into worriers just like you.

The word *virgin* in ancient times did not necessarily have a sexual connotation but spoke of wisdom and righteousness, as in "not altered by human activity." A quality I have seen in many Virgoans is a look of innocence, a pristine countenance, like an angel. Botticelli's beautiful young women painted in vibrantly colored frescoes seem to have all the physical attributes of a classic Virgo.

Classic Virgoans are well-formed, with oval faces and straight noses. All of you tend to have hair that waves gently off the forehead, usually cut in a classical style. Your eyes are alert and intelligent. Virgos often have an old-fashioned look that never goes out of style.

Very fashion-conscious, you are careful with your wardrobe, wearing simple, well-cut, becoming clothes. You have an understated elegance that seems to be natural to you; without even trying, you seem to make a fashion statement. Paris and Milan, two of the world's major fashion centers, are ruled by Virgo. Los Angeles, the city of angels, is a Virgo city and also a city full of technicians who work in the film business.

There are more Virgo beauties in the zodiac than any other sign. They use very little makeup; the first impression you have of a Virgo is of someone well-groomed and in the pink of health. The most famous Virgo beauty of the twentieth century was Greta Garbo. I was surprised when I found out just how many great actresses and ageless beauties were Virgos: Ingrid Bergman, Emma Samms, Sophia Loren, Raquel Welch, Peggy Lipton, Lauren Bacall, and Jacqueline Bisset among them. Model Claudia Schiffer exemplifies all the lovely Virgo traits.

Virgo men are very handsome and seem to have a refined and debonair bearing along with virile good looks. Think of Hugh Grant, Jeremy Irons, Richard Gere, and Sean Connery. Perhaps so many Virgos are successful in the acting field because they are proficient at posing and learning lines as well as being attractive.

The symbol for Virgo is the letter M with a fishlike glyph on the end. The M stands for *mem*, a Hebrew letter for the feminine, and the glyph is reminiscent of the fish symbol of the early Christians. Virgo is a symbol of virginity, the birth of the divine on the earthly plane. Not only Jesus, but also Buddha, Krishna, Osiris, Dionysus, Heracles, and Lao Tzu, are reputed to have been born of a divine father and a mortal mother. Virgos can find the divine in the material universe through nature. You seem to understand this principle in your love of plants and small animals, especially cats, who are ruled by Virgo.

Because of your attention to detail many of you become accomplished artists. The reciprocal action of your opposite sign, Pisces, a sign of imagination, brings the visual concepts that Virgo can put down on paper so well. It has been said that you can accomplish anything you can visualize, and you Virgos are certainly technically accomplished enough if you open up your latent creative ability.

Many of you are expert astrologers, or would be if you were interested.

Being naturally scholarly, you take the time to do all the necessary studying and memorizing, but being prone to intellectual doubt and afraid of making a mistake, you seldom read for the public, thus limiting your joy in sharing your hard-earned knowledge. Your self-critical attitude comes from operating out of your blockage of negativism, for no one is more able to analyze and synthesize than a Virgo.

Virgos also have a wonderful way with words—that is, when you can get your head out of a book long enough to talk. Virgo rules work and production. Consequently, you excel in any field where products need to be made and marketed. Virgo is one of the signs that rule computers, the tools of the information and telecommunication age.

Interpersonal relationships are not your best thing; that's why you are often called old maids. People are very important to you as recipients of your good work, but you honestly do not know how to have intimate relationships. It's easy for you to become married to your work and hide from romance. There is a bit of the monk in all of us, but you Virgos must watch out for a tendency to creep into your narrow bed and take vows of emotional austerity.

Virgos do a wonderful job of entertaining, yet you are so busy doing the preparation for the party you seldom get down and enjoy the fun. You're often found preparing or serving more food in the kitchen or putting dishes in the dishwasher. This is when your transforming power of service goes into overdrive, and your feelings of "I have to satisfy others to be good" create a sterile enjoyment. That is not *true* service. With attachment to the outcome you are creating self-slavery—a prison of your own making. It might surprise you to realize this doership is a technique of control and a way of avoiding intimacy.

Virgos have to bond with others to be happy. You must acknowledge that you need emotional connections to enjoy the fruits of your labors. You are not a machine. True service is not an end into itself, it must come from the heart. You have a tendency to think your life instead of living it; you can become isolated from your own feelings and very egocentric. This can make you very dull and self-absorbed when you want to be just the reverse.

As a Virgo it is very easy for you to see immediately what is wrong—with everything. To think that you know what is correct for others is presumptuous. I call this behavior "New York attitude." There are so many brilliant and talented people in New York, but it seems they are always trying to outdo each other by criticizing everything. This is right up Virgos' alley, for with their ego blockage of negativity it is easier to find fault than applaud. Since Virgo is the master of critiquing, you love to be the one who "knows" and cleverly slashes away at the newest movie, book, or celebrity.

Your wonderful Virgo gift of discrimination can deteriorate into your ego blockage of negativity very quickly. There's always a fly in the ointment if you look hard enough. This doesn't mean you have to put down every situation or product, but use your careful eye to see all the angles in a neutral and nonjudgmental way before making a decision. I am sure the person that created the scientific approach was a Virgo.

As I analyze a chart (a typical Virgoan technique), I have to keep in mind that the negative qualities are the easiest to see, so I always start with the positive aspects first to lay out the groundwork so the client will be receptive to the reading. (Most of you know your bad points anyway, and you need to be encouraged by hearing the good.)

When Virgos learn how to communicate with others and trust their power of productivity they don't have such a need to be in control. Doing what comes naturally for a Virgo means completing a project with a high degree of success and then going off to begin again.

If you are attached to a myopic viewpoint, you totally lose track of the goal of service, which is offering up your work to its higher purpose with no reward in sight. By sharing with others and overcoming your detached attitude you accomplish wonders without being bogged down by perfectionism and your fascination with details. The Virgo transforming path of service teaches you to differentiate between true service and manipulation. Situations will arise again and again until you understand soulful giving without mental gymnastics.

Virgos tend to have hidden agendas. Your acts of service may be to prove to other people that you are good and worthy. Being completely blind to your motivations, you might be shocked if someone mentioned it. Because of your mutable nature you are prone to act as if you approve, when deep down you don't. How can people know you?

The city of Paris is ruled by Virgo. It is probably the most beautiful city in the world, offering the finest of everything, and Parisians have a joy in life that is obvious. Yet they are well-known for being extremely difficult and having a critical attitude. Their penchant for excellence would still be there if they learned how to open their hearts and just enjoy what they have accomplished without such negativity. I say, don't let the Virgoan attitude of the Parisians ruin Paris.

Sacrifice is an important concept for a Virgo, and it doesn't have to be considered negative. Sacrifice means offering something precious to God, making a sacred act. To let go of thinking in a self-limiting way requires a surrender of the ego. You could look on surrender as a new beginning without being encumbered by outdated modes of thinking. When you use your soul power of discrimination and relinquish the ego blockage of negativity, surrender and sacrifice become a noble act with much hope of a favorable outcome. Then you can enjoy the fruits of your labor.

In medieval times devout Christians abused their bodies by wearing shirts that were made of horse hair; they *itched*. Discomfort was supposed to make these sinners closer to God. I tell my Virgo clients they can wear hair shirts like a religious fanatic of the fourteenth century if they want to, but this won't make them better people. It seems such a waste of vital energy.

Your desire to contribute the best you have to serve any situation must come from enjoyment, not a self-defeating attitude. You must broaden your personal motives to encompass what's best for all. The hardness of attitude and negative mind set dissolve when you are free of selfish motives. Then the heart softens. Staying in the critical Virgo mind all the time creates a dry disposition. This transition isn't easy for Virgo and takes a change in consciousness. On the other hand, many Sun signs do not know how to be detached in emotional matters, and this is your forte.

You deserve love; you are loving; you must learn to receive the love you want. When you listen to your heart and know how you feel, your love life has the chance to improve.

Virgo rules the colon in the body and it disperses and distributes the nutrients in food wisely, seeing that they are assimilated in the area that is best served. *The New York Times* printed an article saying that there is a second brain in our gut known as the enteric nervous system. According to the Hindus, the third chakra is based in the solar plexus, the pit of the stomach; it controls our will power and our metabolism. Perhaps the power of the solar plexus that the ancients knew about is what the scientists have just now discovered. Since Virgo rules the colon, it must rule this newly discovered brain that is able to separate and unite, bringing order out of confusion. The brain in the abdomen can learn, remember, and produce gut feelings. This isn't surprising because that area of the body is the source of all prenatal nourishment, and psychic feelings are originally established there. I have noticed that the aspects of the planets are felt in the solar plexus if your mind will comprehend and decipher them.

The Virgo in you seldom knows how to create satisfactory boundaries for your own needs. Your mind is objective and you can see what needs to be done. You know how to take care of it, but how to stop depleting yourself is another story. It seems as if Virgo is born with pencil, paper, and ruler. Virgoans are very old at birth. You start very early sizing things up, and many a Virgoan baby puts his parents on a schedule. There is usually not much frivolity in your personality. You always want to measure up to what is expected of you. Young Virgos don't need much discipline because you are much harder on yourself than your parents would be.

Actually you need a lot of support and encouragement as a child while you precociously learn from your own mistakes. The ruler you were born with is far higher than you can reach; it's all the way up to the Moon, and there is little hope of living up to it. By not measuring up to your unrealistic ideas you are seldom satisfied with yourself, and this adds to your negativity and self-limiting behavior.

What Can Be Done

Virgos are very conscientious by nature. Your goal of useful service is admirable, and you modestly never ask for praise. What can happen without you noticing is that you become a slave to your work. When you work from your soul power of discrimination slavery disappears. You are naturally effective, efficient, and do a very good job with little effort. Work is your thing and when you are connected to your soul power of productivity you can achieve great success. Your penchant for servitude comes from the ego blockage of negativity; often the horrid taskmaster is yourself. The tendency to be self-limiting comes from your obsessive desire to make things right, and being overzealous, you set your mind on petty details and lose sight of the larger picture. Broaden your perspective and lighten up. Your personal happiness is an important factor for true success.

Three Steps for Healing Your Blockage

1. Realize your ego blockage of negativity is often based on a childish fear of competing with adults. Remember you were born with pencil, paper, and ruler in hand. Your parents thought they were doing you a favor when they encouraged your precocious ways. Virgo children are very advanced mentally, and your parents didn't realize they were putting too much emotional pressure on you at an early age.

2. Your soul power of discrimination and productivity is a great gift in life since there are many things that must be sorted out in a single day in any project. Getting things done is your cup of tea. Accomplishing a goal is very stimulating to your fertile brain, and you certainly have the energy to do it. But endless industry without a break in sight seems to show a certain amount of self-doubt. Trusting your worthiness to have what you deserve is important here.

3. Remember, service is an exalted form of worship in many religious practices, and it is your life lesson—your transforming path. This is why it is hard for you to know if it's service or slavery. True service demands self-

lessness, not slavery. You will always be called on to discern what is the right action to accomplish a task in an empowering way.

A surrender to service is a high goal. Yet when you don't like what you are doing and continue without being able to set commonsense boundaries for yourself or to simply say no when you are tired, you are in trouble. Making mountains out of molehills, you lose the ability to lift your work up to the highest good for all concerned. In self-bondage to a project you hate, it is easy to think of yourself as a victim or slave. Service just to prove yourself is a downward spiral, and a prison is created by your own ego. When Virgos enjoy their work they have a very good chance of being successful, and if there is freedom to use their own ideas, even better. If these aspects are missing, a change is necessary.

A Virgo client of mine, a young woman, kept coming back year after year with the same story. She continually got into situations in her career where she was number two in power. Even in a job where she was to take leadership, there always seemed to be a situation that put her in second place. Her goal was to have her own business, but she never seemed to be in position to meet the people who saw her as the powerful and efficient person that she was. She was always behind the scenes. Understandably, her self-confidence was low.

She was at a place in her career where she had enough experience to step into the productive and successful situation she desired, but her perfectionism kept her afraid of making a mistake and being ridiculed. She chose small tasks instead of interaction with the whole group, even though she knew her ideas were good. She was hiding.

How to Apply the Three Steps in This Situation

The answer for my Virgo client was in her vision of herself. She was getting lost in the small picture instead of acting on her bigger vision of her goals. Consequently, she never got around to them. First I asked her to write down what her goals were, especially in business; what her title should be; how much money she wanted to make; and a good daily schedule. She needed to see her goals set down on paper and to look at them often. The basic self is more likely to be motivated if goals are written down on paper. Remember, the basic self controls the desires and owns the physical energy you need to accomplish your goals.

1. Her self-doubt, stemming from her ego blockage of negativity, was keeping her from speaking out.
2. She felt it was her duty to make other people (particularly authority figures) look good. She didn't feel worthy of success.
3. Her fear of being criticized led her to settle for second best. She chose small nitpicking projects when she was capable of much more.
4. Instead of using her power of discrimination for herself, she used it only to help others. She left herself out of the picture, thereby depriving herself of the rewards of her experience and the joy of attaining her ambitious goals.

Only in a dynamic state of interaction with the world (or in my client's case, the office at large) can you keep up the positive contacts that fuel your desires and zest for life. She didn't see herself as powerful because she was separated from her sense of power. Because Virgos have such a tendency to be negative, they sidestep their power of each moment to be 100 percent positive. They nearly always choose the negative—just to be safe. Of course, that couldn't be further from the truth. Our minds create the future in every second we live, and there is always a chance for a positive result if we can see it for ourselves.

Luckily, she had a good aspect in her chart for a new job. I suggested she apply for the position she really thought she could do in a confident way and remember her daily goals. In other words, get real about what she wanted. She needed a job that had many facets so she wouldn't be bored, and working with a group was best for her to offset her tendency to isolate herself. She would have to work on her sense of inner power, her god-given right to have what she needed and wanted.

As a Virgo you must learn that true power comes from within, not from outside of yourself. Knowledge of your soul power enhances, strengthens, and develops your life. It must come from your heart. Know that you are worthy of that which is good—you don't have to do anything to deserve it. Another important aspect of a Virgo self-help program is assisting others. *Unhappiness comes from thinking of oneself.* When you contribute to others, there is a wonderful sense of unity and accomplishment and you move forward on your transforming path of service.

After some conscious planning and working on her vision for herself, my client found that her heart was ready for a risk. She was ready to attract positive people into her life in all areas. She found a new job that was perfect for her, with a small group of people who worked well together. After a successful stint with this company she eventually went into her own business. Just in time, too, for she met someone at the new company she worked with, they got married, and she was able to work at home when her children came into the world. Her fear of not having power over a situation changed as she became more conscious. She learned that her true power comes from trusting her talents and taking a risk. There has to be wholehearted interest and enthusiasm to empower a situation. Put yourself in the right position with a good attitude and Virgo is a winner every time.

The biggest problem you have to deal with is your best trait, the practical mind. The mind is always set to some degree in a critical mode; it has to make the final choice. However, alone and without the heart, it lacks compassion. Compassion comes from the feelings and the emotions, which Virgo steers clear of. The mind can be an instrument of torture without a connection to inner truth. The mind separated from the heart can give a perverted perspective, and your love of order can border on fastidiousness.

You must learn how to protect yourself from overwork and lack of proper recompense. Although slavery has been abolished for many years, people are still enslaved by stringent work ethics and materialistic companies that consider the profit line and depersonalize the needs of the employees.

Virgo, your greatest gift is knowing how to categorize and combine the proper components, creating something good that works efficiently and practically. You deserve your own unique talent. You have much to offer. A Virgo needs contact with others to stay balanced mentally and emotionally. You can thrive by joining others in cooperative enterprises. But you must also pursue your *own* ambitious goals.

Virgo rules small animal, plants, and all the natural wonders on planet Earth. Your love of nature heals you when you get burned out. Enjoying the natural flow of your surroundings gives you the reinforcement you need to let your heart open to just being who you are, a special part of God's grace. A graceful environment is conducive to asking your higher power to give you peace of mind. If you are negative, ask for the positive. If you are tired, ask for energy. You don't have to give anything up. You have to learn to receive what is good for you. You deserve it.

Libra

September 23–October 22

Air Sign Ruled by Venus

SOUL POWER: *Knowledge, Conscientiousness*

EGO BLOCKAGE: *Absolute Perfectionism, Denial*

TRANSFORMING PATH: *Personal Relationships, Unity*

The Libran time of year starts at the autumnal equinox, when the days and nights are equal in length. It is the time when the grain is harvested and weighed. Libra is the sign of balance. Using the scale as its symbol both illustrates the meaning of the sign and honors this ancient tradition.

Libra is the first Sun sign that considers others. It is the sign of marriage and partnerships, and you Librans take them very seriously. In fact, that is what Libra is all about: acknowledging others and forming peaceful and balanced relationships. Libra is the first sign to bring into consciousness the concept of the self in relation to others. The first six Sun signs, Aries through Virgo, are signs of the nighttime; in their approach to life they are primal, subjective, and fundamentally conscious only of their own needs. The last six signs, Libra through Pisces, are signs of the daytime. They are complex, objective, and very conscious of other people's needs and of inter-personal relationships. This isn't to say that the last six signs are more evolved than the others; you are just more complex and have a wider range of interests.

You Libras are very responsive to your environment and the people in it. The symbol of this responsiveness is the ideally balanced scale of serenity. You stay calm when everyone else around you is out of control. You are the one others count on in times of crisis, so you mustn't allow yourself to be swayed by their urgent needs. Stay cool, and you always come up with the right decisions.

Librans are nice people. You are thoughtful and your intention is to bring order out of chaos. With your quick mind you are good at finding the disorder and setting it straight. You are never forceful but can solve a problem patiently and effectively when you have all the facts. Your soul power is conscientiousness, and it pleases you to be concerned with fairness. You are meticulous in your discernment and scrupulous in your behavior. Nothing gets past you. You notice everything around you and take responsibility for your part without hesitation.

Libra is the sign of logic, and although you are very set on doing the right thing, you are still unusually considerate of others. You are often so solicitous that when another person steps into the opposite side of your scale, your appreciation of their point of view may outweigh good judgment and you may give undue consideration to the other person's agenda. Of course, this throws the relationship off from the start. Protocol calls for niceties, but it's not necessary to give up your power for the comfort of others.

Librans are always making comparisons. You have a continuous dialogue going on in your head. No sooner does one thought surface than another, contradictory one is suggested. You like a good debate, but you hate to argue. Your desire on earth is for everyone to love each other and live happily ever after. You like to make choices that maintain your dignity and respect for the other person, and you expect others to do the same.

The power of knowledge, your other soul power, is perhaps the greatest power of all. Knowledge means that through your own experience you have learned an art, a science, a body of work. Your Libran soul helps you associate facts with truth and higher principles. You are capable of knowing all that can be known by an individual. You are knowledgeable and you have a creative mind, so you must trust yourself. Librans are straight as arrows in their approach to life. The Egyptians noticed that an arrow goes to its mark when balanced by a feather. They made the feather the symbol of justice and truth; their gods and pharaohs wore it as a symbol of righteousness.

As a Libran, you can't abide anything that is ill-proportioned and unsightly. My dog Tasha, a toy Yorkie, is a Libra. She is a princess, very concerned about where she is and what is going on around her. One day, we were out walking in our neighborhood in New York when we saw another dog walking with its owner. It was very unattractive, unkempt and shaggy. When I looked down to see what Tasha's reaction was, she looked up at me and shuddered. Astrology wins again! I thought. Even a Libran dog can have its sensibilities offended by ugliness.

Libra is ruled by Venus, the goddess of love, the feminine reactive force that makes life worth living with its grace and charm. Her grace gives you a gentle and kind demeanor. You are compelled to have beautiful surroundings and go to great lengths to have an array of light, pastel colors around you. You are attracted to pale greens and blues, although many Librans love pink too. You want peace and harmony in all things. Music is an important part of your life. You often play a musical instrument and have an incredible collection of beautiful music.

Venus was famous for her romantic intrigues and affairs with both gods and mortals. She has always been associated with romance and feminine beauty and is a favorite subject in art. She is most famously depicted as the *Venus de Milo* and in Botticelli's *Birth of Venus*, rising up out of the mist on a seashell. Perhaps the most beautiful representation of a perfect Venusian male is Michelangelo's *David* in Florence. Its absolute balance and symmetry bring tears to your eyes.

Ancient myths say that Venus was born from her father Uranus's genitals. I guess if Sun gods can be born of virgins, love goddesses can be born immaculately from their fathers. In any case, Venus was born motherless. She descended from the masculine, the thinking function, and as Libra's ruler she makes you very self-possessed, verbal, and in the know. Because you are so gentle in nature, it's hard to imagine how strong you are. But make no mistake, you are leaders and take charge very easily when you set your mind to it. Your approach is direct and objective, and you are impeccable in your discernment—although you take your time when making a decision.

Your logic is best when combined with your intuition. I always think of Librans as being very mental, but there is also a very intuitive aspect to your thinking that can't be missed. Remember Venus is rising from the mist, which is both water and air. Although Libra is classified as a thinker, there definitely is a water element that signifies emotion and feeling, perhaps from Venus's watery beginnings. Maybe this is why you are always caught between two points of reference and have a hard time making up your mind. How many times have you vacillated in a situation, not knowing how to decide. It's because you feel the necessity to make value judgments based on intuition as well as rational considerations. It takes time to weigh your thoughts when they are coming from two different processes.

Since your transforming path is personal relationships, you are inordinately aware of other people and their needs. This sensitivity—looking outside yourself for more information—makes you very analytical and objective in everything that happens. You are constantly weighing information, seeking balance and harmony. Your desire is to be fair and your consideration, particularly of loved ones, is paramount.

There is a decidedly androgynous quality to your nature. As a woman, you think like a man and as a man, you think like a woman. The balancing of male and female makes you an artist in everything you do, even in love and lovemaking. The truth is, very few humans are as balanced as you, so your life lesson is to make adjustments. But you must let go of your ego blockage of absolute perfectionism or you will be perfectly alone.

I'm sure your hesitation in making up your mind comes from your perfectionism. Trying to be careful and not make a mistake, Librans often fall behind and come in late, whereas other signs, like Aries, Sagittarius, and Aquarius, jump in too quickly. There is a cosmic law that is reassuring and comforting, especially for you Librans: *Everything in the universe is in divine order.* The law of the universe says that everything happens at the right time. Astrology is based on that premise. You are always where you need to be for right action to take place. With your soul power of knowledge, you can understand and accept this; by giving up your fear of making a mistake and not being perfect, you can go with the flow.

A desire for excellence is foremost in your mind. Your nature is careful, tactful, and exceedingly courteous. Librans hate injustice, and you pride yourself on your ability to see all sides. How many times have you said, "It's not fair!" or "Is this the right thing to do?" You have to be careful or a lot of time will be wasted in trying to make everyone's crooked road straight or justify your actions. Naturally a gregarious sign, you love all the entertaining that comes with an active social life. Your life is active and you have many chances to learn how to cooperate with others.

Like Cancer, you wish there were a book somewhere with all the answers so you could memorize it and get everything just right. You need to trust your instincts; you're well equipped to make good decisions and mustn't let anyone hurry you. You sometimes get bogged down by getting caught up in outdated social customs and conventions. In trying to do the right thing all the time, you lose your objectivity. You are so easily programmed that you constantly feel the misery of *should, ought,* and *must.*

Being ruled by Venus, your sign is very feminine. Libra women are very beautiful and alluring—even sexy—and the men are classically good-looking. Research done on animals shows that the most perfectly balanced dragonfly has the most suitors. The key to beauty and attraction is symmetry, and Libra rules symmetry. You have elegant bodies, oval faces, beautiful skin, and are attractive people at any age. Most Librans, like Taureans, have dimples, because of their Venus rulership. Look at Cupids in art; as symbols of erotic love they have dimples all over their bodies. Just like Cupid, many Librans have dimpled chins as a sign of beauty.

Libran men are extremely attractive to women. It seems you understand women better than other signs, and with Venus as your ruler you have to come to terms with your feminine side. That is why you are such good lovers. You are the best-looking and most sexual of all the Sun signs. Just look at Armand Assante, Roger Moore, Julio Iglesias, and Yves Montand, all perfectly gorgeous Librans. These guys are always impeccably dressed, with perfect nails, and they must smell divine. Libran men are good businessmen, legal-minded and yet drawn to the arts. You are wonderful actors, architects, photographers, and interior designers and excel at many kinds of creative endeavors. Sting, a Libran and inspired musician, is a wonderful example of a Renaissance man.

The Libran woman isn't to be taken lightly! Your beauty and elegance always has an air of intelligence. Sigourney Weaver, Susan Sarandon, and Angela Lansbury are three such stars that fit the description. There are also some drop-dead gorgeous types, like Brigitte Bardot, Angie Dickinson, and Catherine Deneuve, who never seem to grow old. On the brainy side and just as lovely are Penny Marshall, Barbara Walters, and Mary Beth Hurt.

Libra rules the law of opposites. There is always a certain amount of tension in this process. In Eastern cosmology it is called yin and yang. These two forces are archetypal female and male energies that combine to produce all that comes to be on earth. Even some vegetables are thought to be male and female and should be mixed accordingly. Your sign is totally involved in balancing opposites, and as much as you hate power struggles of any kind, they are prevalent in your life. You are forced to learn how to communicate and negotiate, and you have to learn that compromise doesn't have to be a downer. Libra is the sign of true love, of caring enough to surrender your selfish desires. Combining the needs of both parties is necessary in all personal relations, and a point of real understanding must be reached. You are good at that. Compromise comes from your soul power of conscientiousness. There is always a point of agreement possible if your heart is open to what is best for all concerned.

Libra is the sign of marriage, and with your transforming path of personal relationships, love is always on your mind. Naturally, love affairs are the most important events in your life. You are drawn to relationships like a magnet, and rightly so. The earth is made for couples, and if you're not in a relationship you feel incomplete. Like your opposite sign, Aries, you can be a love addict. You have a tendency to lose yourself in relationships and feel miserable without one. When you feel incomplete within yourself, you look for someone else to fulfill your needs. Urgently trying to fill this void puts you at great risk emotionally. It's a big mistake. You have to become the person *you* want. With your sensitivity you need time to bond with another person. As Nietzsche said, "It is not a lack of love, but a lack of friendship that makes unhappy marriages." Everything in its own good time; keep this neediness at bay and you attract a better relationship. In order to know another person well, a good rule of thumb is to allow two years. This is based on Mars' two-year cycle around a natal chart. That way you can see how your partner responds to negative situations as well as the good. This is still no guarantee that the relationship will work. There is still a risk but you will operate from a more informed position.

The seventh house rules all the other people in your life; ironically, it's considered to be the sign of open enemies as well. It's interesting that from the beginning of a relationship your spouse is already your opponent—before any dissension actually appears. When I first saw this, I was intrigued and started to seek out the anomaly that was hidden in the symbol. Your mate as an adversary implies that relationships are based on disunity. This is a warning that no one see things exactly the same way you do. There is always a potential for disagreement. Ask any lawyer—that's how they make their living. Since your sign, Libra, rules legal matters and court cases, there is a lot to think about. I came to the conclusion that without stress, there would be no relationships. In fact that's what they're all about. You need a point of reference to bounce off, whether it is a person, place, or thing. You would be mentally and emotionally stagnant without it.

I believe that relationships are fated. You can't go to Bloomingdale's to buy one. You can't make anyone love you, and for that matter you can't love just anyone either. But the world was made for couples, and there seems to be a great magnetic force that pulls people together. This great, irresistible force of attraction is affected by your state of consciousness. When we look at our world we see ourselves. Life is a mirror: To have a good relationship, you want to reflect all the good traits you want in someone else. The answer is to get your act together, be as balanced as you can be, and the universe will get your perfect-as-possible mate to you as soon as it can. The odds are in your favor.

Perhaps the reason there are so many divorces in the world today, particularly in the West, is that we romanticize courtship and marriage too much. We aren't prepared to face the difficulties and misunderstandings that are natural to the situation. We are not taught how to solve differences of opinion in a logical sequence. We are still in the "I'm right, you're wrong," win-or-lose mentality.

This competitive way of thinking comes from the reptilian brain, a part of the brain at the nape of the neck that is a holdover from our animal origins. A small part of our brain, yes, but still self-evident in the world, as it rules aggression and self-preservation and lacks the necessary mechanism for communication. It is primitive, with no empathetic response to others. Aries, your aggressive opposite sign, rules the reptilian brain. The second brain, ruled by Cancer, is the limbic or emotional brain, which is a holdover from our mammalian ancestors and rules the tribe or family. There is the later brain, the prefrontal cortex, that is found only in higher mammals such as humans. Are we trapped in a war within our triune brain? It seems so. It is Libra's nature to be emotionally concerned and want everyone to win. Libra rules the prefrontal cortex of the brain, the newest part, the part we're still developing. This part looks inward and finds the empathy, altruism, and moral judgment that consciously links one's well-being with the well-being of others.

It is ironic that as the sign of marriage you often wait a long time to marry or remain single. The ego blockage of absolute perfectionism definitely works against relationships because Libra keeps waiting for that perfect someone. You have a very long list of what you want, and there is no such person on earth. Some really good candidates can go by if they don't live up to your pictures of what you want. Then again, on the reactive side you might jump up and settle for the surface attributes of sexual attraction, good looks, and glamour, forgetting that anyone can talk a good game for a while. Don't believe everything you hear, and don't think that everyone is as pure in their intentions as you are. That's a big mistake.

You must watch out. Don't lose your cool—just getting married isn't what it's about. If you make a mistake and marry the wrong person, it's next to impossible for you to make a decision to divorce. It seems that relationships are fated, and being patient, which is your strength, sets up a vortex that allows the right one to come in.

How married couples get together has always fascinated me. One of my clients met her husband when she got stuck in a revolving door and in forcefully pushing herself through the door, she knocked herself out. Prince Charming came to the rescue and has been there ever since. But the best love story so far is the man who met his wife when he called a wrong number. It turned out to be the right number after all when they started talking. They met for coffee and that was that. God does work in mysterious ways. Remember that your transforming path of personal relationships is always at work in your life; it's your life lesson, so don't be surprised when fate calls.

The teachers of all religions have encouraged similar backgrounds as a foundation for marriage. With this natural opposition in the sign of partnerships, I can see their reasoning. The more alike you are, the easier it is to stand up to the natural pressure of dealing with another person's agenda. Yet the zodiac says growth with your opposite is necessary. We need both: There have to be similarities to be comfortable, but the good old "opposites attract" story still works, especially in sexual relationships.

Libra's transforming path is unity. It is what you fervently seek, and if you are patient you will find it. You are blessed with the ability to look for, find, and understand perfect equipoise, that exact balance of the heart and mind. You will always find that life puts you in situations that require major decisions. It is your life lesson. You're funded for these tests of discernment, and they are far easier if you trust your heart and inner knowledge to help you. If you're not careful, you can wait and wait for more information until the moment is lost. A good rule of thumb is to be practical. Don't sweat the small stuff. What difference does it make in a hundred years if you paint the living room blue or green? Save your mental energy for big decisions, and then take the time you need.

You become so immersed in rules of etiquette and, sometimes, just being glad that someone's there that you forget about yourself. It's hard to believe that someone as intelligent and, yes, sophisticated can be so naive! You are the kings and queens of denial. Face up to it! When things are right in a relationship, it's obvious—you know it in your heart.

Like Virgo, you have a bit of the New York attitude. Virgo and Libra are side by side in the zodiac and much alike. You love to be the critic. The problem is, nine times out of ten you are right. You have an exceptional ability to record reams of information in your brain and to access it at will. You are probably the most intelligent Sun sign in the zodiac. Remember your soul power of knowledge and don't be afraid to use it. Although both Libra and Virgo are very mental and quick on the uptake, Virgos are more clinical; wanting everything to be neat and effective, they focus on the physical. With Libra it has to be beautiful as well as neat, and your focus is on creative concept.

The ability to solve problems is the intrinsic meaning of the seventh house, which rules legal matters and negotiation. A Libra has one major problem: wanting to be *right* all the time. You want to be the judge with a gavel and strike the podium with the final word. This is from your ego blockage of absolute perfectionism. The judge stands alone—and that's where you'll be if you persist in having the final word.

Trying to be perfect places a big burden on you. What if I fail? What if I don't do the right thing? What if I don't know how? All these questions are a waste of time and drain your energy. Own your soul powers of conscientiousness and knowledge. You have a good head on your shoulders, so trust yourself.

You naturally rise to power positions in your career. Being very eloquent, you speak with the wisdom of Solomon. A Libran type, he loved beautiful things and wrote poetry. As a king he mediated with a piercing insight and designed a fabulous temple in Jerusalem. Many famous poets and authors are Libran: the epic poet Virgil, Cervantes, Eugene O'Neill, Heidegger, Arthur Miller, Truman Capote—not a bad list. It really doesn't end there: John Lennon and Gandhi, both Librans, were able to touch people's hearts with their profound and original ideas.

Many times Librans are offered chances to move up in their careers too quickly for their timing and turn them down. You aren't good at burning the midnight oil like Capricorn and Virgo. You like to enjoy your leisure and have a tendency to be a little lazy. (That's Venus for you!) Goddesses like to sip cool drinks and eat bonbons. Staring into space (contemplation) is your way of letting your mind roam, and your best ideas come when you allow time for this. Take the time you need to come up with the right answers. When you feel rushed, you get out of balance. You are late bloomers. Your best ideas usually pay off after age 40. This isn't to say that you aren't precocious in childhood and often act like an adult long before you are; but you like a slow and steady pace, and time is in your favor.

It is a Libran thing to love gracious living. You don't like the rat race. Although you love protocol and festivities such as holiday functions, weddings, and birthdays, you don't like to be hurried. You also want to have one big happy family with everyone in the group or family included.

Since your gift in life is being logical and fair, you are called on by friends and family to mediate when there are differences. Watch out! Trying to please them puts you in the middle, with a good chance of being left holding the bag. Back off and don't get pulled in emotionally; then you can give them your assessment and let them decide. It's not your responsibility to make other people's decisions. It's easy to get stuck if you take things too personally and feel overly responsible. So, with the Libran influence you seem to be the one who takes on the most responsibility, except for Cancer, who is also very family-oriented.

All Eastern countries are ruled by the sign of Libra. In the East they generally revere their ancestors. The East thinks in the long term, and fate is given a chance to have a hand in destiny. This allows a sense of freedom from the urgency and hurry, hurry of the West. In the West we want to see immediate results and appreciate what is active, forceful, and masculine in character, even in our women. The West thinks in terms of cause and effect, of a clearly defined result. It weighs information, sorts it out, selects and classifies it, then—thinking the problem is solved—goes on to the next problem. Although it is said that East is East and West is West, both of these systems of thought have their points and seem to be integrating as we enter the twenty-first century. As the world gets smaller, many people in the West are interested in Eastern philosophy as the East is very influenced by our progressive, productive, and materialistic culture. I think we may be the lucky ones in that exchange.

What Can Be Done

With such a sophisticated and civilized presentation, it is surprising to find you are very naive. Some people call you gullible. As smart as you are, you have a tendency to project your own thoughts and opinions onto other people. This leaves you open to disappointment and disillusionment when they don't live up to your expectations. Since *you* wouldn't do anything wrong, how could *they*? This gets you into a lot of emotional turmoil when the truth comes out. How could they do that to me? I wouldn't have done that to them! You must learn that as humans we all have feet of clay! Don't project what you would do onto others—it's probably not correct. Your ego blockage is denial and your desire to please others creates an illusion, seeing what you want to see, that couldn't be further from the truth.

Librans are wonderful people to know. You are thoughtful and kind and go out of your way to be helpful. You are a responsive partner and love to be in a relationship. In fact, you are very unhappy if you are not in a relationship. Relationships are fated. We can't make anyone love us. Being sociable and interested in a variety of subjects helps to bring new people into your life. A relationship can pop up when you least expect it—particularly when you are content with yourself.

Your biggest problems come from looking for approval outside of yourself and wanting to be right about everything. Put those with a tendency to be overly critical and the constant vacillation of not being able to make up your mind, and it adds up to a form of torture for you and everyone around you. All of these frustrations will be eliminated when you trust your soul.

Three Steps for Healing Your Blockage

1. Your ego blockage of absolute perfectionism is holding you back. How can you make decisions when the results are not going to be the way you want them? This is a depressing thought. There is a way to have perfection in your life but not the way you're going about it now. Your ego blockage of denial confuses the facts; sooner or later life gives you a wake-up call that you may not like.

2. Knowledge and conscientiousness are your soul powers. How do you share your ideas with others? How do you take the risk of deciding what is right for you? The answer to this dilemma comes by sharing your thoughts and feelings with others. Never assume that they respond to the situation in the same way. You only know where you're coming from. Using your soul power of conscientiousness, ask the other person what their thoughts and feelings are, and you have a beginning.

3. Life is a balancing act at best, and it certainly is in your case with your transforming path of unity. Life lessons are stressful, but the answers are available deep inside, already worked out, like the answers in the back of a schoolbook. No one can take your inner convictions away from you. With your transforming path of personal relationships, you are scheduled to learn how to communicate honestly and succinctly in this lifetime.

When a Libra comes into my office for a consultation, nine times out of ten it's about relationship problems. "When will I marry again?" "What is wrong with my marriage?" "I haven't met anyone to date and I broke up with my boyfriend two months ago." I take these questions very seriously even though many times I wonder why they're so worried. Life usually takes care of the man-meets-woman thing, unless you hide out where no one can see you.

One of my Libran clients was dating a Sagittarian. They had been together for five years, but she still wasn't convinced that he was the right one. Of course, she was looking for her perfect soulmate and there were days when he didn't add up in her mind. She had nothing to complain about; sometimes he liked to go off and do his own thing (being a Sag), but by and large he was a wonderful guy. He wanted to marry her and have children.

Her ego blockage of absolute perfectionism and denial were having a fine time. She felt that if she made a decision, her life was over and she was doomed to the unknowable, something she couldn't control. I have seen this behavior in a lot of men and a few women, but Libran women, like most men, listen to their minds instead of their hearts. It's easy for Libra to be separated mentally and emotionally. The longer they delay marriage, the harder it is to make a marriage decision. I personally think the soulmate theory is stretched way out of proportion. There are many soulmates in life. Your best friend may be a soulmate. There has to be an attraction between people to make life worth living. Carl Jung says we have a complete image of the opposite sex within us. When we meet someone of the opposite sex who resembles our inner partner, a kind of scanner goes off. Beep! Beep! Beep! Watch out—when it goes off too much, it's probably an addiction. When the scanner slowly beeps, and the heart comes alive, it's worth looking into—this may be your true partner.

How to Apply the Three Steps in This Situation

There comes a time in everyone's life when you have to make a decision. If not, it may be too late—the party's over, *finito*. The question for my client, of course, is, how does she *really* feel about him? She must get out of her head and into her heart. It helps to be in contact with your soul to make such an important decision. What does she want—chocolate or vanilla? Waiting too long doesn't give you any more information; in fact, the positive energy between you starts to decline. When a decision is made with your soul power of conscientiousness, the heart is there giving you the soulful information you need and a commitment is more likely to last. The last time I heard from hesitant Libra, she had been able to free herself from the need to control the future. She realized that they shared a great deal together and that there was hope for a very good marriage.

The Cabala says that the soul is given freedom of choice and the lessons to learn in the world before you are born. When you are in the throes of a life lesson, your subconscious goes on alert. You have been prepared for this important experience. You do not have to hurry (Librans hate that), but to grow spiritually you have to make decisions. There are no guarantees in life in general, and absolutely none that any marriage will last.

Commitments of any kind have an element of risk. Compatibility between the birth charts of the two individuals helps. It gives you the positive and negative traits of each individual and the way their chart works with yours, but you both still have to live out your life experiences and make decisions for yourselves. It helps to recognize the presence of your soul and seek its guidance. With the wisdom of divine direction, your decisions are easier. The mind alone doesn't have the answer. When I do compatibility charts, I endeavor to lead clients into their soul consciousness. That is where the truth is.

Scorpio

October 23–November 22

Water Sign Ruled by Mars and Pluto

SOUL POWER: *Transformation*

EGO BLOCKAGE: *Domination, Isolation*

TRANSFORMING PATH: *Surrender*

Of all the signs in the zodiac none is so enigmatic and imbued with mystery as Scorpio. The solar energy in Scorpio is beyond ordinary ideas—it is transcendent. You will be transformed many times in this life, and you have the ability to impact others as well. This is a big responsibility and one that must be reckoned with.

As a Scorpio your soul power is transformation. You are seeded with the power to change the status quo, to make things better. Your personality is intense, penetrating, and pervasive and must be used ethically or the results may be devastating. When used with high moral intent, it is a force for the highest good on earth.

It seems that you are always intensely searching and at the same time apprehensively watching to see if you are safe. Perhaps you are looking for yourself—for your own soul.

The first step in spiritual growth is longing for union with the soul. Scorpio is the sign that rules this search. You might think it is for sex or material things, but it doesn't take too long in life to discover that the search is for something intangible, something inside yourself. It's the soul longing to be heard. This longing stays with you until you surrender to a spiritual path of devotion in your life. This path is not necessarily religious. It could be just to help others. When you find your soul power of transformation, the longing and endless search will be replaced with productive activity.

You're an old soul, Scorpio. There is much about you that does not meet the eye, and with a natural desire for secrecy you want to keep it that way. But the question is, do you hide from yourself?

As mysterious as you are, the one thing we know about you for sure is that you like to be in control. With your ego blockage of domination and isolation you look for ways to dominate your environment. You look for a place that is removed so the view is clear and you dig in for the duration. These hiding places can be anywhere, inside your mind or in your physical environment. Emotional avoidance keeps you hidden away from personal contact, and that's a lonely place to be. It's easy for you to be so caught up in your own world that you are unobtainable, even to your loved ones.

If your goals are well-rounded, you can accomplish a lot and many people benefit from your endeavors. But if you live on the sidelines, out of touch with friends and family, you are the loser.

The symbolic rulers of Scorpio are the scorpion, the snake, and the eagle. They like to seek out places of safety. It's hard to find a snake or scorpion if you look for them; they are over in some dark corner, observing their environment. Eagles build their nests at altitudes so high they are safe from predators. The air gets pretty thin up there for you human Scorpions. Symbolically, going to the top of the mountain means reaching success. We have all heard the expression "It's lonely at the top," but does it have to be?

Problem solving is your forte. Your mode of operation could be called an all-out attack—you love a challenge. Being capable of strenuous effort and heroic endurance, you have the ability to clean up a botched job and breathe new life into it.

Scorpio rules the reproductive and elimination systems, the systems whose functions are to release toxins and replenish the body. The deep-seated workings of the mind, the sex drive, and the survival instinct are also under Scorpio rulership. You are the powerhouse of the zodiac, set for great deeds not only by birth but through sheer force of character. By accepting your soul power of transformation as an exciting project instead of a burden, you lighten your load. However, I must caution you not to get stuck in looking for the problem to the point of *ignoring the solution*. The most important part of the transformation of a toxic situation is in the resolution. This entails letting go of the problem and celebrating a joyous rebirth.

Your diplomatic neighbor, Libra, is thoughtful and kindly, considerate of others. Although your presentation is not so mild, you are intuitively just as considerate of others. Also, in times of stress you have the ability to react with a rare combination of emotional empathy and cool detachment.

Many of you are politicians, lawyers, and doctors. Scorpio surgeons can calmly make the proper analysis, then operate on their patients—literally cutting them open to remove the disease. This composed and courageous attitude is your best trait. Through your detachment, you fearlessly do what needs to be done for a healing to take place. Psychoanalysts use the same insight to open up the mind, relieve painful memories, and push their patients gently into a space of vulnerability, where they can be cleansed of old conditioning.

You like to flirt with taboos! What is forbidden or profane attracts you like a magnet. There is a lot of the daredevil in you. This, oddly enough, is how you set yourself up to be controlled: give Scorpios a dare and watch them take the bait. When presented with a project that's impossible to do, you step in, even against seemingly superhuman forces. You don't like authority of any kind but will hold on relentlessly to something you believe in and take charge yourself. Sometimes you don't know when to let go. If you are denied or delayed, your tendency is to hold on. You've heard the expression "hang on till hell freezes over." That's a Scorpio for sure!

With all this stubbornness and determination it's not surprising that your transforming path is surrender. There is a lot of confusion about what surrender actually is. Letting go of something negative isn't losing as long as the higher understanding of the soul is there. Transformational understanding is your gift, it's your power. When you just let go and surrender an expectation and stay softly in the moment, you are at your best. You know naturally how to take things to a higher level. You have an inherent ability to shift a situation to resolution, but no one can force you to do it, not even yourself. The change must come from your own volition, your own surrender of your ego blockages of domination and isolation. The way to true surrender is to transform each moment. This is passion at its highest. Give up the urgency to dominate. Let the soul win.

Paradoxically, it is the same drive to control that gives you the power to be transformed. Daily pressures hone you like a knife and you become the best of all the Sun signs at purposefully slicing through to the truth. Out of this intense self-evaluation comes the dove—the highest symbol of Scorpio, a symbol of a conciliatory attitude and peace. This altruistic consciousness understands negotiation and compromise at its highest level.

The Beast in *Beauty and the Beast* gave off a Scorpion-like aura only to be as a gentle lamb inside. The haunting Phantom in *The Phantom of the Opera*, with his enticing voice and Machiavellian mask, charmed a beautiful young girl. The comic-strip character Batman looks menacing, but underneath his sexy, form-fitting black suit, he is a bookish guy who is a little shy. The Mafia is a Scorpionic institution. Exceptional actors love to play the part of a mafioso and show the good guy inside, acting out the alter ego of Scorpio.

I know a Scorpio who, in his self-styled radical attitude, says, "The devil is never so dark as he is painted."

There are few such Scorpionic female characters in art or history. The only ones that I can think of are Lady Macbeth, Catwoman in *Batman*, and Glenn Close's character in *Fatal Attraction* (a Scorpio film), but they weren't allowed a vulnerable human side that was emotionally acceptable in the end. Perhaps it says something about our culture that when women are painted as dark figures, there is no redemption. Are we all trapped in this myth of black-and-white morality for women?

A positive Scorpion-type female figure that comes to mind is Queen Cleopatra, although her personality was more manipulative than dark. With her alluring sexuality and intellectual genius she enraptured Julius Caesar and Mark Antony, two of the most powerful men in Roman history. Through her guile she brought her country out of a secondary position into equality with Rome. It is said that she wasn't considered to be beautiful but could entrance any man she so desired. According to legend, after Mark Antony's death, with no hope left and facing imminent bondage in Rome, she took a poisonous snake (a Scorpio symbol) to her breast. In Pharaonic Egypt, death by an asp was only available to an initiate of the sacred priesthood. Therein lay her redemption. (Still a little dark for my taste!)

Through your power of transformation your life more than others has dramatic endings or crises that force growth. Elisabeth Kübler-Ross codified the emotional steps that people who are dying pass through. I find these steps useful to process any periods of devastation from loss of job to divorce.

1. *Denial:* Refusing to face the facts is what makes us sick in the first place. It stops the energy flow. The truth is healing and it doesn't take as much energy. Jesus said, "The truth shall set you free."
2. *Anger:* If you know you're angry, it must be expressed. Anger doesn't go away; it is lethal, and when suppressed, it backfires on you every time.

3. *Depression*: Depression comes from hurt and repressed anger. It lowers vitality and functional activity in your daily life. Life events seen as unfair stop us in our tracks. It's important to move past the confusion and the pain, and this isn't easy to do. Sometimes people need professional help.

4. *Bargaining*: God doesn't barter. The way to change anything is to accept the information and be willing to transcend its limitations into a higher order of understanding.

5. *Acceptance*: A new paradigm is set in place. The energy shifts and things move forward again.

The last stage of acceptance is where the process of surrender comes in and there is a rebirth to a higher level of understanding. You can watch these steps unfold at crisis periods, and they can give you guidance to where you are in the process of your transforming path of surrender.

The magic of rebirth occurs daily when you let go of your fear of losing control. You are never in control anyway, and you will be relieved when you can let the natural flow of what's best for all concerned come into play. So many times the fear you experience is not based on reality; it comes from the part of your personality that constantly troubleshoots. You're always looking to solve the puzzle. You feel it is your job, and your first thought in any traumatic situation is exaggerated into all-out survival—Get out the big guns!—even when there's no serious problem and it's not warranted.

As a water sign, you are extremely sensitive to your environment. Your emotions are very reactive. The phrase "Still waters run deep" describes you exactly. Your mind is closely intertwined with the subconscious; there is no break or differentiation. This causes inner turbulence, like an ocean in a storm.

You're an intuitor by nature and psychically connected to the inner workings of your environment. With your piercing insight, always ready for the worst, you become distressed and easily wounded. This can be very draining and keeps you from having what you want. If you're always ready for trouble, the world will accommodate you.

Your conscious mind is very close to your subconscious. You have to learn to allow the subconscious to drop back down and to separate it from the conscious mind to have any relief. If not, the mental turbulence is always with you, making you moody and unresponsive. A Scorpion in retreat, licking its wounds (real or imagined) is a formidable creature, like an injured tiger. The odd thing is that often you turn against yourself and become your own worst enemy, like the scorpion that stings itself to death if cornered. Your eye is constantly fixed on survival. It's always a life-or-death matter to you. Learning how to look at your fears and refrain from radical behavior is crucial. Ask yourself: What's the worst thing that can happen here? This old tried and true question slows down your reactions, allowing the solution to come to mind. There is a dichotomy. Your emotional turbulence can be very disturbing, yet at the same time, it connects with the inner wisdom that is needed to guide you through the crisis. Your soul power of transformation has all the self-control and understanding you need to overcome your overly sensitive nature. Be patient with yourself. An old Chinese proverb says: "That the birds of worry and care fly above your head, this you cannot change, but that they build nests in your hair, this you can prevent."

Sorry, but of all the Sun signs you have the worst reputation. Runners-up are Gemini (liars), Capricorn (cold-hearted and ruthless), Virgos (negative), and Pisces (substance abusers). The extreme description is not true, of course. It's easy to guess why Scorpio is so highly criticized, with your rulership of such mysterious subjects as sex and death. You are called sex addicts. I personally think your reputation far exceeds the facts. Ironically, Scorpio can be celibate more easily than other Sun signs. Aries, Taurus, and Pisces are much more likely to fall into sexual addiction, but if passion is a crime, you have it.

You are ardent and devoted lovers and express intense feeling in anything you do. Sex may not even be first on your list; however, it is rarely totally out of the picture. It doesn't take very long in life to find out how wonderful, sex is, but it does take a mature viewpoint to learn that raising sexual energy up to the highest level of spiritual development is just as wonderful, and you can have both. Sex is the way the universe gave us to have a bodily experience that comes close to God's constant state of joy and bliss. When there is total love on each side and the union is complete, we can experience this state of intense ecstasy. Scorpio's soul power of transformation rules the act of changing physical desire into wisdom.

Many films are made with storylines based primarily on sex, death, power, and money, all Scorpio subjects. Millions are made making films that turn people on or knock people off. Our poor children are so desensitized to violence by the time they are adults that they turn their backs on outrage and condone destruction as normal behavior.

Although sex and death are great transformational powers, they are mysterious and difficult subjects at best. Do you know why you're sexually attracted to one person and not another? What happens after you die? No one really knows! When you don't have the answers, there is fear. Change and the unknown are the most stressful events we have in our life. There is a test that determines what level of stress you are under. The birth of a child and a marriage are just as stressful as a loss of a job and the death of a loved one. With a Scorpio, double the score. You are so intense that change is exceptionally difficult.

These riddles can only be answered by searching your soul and learning more about the inner workings of your mind and the universe. Faith in a higher power helps. You have the soul power to transform your ego blockages—by energizing selected thoughts and withdrawing energy from undesirable thoughts. Your diseased ego (and we all have one) would love to take charge and use your soul power to have what it selfishly wants. We all have the inclination to misuse power—just read the history books. Your values must be impeccable and you must live up to your standards to purify your ego and surrender to the soul.

Scorpio rules differentiation and elimination. It also runs the involuntary systems of the body. It is the sign of the automatic pilot that keeps everything in balance while you're busy living. This silent partner rules the subconscious, which is way ahead of the conscious, having hidden eyes and ears in every pore. Scientists say that we only use a small percent of our brain. It's reasonable to think that the rest of our brain power resides in the subconscious and we can tap it if we know how. You have a leg up on this power with your close connection to the subconscious.

The subconscious was generally ignored until the twentieth century, when Freud, Jung, and Adler, developing a new science of the mind, came up with the theory that deep-seated emotional programs from childhood are stored in the subconscious and control our behavior. (I think past lives are a part of this, too.) Their belief was that the subconscious works to resolve these blockages primarily through dreams, which Scorpio rules. Our dreams are canvases for these strange and fascinating symbols that seem to have no meaning until they are unraveled by a competent interpreter.

Scorpions are not known for their beauty. They are described in old astrology books as thick-set powerful figures, with strong and rather heavy features and swarthy complexions. When I started looking up famous Scorpios I was surprised at how attractive you were generally—Demi Moore, Lauren Hutton, Linda Evans, Jaclyn Smith, and Grace Kelly, not a bad group. I did notice that you Scorpio women all have a very prim, almost Victorian demeanor that is inconsistent with the seductive and smoldering look that comes from your gorgeous eyes.

You Scorpio men are more varied in your looks. Prince Charles, Richard Dreyfuss, Charles Bronson, and Picasso all have very strong, inscrutable expressions around their eyes. This is appropriate, in that the animal rulers, the eagle and the snake, both have enigmatic, hypnotic eyes. Scorpions are not easy to read. You throw people off with your intense reserve and private manner, appearing untouchable. This can work in your favor in a game of bridge or poker or in bluffing you way through a business deal, but it does turn off people whom you would like to attract.

The astrology symbol for Scorpio is similar to the symbol for Virgo: the Greek word *mem* stands for the feminine principle; the symbol is the letter M combined with an arrow instead of the fish glyph. The combination of the feminine and male symbol implies androgyny. Although Scorpio is considered to be a feminine sign, it has a masculine undertone of aggression and attack. The masculine arrow or hunting spear could represent the scorpion's stinger or the focused and intense male attributes of Scorpio. The arrow is also part of the male symbol for Mars, one of Scorpio's rulers.

Mars designates the fiery instinct of action and desire. It is the symbol for passion.

No matter how evolved you are, Scorpio, watch out for your stinger. Eagles are so focused that with a perfect trajectory they're able to dive two thousand feet and hit their prey. Your aim is excellent, so you must know what you want to set your sights on. Beware! Your attack can be lethal and you are responsible for the damage you do in this life and the next.

Trust yourself; the feminine attributes of Scorpio give you the intuitive wisdom of making your mark. The male aspects give you the energy and drive to take the risks you need to be transformed and to transform others.

Of all the Sun signs, Scorpio can be the most unrelenting. This comes from having the planet Pluto as the second ruler of your chart. Pluto symbolizes breaking down energy to its lowest level and rejuvenating it. Although Pluto is the farthest planet in our solar system, it is symbolically the most powerful. One of Pluto's teachings is that you don't have to be in the same room to influence others. Your energy is so powerful it travels all over the world. Your vibration permeates other dimensions. What a responsibility! Pluto rules not only the transformation of your actions, but the transfiguration of your body and soul.

Gandhi was a Libra with a Scorpio ascendant. Hitler was a Taurus with a Libra ascendant, but he also had a lot of Scorpio in the first house. They share the same soul power of conscientiousness and transformation, but history bears out their different impact on the world. Gandhi's was for the highest purpose of freedom, and Hitler's was to manipulate and annihilate. What was the difference in these two men? Both Taurus and Libra are very charismatic and have an amazing ability to sway others. Having the same signs, their transforming paths of unity and surrender were alike but they reacted very differently. Both charts were identical, with the same lesson, yet one reached up and the other selected a path so undesirable and destructive that there is no redemption for his memory on earth. One man surrendered to a spiritual path and the other willfully chose the opposite. Hitler was a self-aggrandizing egomaniac. His only surrender came when he was up against a threat of total defeat. Then he committed suicide, hiding underneath a mountain fortress, a long way from the top.

Although Gandhi brought an ancient message of pacifism to the world politically, he did have a Scorpio ending—by an assassin's bullet. The old astrology books say that only very old souls come in with strong Scorpio placements. They will go through many difficult and transforming life cycles. Scorpio's transforming path of surrender pushes them to fulfill their destiny in the highest way possible. You have a chance *every moment* to work with the highest standards and to transform your life.

There are many theories why one person chooses the highest and another the lowest. This is one of the mysteries of life. Although there are no excuses for his evil acts, perhaps Hitler's ego was so damaged in childhood that his choices were tainted from the beginning and he could never pull himself out of the downward spiral of the dark Plutonian parts of his psyche.

Remember, your transforming path is neutral—it's all in how you see it. Surrender does not mean that you give up your needs in life. It means that you must surrender your ego blockages of domination and isolation, which keep you in a private hell. Surrender is a step up into higher understanding. Your highest destiny isn't something to fight for. It comes to you miraculously at the right moment.

What Can Be Done

Sometimes when I work with a client I want to say, "*Stop doing that!*" It's so easy for me to see your self-undermining habits. It's different with each sign. With Scorpio it's *stop* being so self-destructive, *stop* being blind to the power of your own creative force, *stop* getting stuck in emotional isolation within yourself.

A highly evolved Scorpio is a great joy to behold. You are responsive to information that appeals to your laserlike comprehension. You have the foresight to come out of self-bondage into a quest for your soul power. Putting yourself in situations where you can receive respect and love helps. Being as sensitive to your environment as you are, why put yourself in Hades when you can be in Heaven?

Three Steps for Healing Your Blockage

1. Domination and control, your ego blockages, are just like black holes. There is no light available to see the truth and you are blindly looking in the dark for ways to relieve the pressure. All your unhappiness comes from the continuing stress of projecting power outside yourself, then trying to control it. Impossible!

2. Your soul power of transformation is perhaps the most powerful in the zodiac. It is your higher nature to face facts in altruistic fashion. With intense willpower you go to the depths of the matter and restore it to health or prosperity.

3. Your transforming path of surrender is misunderstood. For anything to be transformed to a higher level or even a lower level it must be released from the consciousness as it is now. Changing your attitude or views is a form of surrender. When these old ideas are released, a better one comes in their place.

A Scorpio client called me one day in desperation. Her voice was full of tears. (I can always tell if the situation is serious by hearing the voice on the phone.) She was separated from her husband and wanted to know if her marriage was over. After some discussion I asked her what had happened. She said, "Well, I had a little affair."

She had been married for ten years and her husband, a Cancer, was a very successful businessman. They had it all—two homes, more than enough money, and an active social life. Their astrological signs were compatible. Why did she stray?

She had given up her career to be with her husband and to support him in his work. The first questions that come to mind when I read for a Scorpio in trouble are, What are they trying to control, and What are they hiding from?

Her husband was a wonderful man. He was her mentor and protector, but his career was really taking off, so they decided she would give up her work to be free to travel with him. She didn't realize at the time how limiting that would be for her and how left out she would feel. Her role was basically undefined.

This is where the ego blockages kick in. One of Scorpio's biggest fears is lack of control. Their ego blockage is domination, so my client's insecurities started to come out. Although her husband took care of her financially and socially, there was very little real communication—he was too taken up in his business. He indulged her financially, trying to make her happy. She didn't know what she needed or wanted in a relationship and neither did he, so they drifted apart. This was what precipitated her "little affair." This kind of marriage can turn into a father-daughter relationship and the sex, becoming incestuous, is a turnoff. Her emotional and sexual needs were not being met; another man showed up with the right looks and the right words to fill the void.

You are only as sick as your secrets, and there is always a 99 percent chance of secrets being found out. Ask a young child what is going on in the household and he or she will tell you. You delude yourself into thinking you are hiding your feelings or your actions. When a couple is in trouble sexually there is a tendency to sweep it under the rug and deny it. But in all reality, you both know it. It's sitting there like a cobra, ready to strike.

How to Apply the Three Steps in This Situation

This is what came through in the reading: The answer for a healing in this situation was in her soul power of transformation. She deserved the love she wanted, but bringing in another man before she had solved the problem with the first one wasn't the answer. The Scorpio woman was unconsciously trying to get even with her husband by doing the one thing she knew would hurt him.

She had to open up to the fact that she might have lost her husband. In flirting with the forbidden, she let her basic self take over and choose a quick fix instead of trusting the transformational soul power that is her gift in life, the power of transcendence. In her ego blockage of isolation, she had dug a big hole and was wallowing around in it.

When a woman marries a father figure there is some unfinished business in her maturing process. Scorpio loves drama, very much like Taurus, but the affair wasn't the problem. The unhealthy codependency of both parties was sitting like a snake ready to strike. Both people were acting out a role of neediness that was lethal to the relationship. The affair could have happened to either of them. Whatever brought them together in the first place was over. It didn't work anymore. It was time for their marriage to be transformed. It was time to start over on an equal footing. Your astrology chart can't make the decision for you. It can give you the life lesson at play here and the possible futures that are feasible at the time. The final call is always up to you.

What you have to do to heal a situation like this is surrender the marriage to a higher power and let time heal the wounds on both sides. There is a lot of good in the marriage if both are committed to building an intimacy of two. A marriage is a creative institution; you can decide how intimate you want to be, what you want to share, and then commit to it. This precious intimacy of two is your creation and can be built on, or changed, at any time as long as you both agree to it.

Scorpio is a sign that is very adept at dealing with the moment. That is where your power lies. Fear takes you back into the past, where you have no control at all. Taking the snake (symbolic of the lower desires that are tempted through sex, power, and materialism) out of the water (emotions) and putting it on dry land (mental process) where it can be seen is immensely healing. When your compulsions and fears are out in the open, you're more conscious of the consequences of your actions.

Because both of these people really wanted to be together, they took the time necessary to heal and started again, slowly building up trust. They were basically compatible but had different agendas on how a relationship should be. He was able to rise above the hurt and rejection. The biggest problem they had was her guilt. Through her self-forgiveness and trusting her ability to transform her life she created a more productive lifestyle. She learned how to be happy within her own self, and slowly her life came back into balance.

Sagittarius

November 23 – December 21

Fire Sign Ruled by Jupiter

SOUL POWER: Vision, Aspiration

EGO BLOCKAGE: Wishful Thinking, Extravagance

TRANSFORMING PATH: Spirituality

Sagittarian personalities are larger than life. You are always seeking the rare, the different, and the outrageous. Asked how your day is, you always say, "*Great!*" You find life an exciting adventure, are rarely bored, and take delight in knowing something new and better is in the offing. You aspire to the highest goals and your soul power of vision gives you a head start in all your endeavors.

As fire signs you enthusiastically embrace life; you rush out to greet the new and delight in the unexpected. You are truth seekers, extremely optimistic, with adventurous spirits. Sagittarius is a sign that rules international travel. You are citizens of the world. You are astute observers of life, seeking a variety of experiences in an attempt to fulfill your curiosity and develop higher understanding. You are looking for the questions, the inner meaning of life, absolutely knowing that the answers will come. You are mentally stimulating when you are at your best, and never boring. You are controversial but never uninteresting.

The Fool card in the tarot is a perfect representation of Sagittarius. The card shows a young lad with his knapsack on his back and his faithful dog at his feet, setting off to seek his fortune. He is calmly about to walk off a cliff, secure in his faith that God will take care of him, create a means to take him safely down to the foot of the hill, and lead him to fortunate situations. The practical meaning of this card is *foolish risks*; however, the higher meaning is that the Fool is about to enter the supreme adventure of passing through the gates of experience to reach divine wisdom. As a symbol for Sagittarius, the Fool means turning your back on the intellect and moving from ego consciousness into the consciousness of your soul power. Sagittarius is the sign of divine wisdom and transcendence.

The basis for your ego blockage of wishful thinking is that although you are often very lucky you can push your luck too far. Then your vision of safety and abundance falls aside, leaving you lost in despair. When you are down there is no Sun sign that can be more depressed than Sagittarius. You *must* live in your soul powers of vision and aspiration to enjoy life.

The natural legacy of Jupiter, your ruling planet, is luck, but positive thinking alone doesn't work. You must commit to a dependable philosophy on which you can build a life. You must be accountable. Sagittarius is the sign of belief systems—how they are applied and then integrated into daily life. As a Sagittarius your transforming path is spirituality, and how you embrace the world is extremely important. You must learn a means of developing faith, or you are lost. Being idealistic, you tend to be positive, even standing knee deep in alligators, much like Leo. Positive thinking is great, but it stands very close to denial. It doesn't serve you well to overlook the obvious. Fear brings about your ego blockages of extravagance and wishful thinking. When your blindness to the facts is opened to reality and you develop faith in your soul power of vision, you become a master of accomplishment. Your soul power of aspiration leads you to great things.

Jupiter is the largest planet in our solar system. It is the only planet that gives out more energy than it receives from the Sun. Jupiter, whom the Greeks called Zeus, is considered to be a fatherly symbol, exemplifying divine wisdom. He is the beneficent and benevolent aspect of God. Jupiter/Zeus bestows grace, blessings, and good luck in your life. In Vedic astrology, the planet Jupiter symbolizes the guru who gives out favors.

Jupiter/Zeus was the supreme god on Mount Olympus, and although Hera was his sister and consort, he had an abundance of partners and fathered so many children they are hard to count. (I read somewhere there were over five hundred.) He generously spread his godly powers to humans: many of his children had mortal mothers. He was a solar god, called the god of Light, and his inclination was for justice and truth. With Jupiter as your ruler you are lucky to share his bountiful blessings, endless energy, and larger-than-life expectations.

You Sagittarians have to be very careful what you ask for because of Jupiter's penchant of giving generously to his subjects, even to their detriment. You, like your benefactor Jupiter, are very generous, to the point of giving the shirt off your back if someone asks for it. This comes from your absolute conviction that it will be returned threefold. You love to be extravagant and include your friends in your enjoyment without hesitation. Your life is an open book and your house is a hotel for all your friends. Being so spontaneous and generous at the same time, your idea of a party is to fly off to some wonderful place for the weekend, inviting all your friends and then, forgetting your budget, extravagantly picking up the tab again.

Although there are stories about Jupiter's indiscretions, he was kindly, judicious, and good-natured. Hera had her hands full with Jupiter, yet their marriage seemed to be perfectly balanced, on an equal footing, and enduring. Jupiter allowed Pluto, lord of the underworld, to abduct the young virgin Persephone. This was terribly upsetting to her mother, the fertility goddess Demeter, who in abject grief over the loss of her child caused the crops to fail, creating a big mess on earth. (Why Jupiter allowed Pluto this favor we can only guess.) After Pluto and Persephone were wed, Jupiter, sympathetic to Demeter's sorrow, demanded that Pluto allow Persephone to go to her grieving mother in the spring; but she was required to return to Pluto in the fall and stay the winter. This is how the seasons were created. Actually, Pluto and Persephone were a happy couple; she became a queen and had a child. Perhaps Jupiter, in his omnipotent way, could see the bigger picture and played matchmaker. Gods don't seem to have the same priorities we earthlings have. This story gives us an indication of the duality of Jupiter. Although he is responsive to prayer, it seems that he is unbiased, and from his solar position your enemies' prayers may be answered as well as your own. Sagittarians, Jupiter-like and reminiscent of Solomon in the Bible, seem to be pulled in many directions in life and are forced to make judgments that consider the best for all concerned. You are required to get out of your own way and move to higher considerations.

The symbol for Sagittarius is the centaur, the mythical creature who is half horse and half man. Perhaps these legendary beings were symbolic of humans' closeness to their horses as a means of work and as vehicles of travel. There is a bond of intimacy that develops when you work with any animal, particularly the ones you sit on.

The centaurs were like big kids, playing with bows and arrows and looking for a skirmish. They were known to be very indulgent and got into trouble from drinking and not knowing when to stop. It is a Sagittarian penchant not to know how to make boundaries. Centaurs are looked on by most people as symbols of power and strength, yet they are a rowdy bunch, wild and lawless, not unlike the cowboys in the Wild West. Sagittarians, like the centaurs, need a lot of space to move around in. You don't like to be fenced in. You are overdeveloped in the "feeling" function and prone to run off half-cocked into one episode after another. This causes havoc in your life.

There are two mythical characters who play a role in shaping Sagittarius, creating two totally different types of personality. The first is Hercules, a real jock who bravely destroyed Hydra, the many-headed monster. You Herculean types are very physical, not intellectual at all. You act out of instinct, you love animals of all kinds (especially large ones), and you are eager for outdoor sports. You excel in physical activities and simply enjoy being alive. You're very coltish in your actions, with vigor, vitality, and insatiable curiosity. You have a playful approach to life. To you every day is a good day, as you are blessed with a wonderful disposition.

The other type is the centaur Chiron, an archer shooting his arrow into the sky, aiming at something far away. Hercules symbolizes physical prowess, while Chiron is a sage renowned for his philosophy. Chiron was also an astrologer, a master of the healing crafts, and is considered to be the teacher of new-age consciousness. Sagittarians can be a mixture of both types, but generally they lean to one or the other, either the physical or the mental type. Great athletes are Herculean types. College professors, lawyers, and judges—often with white hair (symbolic of wisdom)—are Chiron types. The most profound image of the Chiron type is Michelangelo's painting of God on the ceiling in the Sistine Chapel.

Mythology tells us that Chiron was a teacher to the gods. Although his thigh was accidentally wounded by Hercules' poisoned arrow and would not heal, the wound was received during a playful scuffle, so he held no grudge. Chiron is consequently called the Wounded Healer. With an empathetic nature, he symbolizes wisdom, truth, and justice, from the highest letter of God's law. He exemplifies a quest of service, surrender, and liberation. In the myth we are told it was necessary for Chiron to go into the underworld (the subconscious) for his wounds to be healed. Chiron-like Sags have a more sedate type of personality, preferring mental activity over physicality. Although you Chiron centaurs prefer the objective world, when you are emotionally wounded you must take the time to go into your subconscious, with a special teacher or counselor, for a healing. You can heal others with your wisdom, but you can't heal your own wound. There is a hint here of the necessity of therapy to qualify as healers and teachers in the world.

In Greece, India, and Japan, archery was an important psychological and spiritual discipline, having to do with self-mastery. The centaur's bow and arrow is pointed at the sky, aimed at the unknown. Sagittarians are attracted to theories and higher pursuits. Sagittarius rules theology, law, philosophy, ethics, and justice—God's law, rather than man's, which is ruled by Libra. You Sagittarians can't be happy with yourselves if you are not living up to your standards and abiding by the highest morals.

Sagittarian arrows are reminiscent of Jupiter's thunderbolts, which were forged by strongman Vulcan in his fiery furnace on Mount Olympus. Sagittarius is a fire sign, with insatiable curiosity, extraordinary mental energy, and inexhaustible physical energy. This leads us to Sagittarius's ego blockage of wishful thinking. Sagittarius is another fire sign that has a tendency to be overly optimistic, much like Aries and Leo. Fire racing across a field is a picture of fire signs out of control, instead of being a nicely controlled fire in a hearth or temple.

One of your best faults is to race ahead without forethought as to the effects of your actions. You can be very inconsiderate of others as you speed through life. The past and the future are always fragmented in your mind. When you focus on just one fragment of either the past or the future, you can be in total denial about the rest. Try to remember all that happened to you only yesterday. In a way, the future is a fantasy, and although we create the future with our thoughts, it's best to slow down and take the time needed to make a good plan so you can create something worthwhile. Your instincts are good and give you good information, but taking the time needed for a reality check certainly helps the outcome. Creating from a wiser and more informed perspective makes your dreams and wishes come true and have lasting results.

The centaur's arrow has a much deeper meaning: that of questing, aiming at the truth and seeking enlightenment. The long view is natural to you

Sags, and with precision, focus, and concentration, you can set your mark. You must not project your ego blockages onto the path or, worse still, point the arrow inward. When the diseased ego is surrendered to the soul, your life unfolds with a constant experience of God's presence and your path is clear. The present is full, rich with wonder and fulfillment.

Although we don't know his birthday for sure, Socrates, the sage of all sages, was definitely a Sagittarius type. Socrates' method of teaching was casual, a Sagittarius trait. His dual method of argument and discussion has influenced universities and other seekers of knowledge since Greek times. He is mostly known for his admonition "Know thyself," with the definite implication of looking within to the soul.

Socrates wrote nothing, but from what his student Plato said about him, his dialogue had a definite positive note. It was said that Socrates brought philosophy down from the heavens. Today he would be called a spiritual channel. Born in 470 B.C., he was a great moralist in a time of eroded values. A brilliant thinker, he sometimes portrayed himself as a simpleton, very Sag-like, and made people laugh. He believed in the soul; his prayer was simply "Give me what is good."

Although Socrates was a visionary himself, when the Oracle of Delphi pronounced him the wisest of men, he laughed at her proclamation. He never took himself seriously, much to the chagrin of Xanthippe, his wife, who thought him a fool. In her opinion he frittered his life away talking to young men about things that weren't important and not making a cent to support his family. All this seemingly lackadaisical behavior is typical of Sagittarius. But you need to look again to see the real person.

The sign of Scorpio is the sign of emotional longing, while Sagittarius is the sign of energetic seeking. Sagittarius's soul power of vision gives you the pure insight needed to enlarge your perspective and make wise decisions. You naturally feel that the world is yours and that you are divinely ordained to great things in a stupendous way. This confidence sends you out into the world with a prophetic eye that attracts success. You are naturally prosperous and can attract, as Socrates said, "all that is good." On the other hand, your ego blockage of extravagance may far exceed your resources; it is a constant pull, and moderation has to be learned. More or bigger is not necessarily better for you Sagittarians. Sags are often overeaters, overspenders, overeverything. Their lesson in life is to be responsible to the facts. Enough is enough. They must make boundaries that are reasonable to the circumstances.

The-grass-greener syndrome of Sagittarius is a self-sabotage that continues until you realize it's not the place that makes you happy, it's your relationship to yourself and others. Your horse nature loves the freedom of wide open spaces. It's very hard for you to make a commitment for very long. "Don't fence me in" is your motto and many a broken heart knows about the Sagittarian tendency to run at the first sign of a harness.

Sagittarius is a mutable sign. You are multifaceted in your interests and usually have two careers and often more than one degree. A student for life, you constantly look for ways to educate yourself. Long after your classical education is over, you go back to school and get another degree in something totally different. The same is true of your career. After you have been successful in one career, you decide to start another, and are usually as successful in the new one as the old. Sagittarians are risk takers, not afraid of starting over. In fact, they prefer the challenge of new places and would be bored without a dramatic change every now and then. I have a Sag ascendant. After a long successful career in fashion illustration, I became a full-time astrologer. Who knows what's next—perhaps writing?

You are sincere, honest, truthful, and aboveboard. Although you are somewhat judgmental, there is always a bright and humorous side to your criticism. You are very observant of people and can be very blunt. Often when you least expect it, words drop out of your mouth like hot potatoes. Uh-oh! Be kind! You might wish you hadn't said that.

Sagittarius's soul power is aspiration, the strong desire to achieve something high or great. Aspiration stimulates power. It excites hope and expectancy. The word *aspiration* coming from *aspire*, which means "to breathe, to draw in." Sagittarians are seekers, and by aspiring to the highest they draw in the good. In yoga, breath is considered to be the essence of life. When your breath is regular and balanced through meditation or yogic exercise, you develop great powers of concentration. Buddhists call our overactive minds "monkey mind." Since aspiration is your power, you could gain a great deal by taking the time for spiritual training. Sagittarians are prone to burn up their positive energy by constantly being in a hurry. Breathlessly, you want to get ahead of the game. If you are too urgent you're seldom in the present, where the power is. Even if you win the game, you need to learn how to receive your reward without running off half-cocked to the next challenge.

The look of Sagittarius is tall, with a well-made figure. There is a frank and honest gaze from the eyes and a high forehead with a noble look. You have a tendency to stoop, perhaps because you are taller than average, and sometimes you have to watch your weight. You love to overindulge in good food. You've heard of eating like a horse? Horses don't know when to stop eating. Horse owners hang buckets of food on their horses' heads to control their eating.

Although all Sun signs have their beauties, Sagittarians' most outstanding feature is not only beauty of feature but your tendency to glow with good health and express your good nature. Even if you're not really beautiful, you portray it. Some people with these exceptionally good looks are Cicely Tyson, Donna Mills, Jane Fonda, Daryl Hannah, and exceptionally glowy Kim Basinger. Bette Midler is a perfect example of an outgoing Sagittarius beauty, as is vibrant Tina Turner. Chris Evert is the lovely athletic type. It is a joy to see her leggy moves on the tennis court, whether she wins or not.

The male types are varied also, being divided up into two general classifications: the gorgeous Herculean types—John Kennedy, Jr., Don Johnson, Kirk Douglas—and the visionary Chiron types—Woody Allen, Steven Spielberg, Walt Disney. These last three movie men have thrilled millions with their wit and ideas.

As a dualistic sign (half horse, half man) Sagittarius has to deal with internal conflict, and making decisions can be very frustrating for you. It seems like you always attract things in twos: two ideas, two jobs, two lovers. Trying to settle between the two causes you to vacillate and get confused; then it is easy to make rash decisions. There is a tendency to be easily influenced by what others think. You want to be liked and try to please others by agreeing with them when it's really not what you think at all. It is very confusing to your friends when you go off and do the opposite of what was agreed on. All you have to do is tell the truth—just fess up to the fact that you don't agree with them. It may not be a big deal, but friends can be lost from the seeming betrayal.

The problem with adventure for excitement's sake and childish wishing on a star is that no resolution is possible. So where's the gratification? Off in your mind somewhere. Scattering your forces is a problem that you Sagittarians have all of your lives. When your focus gets off center, it's like wild horses running. Perhaps one of the reasons Sags drop the ball is because they look far ahead. Your ego blockage of wishful thinking constantly takes you out of your true power base of being grounded in the present. If you're too far out in left field, as any good athlete knows, it's easy to drop the ball. Philosophy and theory are useful only when incorporated into your behavior, and divine wisdom is available only in the present moment.

Like Scorpio, Sagittarius is a sign of an old soul. You are born strongly connected to your higher consciousness, and if you are deprived in early childhood, you can become very negative. It's a terrible thing for you, and basically not your nature. This depression is caused from saying yes when you mean no. A pessimistic or negative Sag is almost unheard of, but if it occurs, you, like Chiron when he went into the underworld to find healing, have to get professional help.

Sagittarians are very enthusiastic by nature; it's their blessing in life. The word *enthuse* comes from the Greek and means "God within." When you are enthused you are in God's hands. When Sags become disappointed and lose their enthusiasm, they lose their soul connection and everything goes stale. Until there is some resolution within and a coming to terms with your basic spiritual beliefs, you flounder in your life and can become addicted to people, places, and things that are harmful to you. Seeking but not finding what is good and true is very depressing.

With your generosity of spirit you must be aware of a tendency to be a pleaser. Basically, you want everything to run smoothly and everybody to love each other. This can be at your own expense until you learn from experience that *no* is a good word. I always ask Sagittarians to write down the word *no*, put it in their pocket, and when someone asks them for something, get it out and read it. You must learn to set boundaries, or life will set them for you as a default.

Sagittarius's transforming path is spirituality. There is an inner conviction from early on in your life that there is a higher power. A Sag is a very expressive person, classified psychologically as a sensitive type. Feelers are very susceptible to impression. A feeling of awe comes when you see or hear great art, and nature is a religious experience to you. Oddly, though your sign rules spirituality, it takes you a long time to understand it. God seems a long way off and hard to understand in everyday life. A Sagittarius friend of mine once said that he couldn't find his higher power until someone explained to him that God stood for "good, orderly direction."

Even though Sagittarius rules spirituality and religion, you are generally very skeptical. There is always an analytical voice in your head that weighs information back and forth, finding the fallacies and shortcomings. You have a tendency to hold back emotionally, and there is always a part of you that isn't totally committed. You want to be a free agent. Your rational mind tells you that no single system of theology is likely to represent the whole truth about God. But if you do finally, through much soul-searching, choose to be part of a teaching, you take it on with great enthusiasm and purity of mind. There generally has to be some real spiritual feeling involved or you will have no faith in the dogma. Words alone do not impress you, but feelings do.

The truth is, you can never be an atheist. Sagittarius rules the part of the mind that connects to the soul. Your nature is to worship the good (which is a derivative of God). With your transforming path of spirituality, no matter how skeptical you are, you can't discount your need to seek God or higher purpose. You need that *good orderly direction* in your life. If you lose your faith in a higher purpose, your life seems cut off and you can become very depressed.

You Sagittarians set guidelines for what you need and want in life and build your own corral. You like autonomy and moral independence. Perhaps you could start by making a useful schedule and keeping it. Make proper boundaries for your life. Working out or participating in sports is helpful, too. Just walking barefoot on the earth is grounding. Whatever idea you come up with, it needs to be done, religiously.

Your love life is a wonder to you. You're best in singular pursuits. This doesn't mean that you are unlucky in love—quite the contrary. The opposite sex is very attracted to your good looks and wonderful personality. But with your many-faceted dynamic personality, you are afraid of emotional demands. You're also fearful of being tied down emotionally. What if I have to give up riding dirt bikes? What if I can't do what I want to when I want to? You're afraid of being cornered with no escape, or of just being bored, and these fears keep you single for a long time. It is best for Sags to wait until they have matured a lot to get married. You should think about it for a long time. It's very hard to get everything you want in one person. I have a philosophic client with a Sag ascendant who says, "You can't get it all up one tree." There's always something left down on the ground.

You are looking for your twin, or soulmate, and it's best to choose someone who likes to do a lot of the same things you do. It's very important for Sagittarius to marry someone who is like a friend or buddy. You need a sidekick. Since Sag is always looking beyond the horizon, you have to be careful or you could pass this person up. They could be walking or running right next to you all the time and you race by looking for the unobtainable.

What Can Be Done

Of all the signs, Sagittarius is one of the most enjoyable to be around. You are lucky in life and your life lessons are not that harsh. Make no mistake, we are here to grow so be prepared for a bump every now and then. To be objective about yourself is one of the most difficult problems you have. It's easy to fall into wishful thinking when you're so busy you don't have time to think. There is such tremendous physical energy in your sign that you have a tendency to rush headlong into life, acting before you think. Remember the Fool card in the Tarot. You know that God's hand will reach out to save you in some miraculous way. Without this pure childlike trust, life wouldn't be worth living to a Sagittarian.

Sagittarians wake up each day feeling on top of the world. You are blessed with optimism, and yet this can be your weakness. It is necessary to realize that your soul power of vision doesn't work if you are living in the future. Your overeagerness can lead you on a merry chase.

The Crusaders were Sagittarian types and many lives were ruined by their religious zeal. Families were separated for many years, and some children never knew their fathers. You must be united with loved ones and know what you want to achieve right here and now before you can decide on a far-reaching plan. The power of vision is manifested by being grounded in the present. Find your own sacred space in your heart, then the understanding that leads to creative concepts is possible. You must seek it here and now, not off in some far-off land or in the future.

Three Steps for Healing Your Blockage

1. Combining your ego blockages of wishful thinking and extravagance makes you a gambler par excellence. Blind faith in the future keeps you constantly racing on, seeking the impossible with no end in sight. There is no time for you to enjoy the fruits of your labor. All ego blockages are ways of controlling your environment. You control by being unrealistic in your expectations, being scattered, and skirting emotional situations.

2. All power comes from your soul connection to God. Your soul powers of vision and aspiration are truly gifts, in that your sign rules the connection to higher consciousness. It is natural for you to see the good in others, and your concepts for the future are right on target for the best of all concerned—when you are grounded in the present.

3. Sagittarius could be called the Sun sign of soul power. You must surrender to a higher power in this life to accomplish all the good

your generous and philosophical personality is capable of, and you must accept your transforming path of spirituality on a positive level of joy instead of chasing rainbows.

Okay, Sagittarius, are you still here? This story might step on your perfect horse hoofs. A few years back a Sagittarius woman came in for a reading. She was 35 years old, both pretty and in the peak of health, and you could tell that she was very agile and athletic. Although she seemed very feminine, she was definitely the Herculean type, but she seemed depressed and confused and needed to take a good look at herself. I could see from her chart that she was ambitious. She worked for a large international computer company (Sagittarius rules foreign countries) and was advancing rapidly in her company, so business was not her problem.

It turned out that although she was very popular with a lot of friends, *she had never had a date.* She was everyone's best friend, the life of every party. She traveled all the time, which exacerbated her dateless existence. She enjoyed traveling, but it's hard to have a normal lifestyle when you are always on a plane. After I explained her ego blockages and told her what I could see, she left, all charged to change herself.

Six months later she came back again. There had been very little change, so I talked to her even more strongly about her unrealistic expectations. I emphasized that a white knight would not come to rescue her from her loneliness and pointed out that her excessive work habits were robbing her life. I also discussed her tendency to shy away from emotional situations where she wasn't in control. Always being the life of the party is a ploy to escape intimacy. Both the Chiron Sag and the Herculean type shy away from the intimacy necessary to form a bonded relationship. They like autonomy and want to be in the objective position. This isn't conducive to forming intimate relationships. She needed to slow down her life and really do some thinking about why she was afraid of intimacy. I also suggested a counselor to guide her in this soul search.

Six months later she came back, again with very little change in her life. I put down the chart and asked her why she came back. She wasn't gaining anything from the readings and I was feeling guilty about being too hard on her. She said, "I need you to tell me just one more time." Sagittarius can be very obstinate, needing to hear advice more than once before it sinks in, and it's best to let them ask for it. A wild horse isn't good at listening or pair bonding.

This story has many different scenarios. Many of you Sagittarians, male and female, date unavailable people. You definitely need your space even within a relationship, and many times there are two relationships at the same time confusing the issue. You seem to get involved in relationships with people who live out of town or are married; even if they are available, they aren't good marriage material. You also choose people who aren't up to your standards. I know a man who is a recovering alcoholic. He always dates women who drink too much. If you want to get married *don't date someone who isn't good marriage material*. This isn't to say that Sags don't marry; you make wonderful mates. It's just that it's not easy for you to allow anyone to catch you. This is a deep-seated problem with Sag, but it must be dealt with at some time in your life or you could end up alone on the prairie. Even when Sagittarians marry, they have to learn to think of their mate's needs. As often as not, they are out every night. This is not necessarily because you are being unfaithful; your desire to run free keeps you busy in your own pursuits.

How to Apply the Three Steps in This Situation

You horses can be very stubborn, but you are not totally fixed in your ways. It takes a long time for new information to sink in and for you to act on it. You don't take direction easily. It is strange to say that relationships are difficult for you when you have so much luck with them generally speaking. Relationships don't have to be difficult if you get your priorities right and you live up to your standards. If you're single and want to get married, put your love life first. Know what you want. Write it down on a wish list. Be specific and change *yourself*.

The woman in the story was so afraid of rejection that she hid from relationships. There had been some damage in her upbringing—her family was dysfunctional, but aren't they all? Her problem wasn't in her behavior; it was in her motivating factor, a deep-seated fear of intimacy. This is what I told her.

1. You have the cheerleader syndrome. If you think it's your duty to entertain everyone and make all the available men your buddies, this makes your chances of marriage pretty slim.
2. All of this behavior looks perfectly all right on the surface. You're great company but something is missing. Part of this behavior is your ego blockage of extravagance. You overdo it.
3. Your fear of intimacy in relationships is really a fear of being controlled. You fearfully won't let yourself go beyond the safe limits of a pleasant friendship and extravagantly run away from what could be good.
4. Wake up to your ego blockage of wishful thinking and get grounded in the moment with what is really happening, not what you hope will happen. Remember wherever you go, *there you are.* You can't run away from yourself.
5. Your defense mechanism built up from childhood is to please others and make sure they're entertained. That way you feel you are safe from rejection. They love it, but what about you?
6. There is a wonderful affirmation that fits this syndrome: "By pleasing myself I please others."

You Sags like to be free, and you love camaraderie. You often remain bachelors because of this penchant for independence. There's nothing wrong with choosing a life of independence, but you don't have to be alone.

Our Sagittarius in the story didn't know how to form intimate personal relationships because she was focused on herself and her needs—to have fun, to please others. It's fun to have that kind of attention, but it isn't satisfying to your needs. Take the focus off yourself—in this case the need to be liked—and put it on other people. I suggested that my client volunteer to work with underprivileged children, which she did. The last time I saw her she was dating. Now she has to take it from there.

There is a tendency for Sagittarians to get into relationships with people who are unavailable. Then you're *really* safe. All her behavior was sabotaging her needs to have a home and family with a man of her choice. Marriage and relationships are hard work at best, and there is no such thing as living happily ever after. But let's face it, the world is made for couples.

Shelley wrote in his poem "Love's Philosophy":

The fountains mingle with the river
 And the rivers with the Ocean,
The winds of Heaven mix for ever
 With a sweet emotion;
Nothing in the world is single;
 All things by a law divine
In one spirit meet and mingle.
 Why not I with thine?—

The answer for you Sagittarians is to be honest about your relationship needs, then hold a vision of what you aspire to. Don't be afraid of commitments; true love doesn't control. When you take your enthusiasm and curiosity into your everyday experience, then your dreams for yourself and the world come true.

Capricorn

December 22–January 19

Earth Sign Ruled by Saturn

SOUL POWER: *Contribution, Organizing*

EGO BLOCKAGE: *Overachievement, Worrying*

TRANSFORMING PATH: *Responsibility*

Capricorn, you're the tops! Your sign is at the pinnacle, the very zenith of the chart. Upholding divine order in the universe is the most profound function of your duty as a Capricorn. Your soul longs for a higher range of commitment. You honor tradition and enjoy history. Appreciating the past, you acknowledge the present, knowing that is where the power is.

Heights appeal to you. You heartily believe that by learning from the past, you can bring wisdom forward and take it to a new summit. All the great mountain ranges in the world—the Himalayas, the Alps, and the Rockies—are ruled by Capricorn, as are the mountains in Arizona, New Mexico, and even the hill country of Texas.

The ability to rise to the top is natural to you Capricorns. It's your expertise, even though it's usually not sought out consciously. Being reserved, you often need a little encouragement, yet if you're put in a position of authority, you will take charge with capable precision and move up the ladder of success.

The Pyramids are ruled by Capricorn. One of the most thrilling experiences of my Capricorn life was meditating in the pyramid of Cheops after a long arduous climb to the king's chamber. A Capricorn's dream: being inside a mountain of rocks. How appropriate! Rocks are ruled by Capricorn, and I've never met a Capricorn who didn't have a collection, whether crystals or ordinary driveway rocks. My house has rocks in every corner from the places I have visited all over the world. They are an important part of my decoration. They don't have to be very pretty as long as they have an interesting look that triggers a deeper meaning for me. I know a Capricorn man who trades rocks with every country he visits. He takes a special rock to leave behind and brings one home in exchange.

Your soul power of contribution is based on the total conviction that helping others is what makes life worth living. When you awaken to this power and dedicate yourself to this purpose, a world of opportunity opens for you. High standards and consideration are foremost in your mind in all areas of life and, to top it off, you make a lasting and loyal friend.

Life is in your favor as far as success is concerned. Although in early life you are reluctant to push yourself, as you mature, especially in your forties after the period called the middle crisis, you take off. While signs like Taurus and Leo are early bloomers and do a fadeout in midlife, this is when you shine. Like a time-release capsule finally breaking into power, you find that you have all that is needed to succeed. By overcoming your perfectionism and fear of failure, you move up without hesitation. Magically it seems, the best period of your life is then in front of you and continues without interruption all your life.

Just like Camelot's Merlin, who was born an old man in an oak tree (another Capricorn symbol), you are born old and grow young. How wonderful! As a Capricorn, I have found it to be true in my life. We Capricorns wear age very well. It's hard on you when you're young—being so old for your years, it's difficult to fit into your peer group—yet eventually there is a payoff for all the hard work and responsibility. Capricorns take off while others are burning out; you just keep on punching until you achieve your goals.

Your personality is reserved and cautious, yet you are totally reliable, steady, and industrious; you can be counted on. You show up on time with what's needed to do the job. You understand that if your attitude and your reactions are under control, you're in good shape to succeed even though you can't control the world around you. With your high degree of common sense, you learn to observe the rules meticulously, and you are experts in knowing the right form. A little dull, maybe, but effective in most life situations—and it keeps your life in order.

With Saturn as your ruler, discernment is one of your assets, but you have to be careful or you can get stringent. William James once said, "The art of being wise is the art of knowing what to overlook."

You realize at an early age (you usually start working in your teens) that working for someone else is not going to get you what you want, so you devise a plan to be self-employed, patiently put it in place, and skillfully carry it out. You are a master builder, and when you have a plan or goal, you are happy. Still, your success generally comes from plain hard work and being uncommonly good at what you do—it just happens.

As a Capricorn you really can't work at just any old job. You have to love it, and if you love it you will excel in it. That's where your reputation for being a workaholic comes in. Work and play are synonymous in a Capricorn's book if you're in the right profession. Your soul power of organizing blesses you with the ability to have a balanced life. Remember, astrology says that work is only one quarter of your life. There are twelve signs in the zodiac, and each one rules an area of your life, but only three signs relate to work. Taurus rules the money you earn, Virgo deals with the actual work, and Capricorn pertains to what your career is and how the world sees it. You must give the other nine Sun signs their due and consciously make the effort to organize your life in a balanced way. The same thing is true of children. There is only one house, Leo, for children, so they can't be your whole life. Your soul power of organizing helps others as well, and with your soul power of contribution you are able to accomplish your goals with tremendous energy.

Your attitude about money is very complex. You have a big dose of keeping up with the Joneses, even if you deny it. You want success, you love status, and you don't want anybody to get ahead of you. "The best of everything" is your motto, and it doesn't take long for you to learn that real quality takes money—big money. So you work as hard as you can to make it. Intensely ambitious, you want to make your own mark in the world. In fact, you want to make your own money, not have someone give it to you. Beware: As much as you want financial success, in a self-rejecting way you can be contented with far less than you deserve. Capricorns' reserved manners can hold them back. You're prone to be so involved in the goal that you lose sight of the payoff, and you could come up with the short end of the stick financially for all your planning and hard work. If you hold back, you've no one to blame but yourself. Being self-critical, you feel that you're not as accomplished as you should be. Like Virgo, you might let others move past you in the job market when they're not as experienced or capable as you.

Many Capricorns are born with poverty complexes; you have a deep-seated fear of falling short and being broke. This is a part of the born-old syndrome. If you are overly responsible as a child and assume you must compete with adults, you will be overwhelmed and feel helpless. Capricorns often start work early, even in their teens, to have a feeling of financial security.

Capricorn children should be treated like children, even though they are usually precocious. We have a young Capricorn in my family who is such a little man, he cried the day he started first grade. He thought he was required to drive the family car to school, and, embarrassed, he told his mother he didn't know how.

Oddly, with so much fear about being responsible and doing the right thing, you can be a spendthrift. If your desires exceed your pocketbook, you can lose sight of your real monetary worth, but usually not for long. One of your ego blockages is worry, and money worries are the worst. After many sleepless nights you usually come into line with a little effort, but it is a shame so much of your motivation comes from fear of failure. Your life is impoverished by self-negating thinking. The strain of constant judgment is intolerable. There comes a time in life, in your thirties or maybe in your forties, when you have enough experience to know that you are competent and worthy of all that is good.

Although you have a reputation for being materialistic, Capricorn is really not mercenary. You're motivated to succeed, so you work hard—and money usually comes along with that. You are very generous with what you have if the situation has merit. Being a good provider, you see to it that your family is well cared for. You want your children to have a good education and vacations, and a nice living space is especially important to you. But you can be very miserly at the same time and think of yourself as poor when you have plenty. You could drive your family crazy with this unrealistic attitude about money.

One of your fatal flaws is that you care too much about what people think. Capricorn rules the house of career and fame—of how you are seen in the world. In older traditions you were known by who your father was. Your career was indelibly influenced by what your father did, and what his father did before him. Your surname historically told your trade, as in the case of Smith or Butler.

The ego blockage of worrying about what people think is the downside of your devotion to career and fame. If you are totally focused on success in an egocentric manner, you're overly concerned about your reputation, and you allow your standing in life to be measured by what others say. Naturally, you can't be successful in the world without some attention or notoriety. Yet using your success in the world as a measure of your true worth is a shaky investment. There's no way to please people all the time, and if your self-image is based on what others think, you're in trouble. Also this trait is just the opposite of your soul power of contribution—selfless giving to what is needed. It's the diseased ego blockage of worrying taking over, and your ego is convoluting the facts. Contribution is a noble goal, but it is a soul power *only* when there is no preconceived agenda of self-aggrandizement.

Interestingly, the tenth house in the chart, Capricorn, which is the strong parent, is primarily the mother in our culture and many other cultures in the world. When women went into the workforce in the twentieth century, they took on superhuman roles. They did everything. You've heard of Supermom? The Capricorn tendency to overwork and take on double responsibility is not wearing well with women in the 1990s, but what to do? Perhaps you Capricorn women need a little help from your friend your husband. I went to a brunch recently where a young father had his 4-month-old baby with him. His wife was away on a business trip. The little girl had on a beautiful dress and a headband with a bow. She looked very content and so did he.

As we enter the Aquarian age, there's a return to traditional values and a need for relationships on an equal footing. The father may be reinstated as a member of the household again. The young people who have survived all the dysfunction of the 1980s and 1990s will see that for the family's well-being, fathers and mothers are both responsible for creating a home and raising children.

Male Capricorns need to know that yours is the sign of the parent who nurtures the family unit by going out into the world and facing hard realities; but it doesn't keep you from being an important nurturer in the home as well. Dads can cook, clean, and mind the children just as well as moms, but you have to make an effort. You may find that just being the provider is barren and isolating.

Your soul power of contribution indicates a very evolved consciousness. There is a strong desire to serve the highest good. Many great avatars are born in the winter. Christians celebrate Jesus' birthday on December 25, a Capricorn date, although no one knows for sure when he was born.

Generally, there is a turning to spiritual matters as you enter the winter of your lives. This is Capricorn's power period in life. It's possible for this introspective period to lead to the realization of the true power of your soul. Through your hard-earned spiritual grounding you are then able to take charge with experience and understanding and share your wisdom with others, truly enjoying your great Capricornian gifts. One thing that is true about a Capricorn is that you live your life to the fullest. You've been forced to learn from many life experiences. Eventually, if you don't lose heart, at a time when you least expect it, life suddenly pushes you all the way to the top. This period can be the most fulfilling in your life. In your later years your approach to life is youthful, emotionally warm, and you take more time for fun.

You can make things happen. You are a good instigator, particularly if you're satisfied that the project will work, and you like to follow through to completion. You are a master of calculated risk. You definitely won't jump into anything, guessing about where you might land, but you will figure out how to get to the bottom of things and eventually to the top. As great students of life, you want to rise to the summit of truth and knowledge, and you certainly don't want to lose sight of reality. You believe in strong leadership and definitely won't shirk your responsibility.

Oddly, even though you are very respectful of authority, you don't like anyone telling you what to do. So you go out on your own very early in life. Capricorns and Leos are the best entrepreneurs in the zodiac. Leo is a fire sign of great stamina and enthusiasm; you may be a little slow to ignite, but you have more tenacity than your fire brother and, like the tortoise (a Capricorn symbol), your precision and persistence eventually win. Leo and Capricorn have a lot in common: both signs like to succeed and be the head honcho, although their choice of pursuits can be very different. Leo likes to be the king, with a lot of pomp and circumstance, while Capricorns quietly thread their way to the top; you're the CEOs of the zodiac.

In ancient Sumer, six thousand years ago, your ruling planet, Saturn, was called the star of the Sun. This practice of calling Saturn the Sun confused archaeologists for a long time. Yet, Saturn being the planet of law and order certainly describes Leo's Sun-ruled sense of responsibility. Saturn is discipline and whoever enforces it. It rules our transforming path of fate. Still its symbolic connection with the Sun gives hope of renewal as the Sun rules the life force. So it seems that both Leo and Capricorn are blessed by Saturn's benevolence—that is, when everything is in order and other people are considered. Your duty, to behave nobly, is to know that one who leads must follow all.

In the earliest legends Saturn was a war god as well as a Sun god. He battled with Zu, the winged dragon of storms who was in league with the great sea dragon of chaos, in order to recover the stolen tablets of eternal law. When he managed to retrieve them from the terrible monsters, the gods rewarded him by putting the tablets in his custody. Possession of these tablets gives Saturn control over destiny and fate.

In present-day astrology Saturn is considered to be the planet of restriction, essential for growth. His symbol is a cross of life over a Moon-shaped glyph. The cross is a symbol of life, the horizontal line being earth and the vertical line being the spirit moving down through earth. This symbol signifies a combination of spirit and matter. The Moon is symbolic of emotion. Together they represent reality over emotion. Most of us find it a hard task and think Saturn very depressing, when his purpose is only to make you wake up and face the facts. When you know the problem, you have a chance of solving it.

Saturn can be very bitter to his own Capricorn subjects until his limitations are reevaluated and seen as necessary for maturation. He is the teacher who stresses a mature viewpoint; perhaps that's why no one likes him. The truth is, Saturn rules life on earth; he rules time and all material things as well as divine order. As a Capricorn and Saturn-ruled, you have many setbacks in early life. Support from your family is limited, and often your health is poor in early life. After you're older, if you look back with an educated eye, it was the very best thing that could have happened. For instance, a loss in the family precipitates early employment, so you are accomplished much earlier than others. Your company folds, so you have to start your own business. You lose an account, but another that's better comes in with more money. Saturn turns on the overhead lights, dispelling your illusion, and you have to face life as it is. It builds character.

As a Capricorn your most diseased ego blockage is worry. Saturn's gloomy influence makes you feel that you are doomed. He will torment you until you wake up to what he is teaching. After you've been in the same situation three or more times you might take an inventory and see what you are doing to attract such grief. Don't be afraid of changing the situation before it gets bad. Why wait until the worst happens? You've always worked hard and your reputation precedes you. Saturn also rules the wisdom of experience. You have a lot of that to pull you through. You're very capable. It's easy to see that you are first-rate and always come up with the goods. It's seldom as bad as you think.

Capricorn is very accomplished at being emotionally detached; in fact, that is one of the criticisms you get most often from your family and friends. Tibetan Buddhism, Hinduism, and Native American shamanism are all ruled by Capricorn. These religious disciplines encourage self-control, stilling the mind, and detachment. With practice, it is in your nature to develop a peaceful perspective and emotional objectivity. Then you're not so likely to distance yourself from loved ones. You can be accomplished at yoga, a Capricorn practice. (As a Capricorn myself, I heartily recommend it.)

Your ability to be detached is a good trait, yet it can turn very quickly into lack of feeling or coldness to others' needs. The worst thing that can happen to you as a Capricorn is a cool lack of regard for anything standing in your way. Dictators are ruled by Capricorn, and there are many ruthless dictator types in our corporate world today. This controlling tendency comes from your ego blockage of overachieving and wanting to be the boss, at any cost. This is rare (most Cappies are gentle little goats), but it does happen.

Joseph Stalin was a Capricorn and he methodically and ruthlessly committed horrendous crimes against humanity. Paranoia goes hand in hand with dictatorial ethics. This evil disconnection comes when you reach the top, lose your perspective, and trust no one.

Richard Nixon was a great overachiever who cleverly chose his ascent, slipped, then again climbed his way to the top, only to topple when he became so isolated he lost touch with reality. He was great at delegating, as any good Capricorn executive should be, only he created an invisible wall between himself and the public; losing the position he fought so hard to achieve. Capricorn rules the knees, which symbolizes a need to submit to higher power. At some time in your life you are required to bow down and humbly start again.

Traditionally, Capricorn is symbolized by the seagoat—a goat with a fish tail struggling up a mountain. This is not the best equipment for climbing, and predictably the goat slides back down the mountain until it can position itself for another ascent. Nixon definitely had a handicap; he was so absorbed with competition and winning that he lost his soul power of contribution, which motivated him to go into politics in the first place.

Your exhausting compulsion toward perfection holds you prisoner. There is an overriding fear of failure that drives your ego blockage of over-achievement. This fear of downfall rides along underneath your Capricorn love of success, and the invisible pressures of society create an unrelenting tendency to sabotage your hard work. With this self-negating attitude deep inside, you create a self-bondage that only you can change. There is no one else to blame. How you feel about yourself is very important. Only you can deprive yourself of anything. Respect yourself, and others will value what you do. The constant strain of self-judgment is virtually intolerable. Be kind to yourself. These undermining aspects of your personality aren't easy to change, but much is gained when you learn to trust your soul and your natural abilities, which you have in abundance.

In the initiation rituals of medieval times, someone was always picked to play the goat, someone who goes through the whole process for the group. The goat is a Capricorn symbol, and Capricorns seem prone to going indiscriminately through many life experiences just to learn from them. That is, until you learn there are other ways to learn. If there is a snake on the road, you don't have to go over and say, "Hello, snake." You don't have to suffer to be good or smart. Use that common sense that you have so much of!

The old astrology books have nothing good to say about Capricorn looks. Long, thin neck, sparse hair or beard, hard-set face, usually not handsome. Perhaps you are getting better looking every year—I have certainly found you to be a very attractive bunch. Capricorn women have fine features with high cheekbones, full lips, and pointed chins. Marlene Dietrich, Faye Dunaway, and Dyan Cannon, for instance—lovely and so exotic.

Capricorn rules the bones and Capricorn men and women have fine bone structures with small, well-shaped noses and skulls. Look at the small noses and strong cheekbones of Diane Sawyer, Ava Gardner, John Denver, and Humphrey Bogart. Some of the handsomest and smartest actors are Mel Gibson, Denzel Washington, Kevin Costner, and Anthony Hopkins. And we can't leave out Dolly Parton and Victoria Principal—two beautiful, smart, and enterprising ladies.

One of the most beautiful of all Capricorns was Joan of Arc, born in 1412 on January 6 (my birthday). A visionary and mystic, she led France to a momentous victory that was a turning point in the Hundred Years' War. In Paris, across the street from the Louvre, there is a thrilling golden statue of Joan on her horse, dressed in full armor and riding into battle.

Although Virgo is the sign that rules fashion, Capricorn runs a close second. There is always an understated elegance to Capricorns. It could be their desire to win that guides them to select conservative clothes with good lines, the ones that always look good for years. However, I've seen them in clothes from The Gap looking just as dapper or glamorous. My father, a Capricorn, certainly had no interest in fashion, yet he was fastidious with his clothes and always looked like he had stepped out of *Gentlemen's Quarterly*, with a three-piece suit and a becoming hat.

(Whoops! It occurs to me as I reread this section on Capricorn that I too, like other astrologers, have failed to write anything on Capricorn's love life.)

Capricorns often neglect their love life. You are so busy achieving your goals that you forget your emotional needs. Yet as an earth sign, Capricorn is one of the most passionate, devoted, and faithful lovers in the zodiac. Why do Capricorns delay their desire for love and marriage and often marry late or find relationships difficult? Why do you assume that you are the one responsible for the outcome of all your romantic endeavors? Your soul power of contribution must be examined. There is a hint of high position in the word *contribute*; it means "to grant, to decree." This involves carefully weighing the facts and having a set of fundamental beliefs to draw from. The fly in the ointment is the isolation of this separate and untouchable position. Yes, there must be honor and respect for Capricorns to operate out of their soul level in their love life. It is absolutely necessary. But if you don't allow equal footing and vulnerability to your loved ones, you are like Nixon up on the mountain of success, isolated and alone. If you don't grant yourself the power of love that is shared by all the signs, you can end up alone or in a barren relationship. You may always be contributing and never receiving.

What Can Be Done

You would love to live in a perfect world. For a Capricorn that would be with everyone moving up the ladder of success on a path of right action. The problem is, everyone doesn't see it your way. Capricorn is a sign of authority, where someone is always the head guy. We are all moving into new concepts of responsibility in the Aquarian age, and your sense of personal achievement must change. You must see yourselves as part of a unit, not isolated and alone. The Aquarian age rules community and democracy. *We must help each other.* There comes a day when your control tumbles and you are forced into feeling your feelings. That's when your life takes off.

Three Steps for Healing Your Blockage

1. Your ego blockages of overachievement and worrying will go away when you realize you are not alone on the mountain. You *can* ask for help. Worrying is a habit. Your anxieties developed early in childhood when you felt you had to function on the superior plane all the time and there was no room for error.
2. You are always ready to take charge and put complex situations in order. That is your soul power of organizing and contribution. Contribution is a heart action and it is wonderful to share what you have with others. You are born with the knack of seeing what needs to be done. You fit into any work situation with ease.

Many times you start working very early in life. You precociously look for ways to be enterprising while you are still a teenager.

3. Your transforming path of responsibility is like being on a tightwire. Being responsible is a very good thing, so when does it become a burden? Remember that your transforming path is neutral; the lesson seems to show up over and over again until you open your heart to the power it represents, instead of the burden. That is certainly the case with Capricorn, and the continuing call to responsibility is with you in this lifetime. It must be dealt with.

One of my clients, a young matron, came in for a reading. She was totally burned out. She was absolutely lovely and wore the most beautiful clothes—from Armani, Jil Sander, Anna Sui. She was married to a wonderful man who was perfect for her from all outside appearances as well as from their natal charts. You might say that she was married to her soulmate. She had two wonderful children who had never caused her a moment's problem up until now. When she came in for a reading, she started crying as soon as she sat down. (It seems that my office is a haven for suppressed feelings. If you are upset all you have to do is walk in and the tears come out.) I keep tissues available in my desk drawer for just such floods. I handed her the package and waited for her to be able to talk.

Her story wasn't tragic. On the contrary, she had it together as far as her outer goals were concerned. She was a tireless volunteer for nonprofit programs, on many committees, and she was the consummate mother, taking her daughter to ballet classes and her son to ball games and sports activities. Her children were teenagers. Just when they needed her the most, she had set up her life to be so busy she never really spent quality time with them. She was caught up in creating an external image. She had lost sight of her own true responsibilities to her children.

The reason she was so upset was that her son was failing in school, and the school counselor had told her he was depressed. This news had shocked her into the reality of the rat race she had created for herself and her children.

Her ego blockage of overachieving had taken her for a ride. She said that she was tired of trying to be Superwoman. Her husband was on the same frenetic schedule. He spent long hours at work and traveled a great deal of the time. When he had a little time off, he crashed. With all her outer success, she wasn't enjoying her life. Also, she felt that if she didn't look wonderful at all times, her husband wouldn't love her. She was committed to service to the point that she had no life at all. She had to keep up a cheerful attitude all the time and, more and more, she was ready to kick and scream. "*What about me?!*"

How to Apply the Three Steps in This Situation

Life is what you make it. The old saying, "All you have to do is die and pay taxes," could be true. But there are other ways of looking at your life. Mae West said, "Too much of a good thing is wonderful"—but she was talking about sex. The desire for money and position are programmed into our society. Americans are very competitive. Your transforming path of responsibility will work you over pretty good until you get the whole picture of what you need to have a positive and productive life. You Capricorns become very involved in achieving in an external way because you feel you must, instead of having a sense of balance in your life. Your ruler, Saturn, can be counted on to wake you up to the facts of life. Saturn goes around your chart every twenty-eight years. It brings stressful aspects to your Sun sign every seven years to ensure your growth. That is why seven-year cycles seem to show up in your life like clockwork.

All my client needed was a change in viewpoint. She needed liberation from the bondage of her habit of pleasing others to ensure safety, respectability, and love. Capricorns fall into this trap easily with their desire to achieve great heights. She was out of the flow of her life. She was on the right track, but her priorities were off.

Your soul power of contribution doesn't mean you have to take on more than you can do. Overachieving is a subtle blockage—it can sneak up on you. *A Course in Miracles,* by inner dictation coauthors Helen Schucman and Thetford Williams, says, "If you only look at yourself you cannot find yourself, because that is not what you are."

Webster's defines responsibility as reliability and trustworthiness. It is really humanitarianism. The root word *response* means "an act of being called on to answer to a given output." There seems to be an underlying urgency involved with responsibility when your ego blockage is involved. You are very invested in doing the right thing, and you feel as if you're always going to be called to account and will end up short. This adds a tremendous burden, as if life isn't hard enough. When you realize your soul is part of a larger, more powerful source and you are as unlimited as it is, your anxiety, fear, and apprehension disappear.

My client's son's behavior was just a cry for help. It didn't take her long to use her soul power of organizing to get her life in order. Her lesson was to change her perspective from trying to prove herself to just being the beautiful, loving person she already was.

Aquarius

January 20–February 18

Air Sign Ruled by Saturn and Uranus

SOUL POWER: *Originality, Humanitarianism*

EGO BLOCKAGE: *Rebelliousness, Muteness*

TRANSFORMING PATH: *Intimacy*

Aquarius's symbol is the most beautiful in the zodiac. A man from Heaven is pouring water from an urn down onto Earth. He has the face of an angel, and although you think at first it's water he is pouring, on second glance it doesn't look so much like water as waves of air. Aquarius is an air sign, and air has invisible movement similar to water.

After much debate, most scientists in the twentieth century have decided that all energy manifests in particles that fall into the form of waves. The basic form for all the energy in the universe has been disguised for thousands of years, hidden in the symbol of Aquarius, eager to be deciphered.

Our human bodies are made up of whirling molecules. The esoteric teaching "as above, so below" has been handed down for ages as a mantra to metaphysicians. We are told that the universe is made of subatomic particles existing in an infinite source that creates itself in endless variations, no matter how large or small. There is another dimension, one that we can't see with our eyes, that is just as real as the one we live in. Aquarius rules this cosmic dimension.

Cosmos means "order" or "beauty." The universe is intelligent and alive, and you are not removed from the equation. Aquarius is the Sun sign of hopes, wishes, and goal setting. It rules abstract thinking. You are tuned to this creative source, in the highest level of your mind, giving you an extraordinary breadth of vision. Our minds are like wonderful computers that have endless amounts of information filed into memory banks, everything from genetic coding to the constant daily imprint of our lives. Aquarius rules the fifth dimension, where there is limitless power. It's where the future is created, and your attitude has a lot to do with it. You are a master of mind control when you get the hang of it. It is your mind that creates matter. Einstein said that matter is gravitationally trapped light. You are truly a light being with divine attributes.

We are entering the Aquarian age at the beginning of the twenty-first century. The first time most people heard about the Aquarian age was in a musical called *Hair*, which was popular in the 1960s. It had a haunting song called "The Age of Aquarius." At that time, few people knew what they were talking about. Now it is mainstream news.

Although many people have set the year 2000 as the time of entry into the new millennium, the exact date is arbitrary. We may not be fully into the new age for another hundred years or so—the changeover in these great precessional ages is slow. The gradual changeover can be seen as the electronic age, ruled by Aquarius, grows stronger every day. Television, an

Aquarian enterprise, covers the world with news. You can watch a war in your living room. People are becoming more and more individualistic all the time. Science, electronics, and personal freedom are characteristics of Aquarius.

And although we can see a war on television, we don't have the slightest notion how to stop war. The Aquarian age will necessitate an evolution of consciousness. On a soul level we are all alike—no one is different in the universe. Great spiritual texts speak of being made in God's image. The possibility of extraterrestrials appearing on Earth is also likely. How can we hope to assume diplomatic relationships with them when we still don't trust our earthly neighbors?

A complete precessional cycle is about twenty-six thousand years. This cycle is divided into the twelve Sun Signs, each lasting approximately two thousand years. The cycle moves counterclockwise, with Aquarius coming after Pisces instead of before, the reverse of the normal order of the signs. Civilizations don't last long enough to record these cycles, even though it is apparent that ancient people were aware of them. In the Temple of Dendera in Egypt, there is a zodiac on the ceiling. If you look closely, the signs are arranged in a spiral with Cancer at the center. This implies that the age of Cancer, which was eight thousand years ago, was probably the beginning of the Egyptian civilization (which is further back in time than Egyptologists want to admit). The Sphinx, the oldest monument on earth, symbolically signifies the Leo age. Perhaps it was built through knowledge held over from prediluvian time, some twelve thousand years ago.

We are now leaving the Pisces age, which we entered two thousand years ago in Christian times. The biggest contribution of the Pisces age has been the education of the masses, primarily through Christian missionaries. It's sad that so much of the Piscean message of unconditional love has been misconstrued, making this last two thousand years the most bloody in recorded history.

The Arian age held sway during Old Testament times, when rams were sacrificed by the biblical prophets. When the Arian age commenced in Egypt, a new dynasty was ushered in—that of Amen-Ra. This age was preceded by the Taurean age, when the people of Egypt, Sumer, and India worshiped the bull. If you read history or the Bible, and travel over the world, you can still find the remnants of these great ages.

Aquarian soul powers are humanitarianism and originality. As you Aquarians enter your age, you, more than any other sign, may feel your time has come. You have a chance to change the world with new ideologies and inventions that can help humanity struggle with the plight of survival in a small world of plenty. We have never had so much and so little. So much trivia and so little of true value. The one thing that we need to learn as these great changes are sweeping us all along is how to hold on to discernment and good taste. If we don't watch out, all that is good and true could be lost in a whirl of multimedia fragments as tasteless as breakfast cereal. More is not necessarily better.

Aquarius rules electronics and all modern inventions. Every day new electronic gadgets are marketed to make our world more convenient. Many of them have transistors and some are small enough to put in our pockets.

The world keeps getting smaller. Aquarius rules anything that comes in multiples, such as products or ideas that can be projected mechanically or physically all over the planet. With the introduction of cyberspace, communication with people halfway across the world is at your fingertips. The Internet connects millions of people who never would have met, yet there is more loneliness than ever as we sit for hours at our computers and eat dinner alone. We can have a relationship with someone we've never seen and probably wouldn't be attracted to otherwise. There are many pros and cons as we enter this groundbreaking time. We have much to learn and more information than we can absorb in this, the Aquarian age of information.

There will be great discoveries in the next two thousand years. The main intent of Aquarian consciousness is to teach us that we are all connected—that is what the angel in the symbol is telling us. We are vibrationally connected to earth, no matter the color of our skin or our religious preference. We breathe the same air and drink the same water. If one person is sick or hungry, we are all sick and hungry. The same Aquarian Sun shines on us all.

In the Aquarian age we have a chance to be totally grounded in our soul power. As we transcend our ego blockages and live through our soul power, our intellect is genius, our will is virtue, and our affection is love. The more we can transcend our feelings of separation and fear, the more positive the entire vibration of our beautiful planet will be.

Your most important evolutionary statement as an Aquarian is in desiring liberation and individuality. As you enter the Aquarian age, the soul-searching messages "Love thy neighbor as thyself" and "Do unto others as you would have others do unto you" may be understood and embraced. To care about others doesn't take away your freedom. If we listen to the news, however, it seems just the opposite of what should be happening. Nevertheless, humanity does have two thousand years to accomplish this goal.

You Aquarians have a beautiful soul power, humanitarianism. You are dedicated to truth and you recognize instinctively that all men are brothers. Of all the signs, when you express your soul you are the most open-minded and unbiased. You delight in social interaction, and you like people of all kinds. You are truth seekers, beautifully objective, seeing all parts of a situation without prejudice.

Like folk humorist Will Rogers (a soulful Aquarian type), you never meet a person that you don't like, and you definitely care about another person's right to pursue life in the way he or she sees fit. As an Aquarian, you march to a different drummer, and you enjoy people who are as eccentric and eclectic as you are. However, you don't like dissension or violence and will make a major stand to stop dysfunction and injustice.

You Aquarians are naturally modest and never brag about your accomplishments, even though you have great skill at seeing through to the truth and are at your best when there are problems to solve. You are a great analyst, instantly perceiving what needs to be done, yet you hesitate to interfere with the workings of fate. "Live and let live" is your motto.

On the other hand, with your ego blockage of rebelliousness, you can be prejudiced, even though this is the antithesis of what your sign stands for. When you allow yourselves to be narrow-minded and caught in negativity, you Aquarians are extremists and can even be revolutionaries. This destructive mind-set is generally not the rule. Prejudice is taught, not inborn, but Aquarians more than any other sign can fall prey to this thinking and block yourselves to the joy of other cultures and other people's ideas. Democracy is ruled by Aquarius, but so is communism. It's your choice. What do you choose—order or anarchy?

I'm convinced that our American superhero, Superman, is an Aquarian even though he was born on Krypton and his birthday isn't in the script. His two-part character is a good example of patience and modest optimism on one hand and the superhuman goals of cooperation and support that make things better for everyone around him.

Superman's character is also a perfect example of the dilemma you Aquarians suffer in your love life. In the love department you are strangers in a strange land. As Superman you're untouchable, and when you turn into ordinary Clark Kent you hide out, afraid of rejection, not knowing how to make the small talk of romance. Aquarians are more in love with ideas than with individuals. You don't fall in love easily. You're too much in your head for such heartfelt endeavors, and often you let a relationship die even though you are really interested in it. The truth is, you don't know how to communicate your feelings. The words are there ready to be spoken, but when you feel emotion, your mind goes blank.

Intimacy is your transforming path. It will always be a lesson for you, so you might as well get to the bottom of it now. The cosmic truth is that Earth is made for couples. Everyone on Earth is continually drawn to his or her opposite. As the song says, "Love makes the world go round," and you are not immune to its allure. Yet when you do fall, it comes as a lightning flash of illumination and usually lasts for life. Once committed, you make wonderful mates because you are basically so congenial. Here's a warning for you, though: You have a tendency to see only the good, so be careful. If you are hit with the thunderbolt of love, be sure you're not saddled with a nightmare instead of a dream. It is very hard for you to get *out* of relationships. Your Aquarian viewpoint lies in your soul power of originating something of value; breaking up was left out of the picture. You don't like to be unhappy or make anyone else unhappy, and criticizing others isn't something that you are comfortable with. That's why you wait until it's a big emotional deal, too upsetting to hash out, and the pressure finally forces a split. The problem could be worked out peacefully in the beginning, if you could learn how to speak your true feelings. When your heart opens, your mind is clear and the perfect words come forth.

With the gift of originality your mind is capable of great feats. Aquarians are advanced thinkers and often have photographic memories. This is especially true of areas that you are most interested in. My brother is an Aquarius. Since boyhood, he has known the names and statistics of the top baseball players in the world. Usually an Aquarian has to be very interested in a subject to learn it at all, and many an Aquarian with a high IQ has been known to flunk out of school because of a rebellious attitude toward the educational system as a whole. Aquarians love to challenge the status quo, and changing the principal's rules doesn't go over too big in high school (or in any other established organization) until you get the support you need from others.

Originality and rebelliousness can go hand in hand, so they must be balanced. Your ego blockage of rebelliousness for egocentric reasons is a downward spiral. Authority doesn't impress you, and your gift of originality stirs you to see what can be changed. When you are stuck in a barren environment, you have to watch out for the urge to ruthlessly tear everything down so that the new can come through.

The foresters at Yosemite National Park, in California, learned that if they put out the fires that started naturally from lightning, the forest would die. The fire was part of the process of birth, death, and renewal that is necessary on earth. Also the nitrogen from the fire was necessary for the growth of the trees. If you don't have a certain amount of chaos and change, you have dead wood. Even Thomas Jefferson said, "A little rebellion is good for the soul."

Aquarius was ruled by Saturn alone until Uranus was discovered in 1781 and designated a co-ruler by the astrologers of that time. Saturnine Aquarians are scholarly, traditional, and predictable, maybe a little stuffy but ready to make changes if necessary; Uranian Aquarians are just the opposite. Tradition and authority do not impress Uranians; they love to try new ideas and shock people. A Saturnine type generally works in some conservative business but adds a lot of originality to it—as a stock broker, banker, college professor, or computer specialist. Uranian types choose more unusual pursuits. They like to work on subjects that require a lot of analysis. They like to form their own hypotheses. They enjoy being consultants in scientific research, astrology, or psychology, and they excel at product development in any area. Uranian Aquarians are attracted to computers, television, and any business that works with electronics.

A lot of Uranians are attracted to politics. Ronald Reagan was an Aquarian who broke a lot of rules during his political career. He even had an astrologer in his early acting years, Carol Richter, though Nancy took the rap for believing in astrology. After he was elected governor of California, he was inaugurated at midnight. You *know* an astrologer had to have picked that unusual time!

You Aquarians have a serious communication problem. Your mind works so fast that you talk in shorthand. Your ego blockage is muteness. It seems odd that anyone with such a good mind can verbally shut down, unable to speak at all when it comes to discussing your feelings. If the conversation is about an abstract subject, you can pontificate for hours and put your point across very well. However, when it comes to your own needs or personal feelings you turn into a stump. Your transforming path of intimacy and your ego blockage of muteness are interdependent. When your emotions surface, your electrical mind gets waterlogged and shorts out. You're almost always in analytical mode. You are stuck in your head and find it difficult to express your deeper feelings.

The answer is, of course, to get back into the present instead of jumping ahead into thoughts of the future. As a thinker, you have a tendency to project your energy onto the outcome and lose the power of the present. This sets you up for false expectations. Get back in your body! When you're having an out-of-body experience, you might have a great overview but you can't feel your feelings. What's the point?

When you Aquarians conquer the insecurity and fear that is at the base of this dilemma, you are the best communicators of all. The ego blockage of all Sun signs is primarily the desire to control. Each one has its own specialty. Yours is wanting to be in situations where you make all the decisions and call all the shots. It's strange that your sign rules change and yet you're so afraid of it. Another enigma is that although Aquarius rules all the new electrical appliances on the market at this time, none of them move of their own volition. They all do marvelous things, but they have to be moved by someone else. It seems as if you need a stick of dynamite to be moved—then, when it's least expected, you are changed by a word, a thought, or a mood. Most Aquarians live in God's time, a realm of the ever present, so your perspective is often from another dimension.

Aquarius is a very attractive sign. You always have a distinctly different look and like to stand out. You are usually very tall and slightly androgynous in your looks. A female Aquarian has a markedly masculine look to her head and is very forthright in her presentation, while an Aquarian man may have an unusually handsome face that borders on the feminine. These beautiful people with high foreheads, clear eyes, and aristocratic looks are the Uranians, and they are seen more frequently now at this time of the Aquarian age. The Saturnine Aquarian is just as handsome but much more conservative in demeanor. Paul Newman is a perfect example of this type; look at his piercing blue Aquarian eyes. Although he is one of the most respected actors in the world, he has a quiet and gentle manner and his philanthropy is well known.

With the advent of the new age, fashions have become more androgynous; there is very little difference in the clothes men and women wear. It all started with blue jeans in the 1950s. Fashions may come and go, but jeans are still in and go everywhere in our cross-cultural Aquarian world. I was told in 1980 by spiritual teacher Ella Vivian Power from Santa Fe, New Mexico, that a new root race will evolve in the Aquarian age. They will be the Golden People. The cover of *Time* magazine in 1993 had a composite picture of seven young adults from all cultures; the outcome was decidedly androgynous and golden. We are closer than we think.

Generally, Aquarians are known for their eager minds and independent outlooks. Classical and striking, Aquarian looks are exemplified beautifully by Vanessa Redgrave, Cybill Shepherd, and Farrah Fawcett. Television genius Oprah Winfrey is everyone's favorite Aquarian. Nick Nolte is a quintessential Aquarian with his high forehead and casual approach. Other attractive and exceptional Aquarian men are Alan Alda, Clark Gable, and Robert Wagner.

The symbol for Aquarius is a glyph of two undulating lines. These waves are representative of male and female energy moving forward in time but never coming together or drifting apart. Like the wave symbol, radio and television bands of energy do not overlap. You have the right to your own wavelength, yet you must learn to connect with others in soulful consciousness, where there is no separation.

Scientists say light becomes wave simply when it's observed. Unobserved, it reverts back to chaos, or randomly moving particles. All that's needed to change light's form is consciousness and focused attention. The flowing symbol of Aquarius illustrates the free will which shapes our conscious world. Thoughts have power.

This connective link between the male and female meridians is represented in the brain by the corpus callosum, a band of fibers that connects both sides. This bundle has undergone a steady thickening over the course of evolution, suggesting that we are moving toward greater synchronicity between our right and left brains. Early humans were primarily right-brained. Their lives were nonlinear and their language was limited. Later, from the Iron Age to the present, there was a shift toward left-brain rational and verbal thinking. Through research in humanistic psychology we are beginning to realize that both halves are of equal importance. Too much dependence on the left brain focuses the mind on the outcome rather than being centered in the action. You lose your sense of control, and this causes obsessive thought patterns and repetitive head talk. Too much left-brain emphasis pushes you to be anxious and overly competitive. Your life is full of urgency, trying to win or just to catch up. This feeling of not ever being finished or complete produces a state of helplessness, even depression, as the mind never finds satisfaction. Remember, *there is no real satisfaction outside of the present moment*. This is not to say that goals are wrong. You need to know what you want in order to accomplish anything, but you need to feel closure and completion to be content. What good is finishing if you never stop to enjoy it?

In the two centuries since the planet Uranus was discovered, scientific method has taken precedence over God. Everything has to be identified, measured, and weighed. We have gained much from this process, yet science with all its power is limited. Love can't be measured.

Many of the children born at this time have right- and left-brain synchronicity. They aren't able to buy into the competitive psychology of their parents. Our school systems will have to change from Saturn-type schools with left-brained teaching, where the children are led to a predictable answer, to Uranian-type schools that teach problem solving in a holistic way. The answer is found in a creative process of possibilities. Aquarius rules multiplicity and choice.

What Can Be Done

Aquarians, you are very advanced. You have what is needed to be balanced and to create an original and exciting life. Your basic virtues of tolerance, honesty, respect for truth, cooperation, and compassion will be more self-evident as you break through your fear of being controlled. Your desire to blaze new trails and be original at any cost can be tempered, and your mind can holistically channel a positive future.

When you are comfortable with your feelings, the tightness in your throat opens up and your muteness disappears. Your soul power of originality is the key to learning new methods that overcome the fear of intimacy and the silence that holds you back. Whole-brained consciousness is connected at the heart. The mind is a wonderful thing but without the heart it is dry.

Three Steps for Healing Your Blockage

1. When you get stuck in the brain you are caught in mind-sets that trigger a deep desire for control at any cost. Your normal way of thinking, which is kind and considerate, falls away. Then revolutionary and destructive ideas are formed that set you off on a destructive path. Whether you act on these thoughts is immaterial. You become very nervous and your entire electrical system shorts out. This is your ego blockage of rebelliousness. When you are disturbed emotionally you can't speak or say what you really mean. Often Aquarians talk in shorthand, because stress causes

the synapses of the brain to short out. Your ego blockage of mute-ness can be obvious or hidden. It's still there until you can resolve the fear of change and loss of control.

2. You are gifted with being whole-brained. You are a harbinger of the future, where humanity will have more brain power than we do today. As you balance the meridians of your brain you are operating out of your soul power of originality. Your understand-ing of others is your soul power of humanitarianism. Your soul becomes a living impulse that carries transforming power.

3. You must learn how to be in harmony with your transforming path of intimacy. You can't hide from other people. You're a peo-ple person anyway. The discrimination you are capable of is at your fingertips—it just takes some effort on your part to put it to practical use. Aquarians are just as capable of affection and need "warm fuzzies" as much as anyone.

All right, Aquarius! Turn on your computer mind for a minute. Let's look at what you need to do. Your humanitarian soul power of caring for others and being so resourceful by creating original processes that help others is noble and desirable, but what about yourself? Don't leave yourself out.

I had an Aquarius client who came in for a reading every year like clockwork. She had been in a difficult marriage for years and was always wanting to know when her problem would be solved. Her husband was a wonderful man, but his life was totally taken up with his work. The problem was, she was pulled in two directions by what she wanted from her marriage. Aquarius's symbol of two wavy lines is really a dual sign, much like that of Gemini or Pisces. Aquarius can vacillate a long time before making a decision. My client wasn't unhappy with her husband, but she was afraid that when her children went off to school (she had twins, a boy and a girl), she would be left alone.

Many times you Aquarians fall into the trap created by your own self-sufficiency. You are powerhouses when it comes to helping others. You appear so independent and capable, but when the chips are down, you wake up and find that, in your overly independent way, you've created a world without a support system.

Aquarius wants a best friend for a mate. Although this is all well and good, there are traps in this pattern. You don't like to upset the boat with emotional confrontations and let important feelings go by the way. With friends outside of the home, you can clear these problems easily because you don't have to live with them every day. With your partner you need to stay emotionally connected or the bond you have created together at the beginning will dissipate. Your mate wants to share your life in all ways. You're not just friends—you're lovers and emotional partners through life.

On your life path, you need to be alert to what's really happening, and to ask questions. You need to stay very conscious of your communication with others. You must be clear about what you want and share your needs with your mate to keep a relationship growing. My client's ego blockage of muteness was responsible for her dilemma. Up in their ivory tower, Aquarians tend to overlook the obvious. It seemed to me that her marriage problem dealt with her *own* denial, *her* muteness, not her husband's. There was also a touch of her ego blockage of rebelliousness here. She didn't need anyone! Ha! Look again.

How to Apply the Three Steps in This Situation

The real issue here was my client's transforming path of intimacy. An Aquarian can't see the trees for the forest. You like to see the big picture and don't want to be caught up in trivia. The first thing my client needed to look at was what she wanted and needed in her relationship with her husband. It is senseless to make conversation without some idea of what you want to get across. I think writing these things down helps to impress them in your mind, as affirmations.

My client finally realized that her husband was a really good guy. She had taken him for granted for years, and, to be honest, he had done the same thing with her. They reinstated their marriage as the most important project in their life, and the last I heard, they were doing just fine. Although she did have to learn to play golf!

Pisces

February 19—March 20

Water Sign Ruled by Neptune

SOUL POWER: *Imagination, Compassion*

EGO BLOCKAGE: *Escapism, Self-Delusion*

TRANSFORMING PATH: *Illusion, Transcendence*

Pisces is the last sign in the zodiac. It is the journey's end, and at the same time, it is the beginning of a new cycle. Pisces is the culmination of the quest for liberation of the soul, which starts with Aries and reaches a zenith of surrender and peace in the twelfth house. Pisces' true home is in what Carl Jung called the collective unconscious, or group mind. It is absolutely necessary for you Pisceans to acknowledge the reality of your vision; it is beyond the ordinary mind, very real, powerful, and complementary to your nature. Without due respect for your soul power of imagination, you give up your greatest gift and can stay lost in a desert of self-induced boredom.

You are very impressionable. Your soul power of imagination opens boundless worlds for you to explore, filling your life with creativity and mystical experiences. But as visionaries and mystics you may find it hard to stay grounded in the ordinary world. Your head is in the clouds, so your feet must be planted firmly on earth or you will drift with the current of the collective, never physically manifesting all the wonderful things you are capable of. With your soul power of compassion, and being so receptive to subtleties, you are loving and nurturing to others' needs. You are naturally endowed with the ability to enjoy wonderful moments of expanded consciousness, to literally be blissed out. But what good is it to have this gift if you yourself aren't transformed by these wonderful revelations? You must learn how to ground yourself in the present moment or you could drift in a psychic sea of illusion. It is imperative that you seek out positive people and situations, for you are easily influenced by your surroundings and you must take responsibility for your ability to affect others. What good is a mystical revelation if it can't be applied in real life?

You don't have the firm mental boundaries of the preceding sign, Aquarius, or the fiery will and action of the next sign, Aries, but your soul power of compassion opens a sense of unity that other signs can't imagine. Anything is possible for a Pisces. You are sensitive to superphysical influences, and in your intuitiveness, you also have the attributes of the mystic. You are drawn to your own personal spiritual experience.

Neptune, the god of the sea, is the ruler of Pisces. His planetary message is the principle of dissolving and unifying in the universe. Neptune washes away all that is no longer needed and creates a longing for union with the inspirational. The perfect application of this longing is shown by your soul power of imagination and compassion. You are a soulful person. Your purpose is purification. To recognize truth is your highest goal, and your biggest lesson in life is discernment. With good judgment and a desire for the authentic, you are able to separate the pure from the impure.

Neptune, your ruler, disciplines his watery subjects with a trident, a three-pronged fork, as his scepter. He rules the psychic, the collective unconscious, a level of knowledge that is above reason and to which you are connected through your emotions and feelings. Piscean Edgar Cayce, a great visionary from Virginia who lived in the early part of the twentieth century, was called the Sleeping Prophet. When he went into a trance, he was able to enter the collective unconscious and give people information about their health and other matters. In this consciousness, past, present, and future are all connected; there is a sensitivity to superphysical influences and a sense of harmony with all life.

As a Pisces, you live in both the physical world of the body and the psychic world of the soul, interrelated and interdependent. Beyond these two personal worlds is an even higher world of the spirit, which is also woven into the fabric of your being. Your body and soul are parts of your ego identification and are yours as long as you have lessons to learn on the earth plane. Your spirit is the eternal force of life that never dies and is impersonal, being connected to everything in the universe. You are body, soul, and spirit. Pisces rules the understanding of these unseen worlds. Neptune's trident stands as a symbol of these three principles.

Neptune rules the worlds of fashion, music, and art. Sweeping cultural trends are formed in subtle levels of consciousness beyond logical understanding. Why does everybody want to paint the living room yellow when for the last two decades peach has been the rage? With Neptune being so illusionary, it's hard to predict these trends logically; it is much more fun to watch new trends and fads as they unfold. Popular music, fashion, and slang come out of this area and make an interesting study. Movies are definitely Neptunian, thus Piscean. They are the biggest art form we have in the world today. How many times have we all cheered on the hero and cried over a sad story at the movies? I cried so hard in *The Color Purple* that I thought I would have to leave the movie. Being a moviegoer all my life, I find my mind is filled with movie memories as much as with real-life events. At their best, films deal with social issues, and much can be learned by studying them. Movies are our myths, our waking dreams, and can do great service when they put cutting-edge information out to the public. They are also symbols of deeper cultural processes.

Pisces is a sign of duality. Its symbol is made up of two fishes. Some astrological sources say the fish are dolphins. I think dolphins are a good choice. They are really mammals that have a developed limbic or emotional brain; some believe that they are the single most intelligent animals on earth. The limbic brain gives the dolphin the ability to nurture and vocalize for the purpose of maintaining contact and playfulness. Fish have only the reptilian brain, which is primarily concerned with territorial dominance and self-preservation.

The Piscean symbol of two fishes facing opposite directions shows the duality and conflict that stirs Pisceans into continuous action. The fishes are symbolic of the mind swimming around in the emotional ocean of the unconscious. Fish are never still. They are continually in motion, and like chameleons, they change color according to the colors of the water. You Pisceans, like your fish symbol, are constantly moving and swimming in all directions. Accomplishing your goals takes great determination.

The fishes are drawn as two crescent moons. One signifies dissolving the old form, the other beginning the new. If the crescent moon glyphs were turned around, they would form a circle or an egg shape—a symbol of wholeness. With your transforming path of transcendence, you are constantly put into situations where you are swimming against yourself. Your soul power comes from inner conviction, not pleasure seeking, and you must allow your gift of inner vision to make a safe environment in the real world.

According to Greek myth, a dolphin allowed an orphan boy to ride on his back. One day the boy drowned while swimming out to meet the dolphin in the ocean. The dolphin brought the boy ashore and compassionately remained with him on the beach to die himself, a fish out of water. Many Pisceans are so emotionally affected by others that they give up their own happiness in sympathy to others' needs. Neptune and Pisces rule unconditional love. Your empathic nature is one of your best traits, and many people are helped by your soul power of compassion. Other signs have to learn compassion, which is as natural to you as breathing.

In ancient Egypt, the universe was considered to be an egg, "conceived in the hour of the Great One of the dual force." This analogy represents the vast potential inherent in the cosmos. Anything is possible. Perhaps that is where the two dolphins come in, representing equipoise, dual cosmic streams, one of *involution*, which means "to absorb or envelop" and the other of *evolution*, which means "to grow into a different and more complex form."

With Pisces, there is a lot of symbolism dealing with water and the feet. The feet in India are considered to be the source of grace. The feet of great gurus are venerated. I have always thought this was symbolic of the grounding of universal power. Jesus walked on water. His feet, which symbolized his understanding, were firmly supported on the water, symbolic of his bond with the unconscious. He understood the interconnectedness of the universe through the principle of love. Since Pisces rules the feet on which we stand, Jesus' washing his disciples' feet was an act symbolic of cleansing their understanding—their stand on truth.

The birth of Jesus heralded the precessional age of Pisces two thousand years ago. This great age has been threefold in its Piscean nature. One effect has been the advent of a great spiritual teaching, although Piscean-like, it is much misunderstood. The second stage has been the dissolving of continental boundaries. All major exploration of the world has been accomplished and recorded in the last two thousand years. Territorial boundaries are being dissolved by competition and materialism. Perhaps in the future there will be even better integration with higher principles and standards. The third and most important aspect of the Piscean age has been the education of the world primarily through the missionaries of the Christian church. This dissolution of cultural boundaries through education has had both positive and negative results—again, the two fish swimming apart.

Water has the power to transform by cleansing or washing away the old. One of the most important things you Pisceans can accomplish in this lifetime is to see through your ego blockage of self-delusion and deal with solid facts. Wake up and smell the coffee! Remember the other fish is there offering a different perspective and a new beginning. Confusion always precedes a decision. Have heart, no matter how bewildered you are, for there is clarity waiting for you when you center yourself and logically sort out the details.

Pisces is at home in the vague and uncharted ocean of the unconscious. The colors of Pisces are sea green, pale aqua, shades of lavender and violet. You see life events as a mixture of soft colors, like an impressionist's palette. Born psychic, you are tuned to life's subtleties and with your soul powers of empathy and imagination, you make first-class clairvoyants. However, in an overly emotional world of reactivity there are no boundaries between one area and another, and your nebulous vision causes a lack of confidence and promotes procrastination.

When your ego blockages of self-delusion and escapism surface and manifest as fear, watch out! The diseased ego is always frightened. You may see only what you want to see. It's hard for you to separate your feelings from those of others. Pisceans are prone to shed tears at the drop of a hat if the story is good enough. Affected by others and vacillating back and forth, you allow yourself to be dependent on someone else's opinion. Then hooked just like a fish and taken out of your watery environment, you do as they dictate. There is a tendency to be a victim and allow other people to control you. You make bargains to feel safe and put your own needs in jeopardy. You must take responsibility for yourself.

It is very healing to sit down and have a good cry, and Pisces is always very close to tears. The strength and resistance needed to stop the flow of your natural emotions is very destructive and unnecessary. As human beings, we live our lives primarily through our emotions, but we must learn that our feelings are only a part of the story and not always true. Knowing how to tell the difference is something you have to learn.

Like the little mermaid, you find it torture to survive in the harsh world of reality without the illusionary bliss and creative imagination that's possible in your watery home in the sea. Pisces rules dancing, but like the little mermaid who decides to go back to her fish tail and the sea, you have to avoid dancing on your toes when human anatomy dictates that you are more comfortable flat on your feet. I'm constantly telling my Piscean clients to get into their feet, stand on them, have the courage of their own convictions.

I once read a chart for a beautiful Piscean woman with two little children. I could see from her chart that she was in a very negative relationship, and actually was in danger. My advice to her was to leave the man as soon as possible for the safety of her family. She made up all kinds of excuses, which boiled down to the fact that she was afraid of him. Seeing the circumstances, I suggested ways to protect herself emotionally and physically. The next year she called me and said he had put a gun to her head in front of her children before she woke up to reality. She said she saw me in her mind's eye telling her how to get out of the situation. Using her strong psychic and spiritual connection, she took her soul power back, walked away, and created a new life.

In the great age of Pisces drugs and alcohol were released for public use. Before that time, priests and shamans were the only ones who had the right to use hallucinogenic substances, which they did in religious ceremonies. Most alcoholic use took place at holidays and celebrations. When Neptune was discovered in 1846, and the hidden world of microscopic germs was found, a period of medical research and drug development commenced. Pisces and Neptune rule drugs of all kinds, including coffee and cigarettes. Now, the discretion is in our own hands and we seem to have failed. Most of the world has a problem with alcohol addiction, and drugs are destroying many people's lives; particularly alarming is the drug use of our children at such early ages.

Love and sex addictions are also prevalent with Pisces. With your ego blockage of escape and your tendency to be in denial, you are a sitting duck for addiction of any kind. The underlying objective of such addictions is looking for your soul. You are, as Willie Nelson sings, "Looking for love in all the wrong places."

You are a water sign and your consciousness flows easily from one dimension to another, trying to find the answer in a sea of probabilities. You are connected to a fountain of endless possibilities and your creative endeavors never dry up. You don't need alcohol to be imaginative: it's one of your soul powers, and mind-altering drugs are definitely *not* good for anyone. They deaden your connection to your soul. Although many artists claim that drugs enhance their creative performance, they are only deluding themselves.

It's very important to take good care of your health because your sensitivity to prescription drugs can do you as much harm as good. Vegetarian diets are good for Pisces, as is any carefully thought-out diet of nontoxic foods. Pisces is susceptible to toxicity in any form, and you should carefully consider where, how, and with whom you spend your time.

You are often confused in your identity. Many times, thoroughly confused about what you think, you're caught in a cosmic ocean of feelings without clear direction. This creates your ego blockage of escapism. You can live your entire life as if you are in a rudderless boat floating aimlessly on an ocean of events. Your soul powers of empathy and imagination are obscured by this confusion, and your ego blockages of self-delusion and escapism take over.

Seeking stability, you Pisces often mate with earth signs, only to find that their dry, realistic world stifles everything you see as holy. You have to be more grounded yourself before you can abide earth people. You are also attracted to Leos because you both have an attraction to the dramatic—but you may find that their fiery nature is incompatible with your watery sensibilities. Your own water sign cohorts, Cancer and Scorpio, are best for you. I have also found that Pisceans can be very happy married to each other when they have learned to be more reality-based.

The biggest lesson you have to learn is discrimination. This is available to you at all times through the reciprocal power of your opposite sign, Virgo. You have to learn to stop putting energy into things that are a waste of time. Your power of imagination can turn into fanciful notions very quickly, and a total loss of what is good and true for you ensues. Eventually the party will be over, the overhead lights will come on, and you will have to pay the fiddler. Saturn, the planet of reality, takes precedence over emotion and confronts Pisces more than any other sign. It is your antithesis. I have a Pisces client who wants to form a group to buy a missile—and shoot Saturn out of the sky. I wish it were that easy.

You need to do a reality check every day. Escaping in any way really turns you on. It's a constant pull, but your soul powers aren't open to you without surrendering to reality. We live in a three-dimensional world and have to be grounded to be truly happy. You have to have a stable idea of what you need and want at all times to keep you on solid ground. Your soul power of imagination (tapping into the superconscious) can save the day and overcome the confusion that hangs you up. See yourself as possessing all you need in life to be the powerful person you want to be—and remember, there is a level of the mind where the imagination is true.

On the other hand, being so impressionable, your tendency is to overempathize with what others need and leave yourself out. With such an open heart, you are a sitting duck for abuse. It's difficult for you to separate your feelings from those of others. This self-sacrifice contributes to your need to feel overly responsible, to the point of wanting to withdraw, to seek seclusion, to escape. It is necessary to clearly define your boundaries. Again the two fishes of Pisces show up, both in the desire to be secluded, to meditate, and in the denial of self, the willingness to be the victim.

When you envision yourself as a whole person, worthy of the highest good, your divine will takes over and washes away the tendency to let yourself be victimized. Your lesson is twofold. You must steel yourself to the cold hard facts; at the same time, you must continue to put your faith in your soul and spirit, and not in the material world alone. Watch out! When you lose touch with reality, you're riding for a fall. It is so easy for you to slip over into illusion.

Modern physics is changing our ideas about the structure of the universe. Now it is said that the physical world cannot be separated from the invisible world. You can't separate your outer consciousness from your inner consciousness anymore. You live in a continuum of possibilities and your soul power of imagination is a great asset. In fact, you're actively creating your world at all times. Pisceans like this multidimensional approach and naturally go with the flow. Your healing comes from being grounded in the moment, fully aware of the possibilities and taking responsibility for your part of the action.

The key here is not to be fragmented: reality versus emotion. As with the other mutable signs, Gemini and Sagittarius, the dual properties of adaptability and variety of interests can be a detriment. You can go from pillar to post, being drawn into one draining situation after another. Each moment of your life is precious, and to attract all that is good, you must be centered in your heart with your feet firmly planted on the ground.

Your transforming path of illusion is comfortable, like an old shoe. Your life lessons are as familiar as your face in the mirror. It is true that you must be in harmony with your own life lesson, as it is played out in the physical world, yet it is easy to overlook what is so familiar. When you are prepared to overcome your ego blockage of escapism by facing the truth, your transforming path of transcendence spirals you up into a world of harmony with your highest principles. You pass beyond the ordinary scope of your mind and enter a knowing place in your heart, where the soul resides. This is an emotion that transcends understanding, passes beyond human limits, and brings "the peace that passeth understanding." To experience anything to its fullest, you need total trust, and your sign, Pisces, is the sign that rules this unconditional love. It is your natural propensity to reach great heights of spiritual understanding and to be a healing force in the world.

Pisces is one of the beautiful signs. Your eyes are one of your special features. Ruled by the sea, your eyes are often blue-green or hazel, but if they are brown, they still have a dreamy psychic look to them. You usually have a sensual mouth and a narrow, piquant face. Usually your hair is thick with lovely natural curls, like the waves of the ocean.

The most famous Piscean of all is Elizabeth Taylor, known for her violet eyes and lasting beauty. She has the Piscean tendency to see the world through rose-colored glasses, especially when it comes to her love life. All her love affairs have had dramatic beginnings and turned into fabulous fantasies. When the bubble bursts, as it always does, things go back to normal and the party's over. In love with love, you Pisceans need to wait a while to know if your relationship has a chance. The truth is more romantic in the long run and doesn't need to be embellished. Oh, Pisces, will you ever learn?

Many Pisces are plagued with weight problems. It's hard for you to stay on a diet, with your penchant for physical pleasures. Pisceans have to watch indulgences of all kinds. You have a reputation for being the alcoholics or drug addicts of the zodiac, so watch it. Shopping, eating, and sex are all high on your list, and many Piscean types need to be in recovery right now for their addictive habits.

Of course, there are always exceptions, famous Pisces beauties who are at the top of their form. Cindy Crawford, Sharon Stone, and Vanessa Williams, for example: they don't have an extra ounce on their body. Kurt Russell, William Hurt, Sidney Poitier, and Bruce Willis are dream-boat Pisceans who certainly capture the imagination.

What Can Be Done

Pisces is a water sign, and water symbolizes emotion and feeling. In our world today we are prone to materialism and lean too strongly in the direction of science, the rational mind. This started back in ancient times when we were changing over from the age of Taurus (the age of the goddess) to the age of Aries, the Old Testament period. Right now we are going through another transition, from the age of Pisces to the Aquarian age.

The Aquarian age will balance male and female polarity. Since the advent of the Arian age four thousand years ago, our world cultures have been dominated by the male archetype; the female archetype has been suppressed. This may be why so many women (as a means of survival) have become so strong in our society today. Men and women are going to be more balanced mentally, emotionally, and spiritually in the future. A shift is taking place in the 1990s as we move into the Aquarian age: men will step out of the safety of their imaginary male dominance and get in touch with their inner female, their *anima*. One good sign of this: For the last decade, men have been showing emotion in films, even crying.

The lack of respect for feminine inner conviction and intuition has created a materialistic society where men and women feel cut off from emotional expression. The psychic is generally portrayed as evil, and our school systems are set up for left-brained teaching, leaving out the right-brained, creative, and intuitive element. No wonder so many are addicted to escaping into nonlinear worlds through drugs and alcohol. Our mystical and artistic natures must be integrated into our personalities, whether we are male or female, if we are to use our soul power.

To truly merge with the collective unconscious, wherein lies the balance of mind and feeling, we must surrender our personal ego. Surrender is an important part of Pisces' consciousness. When you surrender the ego, you enter the divine, the cosmic; this happens through grace. Pisces' soul power of compassion reflects this great law of grace. Grace is greater and more powerful than the laws of the physical world. Even your transforming path of illusion is cleared up when you have the grace to trust yourself. Self-confidence is crucial to your dreams. When you feel you deserve the good in life, you draw it to you. The mist of unresolved emotional crisis melts and you can see clearly, transcending your blockage of self-delusion. This level of hopefulness is available at all times, but it can't be seen with physical eyes. It must be seen with the eyes of the soul.

Three Steps for Healing Your Blockage

1. Self-delusion and escapism are your ego blockages. It is very draining to be groping around in never-never land. When you don't know who you are or where you need to be, you are giving up the most valuable asset you have—the moment you're living right now and the power to create the future with your thoughts.
2. Compassion is the highest form of love we have on the earthly plane. It is your gift in this lifetime, your soul power. You are born with the gift of being able to feel the needs of others. Your other soul power is imagination. Two great Pisces men who were inspired and guided by their inner vision and imagination were Michelangelo and Albert Einstein. Their artistic vision and scientific accomplishments were monumental, and continue to inspire the world.

3. Your transforming path is your ability to see beyond normal limits, and your lesson is how to use it positively. With your ability to visualize the possibilities of the future and to draw on the past, you can accomplish the near-impossible, you can transcend the ordinary. Learning how to stay grounded in reality is the key. Without the ability to use these mystical and artistic ideas productively, you slip back into your ego blockages of escapism and self-delusion. You are lost in a world of illusions with no real objective and are out of touch with your creativity.

I have a Pisces client who is an artist. Her canvases are magical; she paints the most wonderful organic scenes. Could the vague figures be animals, flowers, people? It's hard to say exactly, yet they intrigue and capture your mind. As you look at one of her paintings, it's as if a story is hidden in the rainbow colors rising up from the softer hues. It's up to you to see it as it unfolds within your imagination. It's all in the eye of the beholder. Very Piscean! Very wonderful!

On the surface this is all well and good, but she has a serious problem. Her father was an alcoholic and she has a lot of resentment toward him. He left when she was 3 years old. Her mother became her primary parent and, being overwhelmed with responsibility, suffered from depression. My client was the third child in the family. Distressed by never feeling safe and always waiting for the next harangue, she shut herself off. She had shut so many doors on people, places, and things that her whole life was based on keeping everything out. That kind of situation eats up a lot of emotional and physical energy.

In families that are wounded by alcohol abuse, each child takes on a role that she unconsciously feels will heal the problem. The first child is the hero and unconsciously achieves, hoping to heal the family. The second is the rebel or scapegoat, often acting out to change the family dynamics. The third, the lost child, is lost in the shuffle and learns to entertain herself by spending time alone, where it seems safe. The fourth is the mascot, the cute one who thinks that the world owes him something. Many times the lost child develops artistic talent instead of repeating the family pattern of alcohol abuse. She creates her own private world. This is not to say that all artists—or even psychics, for that matter—are dysfunctional, but their gifts are often developed in dysfunctional situations as defense mechanisms.

Although my client was encouraged by everyone who saw her paintings, she wouldn't allow her work to be publicly displayed. She couldn't stand the thought of having anyone intrude on her privacy. Her studio was full of finished paintings that no one had ever seen. Her blockages of self-delusion and escapism were in full force, set off by events in her life that she couldn't control. She was a prisoner to her fear of being exploited and disappointed by others.

How to Apply the Three Steps in This Situation

Abandonment by her father was central to my client's fear of showing her paintings to the world. When the father figure is negative, either through abandonment or abuse, it has a very destructive impact on feelings of personal worth. Symbolically, our father on earth represents our father in Heaven, and the child fears being unworthy in God's eyes. Naturally, the mother is part of this dynamic also and seems just as godlike to a child.

When Pisceans feel unsafe as children, they become very creative in building up defenses to protect themselves. My client's defense mechanisms were hiding her innermost thoughts and creating her own world. As the lost child, she was limiting herself to her own detriment, and isolating herself from the rest of the world as a result. As she faces her ego blockage of escapism and cultivates intimacy with others, she will be open to the fame her work can bring. I suggested that a twelve-step program like Adult Children of Alcoholics might help her with her issues around overachieving, perfectionism, and lack of self-esteem.

As a Pisces you must remember that your transforming path is illusion: there is always a dreamy and unrealistic aura to your life. Staying grounded isn't easy for you, but it has to be your first priority. You must know your limits. With your soul power of compassion, you are very aware of what is happening at a deep level. This psychic gift must be directed to self-healing before you can help others. Until you have the understanding needed to help yourself set the proper boundaries, you will constantly be in a state of self-delusion.

The Pisces artist has to bottom out just like an alcoholic. Her case is hard to crack because in her isolation there is no one to confront her. No resolution is possible until she hurts so much that she is willing to do whatever it takes to be okay. Her bubble must be broken—and it will be. Life is a great teacher, and sooner or later our problems must be faced.

Life is continually coming at us, forcing us to transcend the situations we find ourselves in. The quest for truth and beauty, which is the very breath of a Pisces, will eventually take you to reality.

Part IV

Your Sun Sign and Its Opposite

Duality

Who hasn't heard the expression "Opposites attract"? The French go a step further and say it another way: *Vive la différence!*

Chinese Taoists realized long ago that in the universe like attracts like and opposite attracts opposite. They understood that this magnetic principle, which they called yin and yang, was dramatically creating the tension and passion that makes life worth living.

In India, the creator god is called Shiva and his female consort is Shakti. This is how Jnaneshwar Maharaj, an Indian mystic, describes the union of Shiva and Shakti:

> They sit together on the same ground
> Wearing a garment of light.
> From time past remembrance they have lived thus . . .
> United in bliss.

Difference itself merged in their union
When, seeing their intimacy,
It could find no duality to enjoy.

Because of God, the Goddess exists,
And without Her, He is not.
They exist only because of each other.

When the Master of the house sleeps,
The Mistress stays awake,
And performs the function of both.

When He awakes, the whole house disappears,
And nothing is left.

Although He is manifest,
He cannot be seen.
It is only by Her grace
That He appears as a universal form.

Jnaneshwar says that when Shiva and Shakti dance, the creative process and higher consciousness become involved in nature.

If you observe closely, you can see this dynamic of yin and yang, Shakti and Shiva, at work in your daily life. There is a great unifying principle in the universe that affects us all.

It's apparent that there is more to personal relationships than meets the eye and that some experiences have more *pow!* than others. The X factor, what you might call chemistry, is needed to delight in another person. It is the same with friends and family as it is with a lover—there has to be a deeper connection.

All relationships are based on this X factor. We don't understand it; we can only feel it, but if it isn't there the relationship is a dud.

Your relationship with yourself can be just as full of joy as a romance. In fact, it is the most important relationship you will ever have. You need to be as loving and considerate of yourself as you would be to the biggest love of your life.

As long as you are on Earth, you are confronted with dualities in every area of your life. Carl Jung says that men have a hidden woman inside of them called the *anima*, and women have an inner man called the *animus*. You are constantly involved with the compelling and interesting opposites of male and female in the world and also within yourselves. Your *anima* or *animus* is a part of your soul and must be treated with the greatest respect.

Life is a constant fusion of opposites. Without these subtle stresses, you would be mentally lazy, contented with things just as they are, and life would be very boring.

The Sun

The symbol for the Sun in the chart is a circle with a dot.

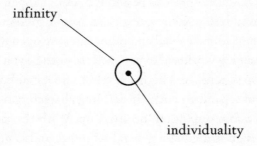

This is a symbol of consciousness, of ongoing creativity, and this is where the duality starts. When you look at the Sun sign in your chart you may ask, Is the Sun symbolic of the ego or the soul? It is both, and you are constantly in the throes of balancing the soulful *circle of infinity* with the ego *dot of individuality*.

Consciousness in its original nature is quiet, pure, and above dualism. It's our minds that are dual in nature. The dot in the circle symbolizes the spark of life that animates your sense of self. The ego immediately starts thinking and sorting things out. Much of your life is spent reuniting the dualities of timeless consciousness, which is God's time, and individuality which is your time, into your personality. Huston Smith, a renowned scholar of religion, talks about a Buddhist master who gave him a definition of Zen, which is involved primarily with the union of opposites. The master said, "We can put it in a formula: infinite gratitude to all things past; infinite service to all things present; infinite responsibility to all things future. That is Zen." Gratitude, service, and responsibility take us to wholeness.

As we enter the Aquarian age, we are going to have astrological charts that are solar: the Sun, not the earth, in central place. Your Sun-centered chart is something you grow into.

As you grow in consciousness and learn to balance the ego's confused and often self-destructive patterns with your own Sun sign's soul consciousness, the energy of all twelve signs is available to you. This is called solar or heliocentric astrology. Your soul power is connected to all the other signs. This is a wonderful place to be and it doesn't happen overnight. The first step is surrendering your ego to your soul's guidance. Your soul's boundaries are multidimensional and other signs are open to you. Through your imagination new worlds of experience are open to you.

After this leap of faith, at a higher level of understanding, you are able to free yourself of separating and self-defining characteristics. The egocentric nature of the Sun sign has to be given up. With the merger of all the signs, your Sun sign is used as a general reference and is not so confining. As you unite with the solar perspective, you can live with all there is to offer here on Earth as a free soul who is not confined in any way.

Your soul is not limited; it's your ego that sets the boundaries. The Latin word *mediator* means "go to the center." This is another clue to the fact that harmony comes from meditation and contemplation. The center is calm; even a hurricane has a central point where there is peace. To access the power of the center we must change our perspective. We must feel full instead of empty. When you feel complete within yourself, it's easier to stay centered. Solving problems doesn't take as long, and you lose the need to identify with them so much. How many times have you heard yourself or others say *my* bad health, *my* money problems, *my* bad marriage?

To achieve harmony you must accept conflict as a creative principle, a moment full of potential; then life is an opportunity for wholeness. When you enter a harmonious state of consciousness you wear your ego more lightly, as a coat effortlessly draped on your shoulders.

Six Sun Signs

The first step in solar consciousness is to unite with your opposite sign. Two heads are better than one and the same is true of the Sun signs. Each sign has attributes that are not complete until the meaning of its opposite has been recognized and consciously drawn into the personality. You have to look at the zodiac as if there were only six Sun signs: Aries/Libra, Taurus/Scorpio, Gemini/Sagittarius, Cancer/Capricorn, Leo/Aquarius, and Virgo/Pisces.

The Opposition

Astrology is a holistic system; the Sun, the Moon, and all the planets are in a complex web of interrelationships. These relationships are called *aspects.* Your nervous system is sensitive to these patterns, and you can expect certain reactions based on the aspects of the signs.

As a student of astrology the first things you learn about are the Sun signs. Then it is necessary to learn how the planets are related to each other in the chart and how these relationships affect your behavior.

The aspects are determined by the number of degrees that fall between the Sun signs and the planets in the zodiac. These patterns can be seen and memorized easily as you become familiar with the zodiac.

An astrology reading tells you about the personality traits you were born with and how the planets are affecting you today. Astrologers use aspects in analyzing charts of individuals as well as compatibility charts for couples. Also, the best days for important events are found this way.

There are many kinds of aspects involved in the interaction of the signs within your chart. Some are positive; some are difficult. In Sun sign astrology, there are signs that are more compatible than others. This has to do with the aspects between them. A trine (120 degrees apart) is thought to be a good aspect that brings luck, and a square (90 degrees apart) is considered to be difficult, bringing life lessons.

Aries is trine Leo, and relationships between these two signs are considered to be favorable, yet the aspect of Aries square Cancer causes conflict and stress. In relationship charts, the trines indicate compatibility and the squares show sources of conflict. With a little study it is easy to know which signs are best for you.

Many books have been written on the subject of compatibility. The astrology columns you read in newspapers and magazines use this system. I personally believe that all signs are compatible on some level, but it is true that there are combinations of signs that seem to be more favorable, making communication easier.

The aspect we are concerned with at this time is called an opposition and is usually considered to be stressful. An opposition is just that, two points, two planets, or in this case two Sun signs that are directly opposite each other.

There would be no relationships without the stress of an opposition. Consequently the way to look at oppositions is as a complementary force, with the possibility of combining both energies and having more power to work with.

When I first started the study of astrology, I noticed that as a Capricorn I had a lot of Cancerian characteristics, even to the point that many people thought I was a Cancer. Having a home and spending a lot of time there with my children was very important to me.

I was *such* a homebody; I loved to decorate my house and cook, and I even worked at home as an artist and astrologer. I realized later that I had overdeveloped my opposite sign of Cancer, and because of my transforming path of responsibility I was house-stuck. I was not using my soul power of contribution in a well-rounded way in my career. It was necessary for me to integrate both home and career—Cancer and Capricorn. So I started traveling some to balance out the polarity and also to have a more busi-nesslike attitude in my career. That is when I started being a professional astrologer and saw myself as having a career instead of just doing charts for friends.

(By the way, my ascendant is Sagittarius with the polarity of Gemini—both signs of travel—so the solution came from integrating the polarity of my ascendant as well as my Sun sign!)

The same principle of opposition applies to your ascendant and Moon positions. You have your Sun sign, the ascendant, the Moon sign, and their opposites at your disposal. So what you are dealing with is a possibility of using the powers of half the zodiac circle. I say possibility because you might have the same Sun sign, Moon, or ascendant, not always three sepa-rate signs.

When you balance the polarities of the Sun sign, the ascendant, and the Moon, your personal vision is expanded. You are released from the narrow ego boundaries of your Sun sign, and the other signs open their doors with all their traits available for your growth.

With this expansion, a broader self-valuing system is put into place that helps you challenge old self-limiting beliefs and opens the doors to new and varied ways of seeing yourself. If you are a Pisces and continually get stuck in victim situations, be an Aries and stand your ground. You have the wisdom of Libra at your fingertips and the depth of Scorpio. Life can be much richer if you move into it without fear.

Opposing Points

The opposition is composed of an activating force and a restraining force that shift the balance of power back and forth. The stress of this polarity keeps throwing you off until you've learned how to see the opposites as complementary.

From the perspective of the basic self (the part of your personality that doesn't reason), the stress between these two forces is impossible to resolve, and although the polarities are mutually dependent and facets of the same unity, there must be a shift to higher understanding to achieve this new state of balance. To accomplish this, you have to really *want* to grow, and you must be open to a broader viewpoint.

The key to success lies in your desire for harmony. Until you develop tolerance, there will be many power struggles coming from opposite viewpoints. This is what makes life difficult. While you can't totally get rid of the stress of the opposition, you can channel the energy into positive attractions and appropriate sexual tension and avoid endless apathy or anxieties. Your goal here is to bring the dynamics of the opposition into balance. Physically, there must be a body-mind connection to see harmony in all things. Close observation of your body helps to know if you're centered or not.

It's obvious if your heart is pounding and you can't catch your breath that you aren't centered. Back off until you feel emotionally clear before you make major decisions. Another way to check yourself is to see if you are feeling numb. Feeling nothing is just as dysfunctional. Constant conflict can burn you out and make you emotionally dry. Either way, observing the body is the best way to know how you feel. The mind can be in denial, so be careful.

Integrating Your Opposite

The soul power and ego blockage of your opposite sign already exists within you and waits to be brought into your objective awareness. You have to use your imagination to draw on the qualities of your opposite sign. It is important to learn what your opposite signs are and what their traits are. Your Sun sign and opposite sign have distinct lessons to teach you. When you are emotionally detached enough to observe your feelings of anxiety and delay action until a good decision can be made, you are already halfway there.

By honoring your opposite sign, you can benefit from its soul power and enlarge your conscious awareness. When you take the time necessary to understand the characteristics of your opposite sign, it's easy to integrate them within your personality. The opposite pattern is part of your unrealized power already there deep in the subconscious waiting to be drawn into your conscious mind.

For instance, if you are a Capricorn, there is a soft tender Cancer inside of you, waiting for you to get in touch with your emotions. You analytical Virgos have the power of the psychic at your fingertips—you must look within yourself for these wonderful Pisces skills. Each sign has a wonderful gift waiting to come into your consciousness and to open up new sources of enrichment and deeper understanding.

Equipoise

The signs of the zodiac are divinely inspired and are coded with a spiritual message for your personal growth. Astrology is unique in its ability to symbolically connect what is going on in your outer world with inner meanings of deep significance. The Greek word *symbolos* means "bringing together." Using a symbolic system like astrology for personal growth leads you to deeper understanding and wonder at the miraculous way our world works. When I first started studying astrology, I saw how very fine are the workings of the universe. I realized that, as humans, we want to make God in our image because it is so hard to comprehend the multidimensional qualities of that state of consciousness.

You have the opportunity to stand on the midpoint between your Sun sign and its opposite and have the benefit of all the characteristics. The alliance that is created by the polarization of two opposing signs is very powerful. It is the beginning of your spiritual path of oneness.

There is an exact midpoint in an opposition that is geometrically perfect and could be described as a perfect point of enlightenment. This is a law of spiritual geometry: *Perfect balance brings perfect symmetry.*

Appreciation for the opposite sign's position helps you meet halfway and find a solution. As you find balance between the two points, you are naturally lifted up to higher reasoning, to a state of equipoise.

Couples who have been married successfully for many years seem to radiate this state. They may even look like each other. You have a feeling when you find this sort of commitment that the enmeshing is kind and loving and the trials of life have been met and conquered.

Wholeness

You are a combination of all twelve signs in the zodiac. Your opposite sign offers the symmetry necessary to join the other signs. When and if this polarization occurs, you are able to integrate the soul power of the other ten Sun signs and experience fewer limitations in mind and body.

You will be able to accomplish something quite extraordinary. You are coming into wholeness where you are not separated into dualities, the male and female, the dominant and the weak. Moreover, wholeness, the joy of absolute oneness with God, expands your conscious awareness, giving the patience and understanding you need to continue growth on higher planes. This is the marriage of body and soul. Instead of being trapped in the body with feelings of fear, shame, anger, and confusion, you know your experiences are only deepening your knowledge.

With these extraordinary gifts of awareness and energy, every thought you think is a force in the universe. At this state of wholeness you can see your responsibility to your world and to others.

You are the seeker on a sacred quest, one who is liberated from a sense of separation from God, one who honors the unknown. Like the galaxies, you are without boundaries.

Aries and Libra

Responsible Action

The perfect balance point between Aries and Libra is responsible action.

Aries instigate new ideas, continue until they have satisfied their interest, then move on to new challenges. In contrast, Librans find a challenge, follow through resolutely, and complete the project without any need to hurry. While Arians tend to see the project as an exciting adventure, Librans are able to sustain the idea with a linear process necessary to complete the task. Aries and Libra are about starting and finishing, and they need each other to accomplish their goal. It is a wise Aries who learns how to temper his impatience and allow the balancing energy of Libra to bring the project to completion. Libra benefits from Aries' courage and ability to take risks.

Aries' need for constant activity, combined with a short attention span, is directly opposed to the painstaking process involved in success. "I'll do it my way," an Arian motto, is their ego blockage of self-gratification, full-blown, without the integration of Libra's soul power of conscientiousness.

Yet Libra, being so cautious, needs the initiative energy of Aries' soul powers of courage and instigation to manifest something new.

When it comes to decisions, Librans get bogged down in trying to be perfect. There is a law of divine order at work in the universe: All things come to those who wait. But Libra's perfectionism doesn't trust this. By wanting more time and information to make a decision, Libra misses the boat. On the other hand, Aries jumps into situations too quickly only to find out more time was needed to correctly assess the situation.

Both of these signs rule relationships. Aries rules the relationship you have with yourself, while Libra rules relationships with others. Aries desires the excitement of the unknown, and Libra loves to do things exactly as they were done in the past. Each sign requires the other's attributes to be more productive. These two different mind-sets initially repel each other until you understand your opposite sign is complementary and has what is needed to come into balance.

Each sign appears to be an opposing force for the other until you see that you value the very same things but from a different perspective. This new perspective broadens your horizons. Gandhi, a Libran who was the leader of a nonviolent revolutionary movement in India, said: "Love is the subtlest force in the world." This statement exemplifies the perfect combination of Aries and Libra—the beginning of a soulful alliance of action and mind. Peace is achieved in daily life when every action is done with compassion. The Aries hyperactivity becomes focused and the Libra perfectionism is overcome! The war is over. Balance and beauty prevail, yet much is accomplished.

To enter this portal takes time, patience, and great courage, principles that are innate in these two Sun signs. In the evolved Aries/Libra combination, one of the most powerful in the zodiac, love and understanding triumph—and *responsible action* is at work in the universe.

Taurus and Scorpio

Transformed Values

Taurus and Scorpio rule personal resources; they are concerned with ownership.

Taurus rules manifestation in the physical world, whereas Scorpio is concerned with inner resources. Scorpio deals with things unseen. These can be financial agreements, such as inheritances and investments, as well as psychological and soulful resources. To integrate the power of both signs, you need to make a change in values.

Taurus is a sign that likes quality as well as quantity. Taurus always wants the best, and your goal is to enjoy beauty and peace in a safe environment. Although abundance comes to Taurus naturally, a fear of invasion stops the flow of nourishment.

Scorpio, on the other hand, is an extremist. You can be very evolved, a spiritual teacher like Billy Graham, or the worst of the worst, like Charles Manson. Scorpions like control for personal gratification. This can entail sex, power, and money, and yet it can be psychic powers as well.

This makes us think of Hitler, who was a Taurean with Scorpio influences. He combined the ego blockages of Taurus and Scorpio perfectly—

self-gratification combined with domination. Taureans are the charmers of the zodiac. Hitler's ability to charm the multitudes was on a par with the cult heroes and movie stars of our times. He was very interested in the occult and could have been helped by its wisdom if his greed hadn't colored all of his decisions.

What Taurus needs is Scorpio's concentration and focus. Taureans' extreme sensitivity and tendency to overreact can be balanced by Scorpio's long attention span and intensely reliable commitment. In traumatic times, Taurus runs away in fright while Scorpio has a position strategically staked out. Taurus's flight must be tempered by Scorpio courage and the ability to face foes. This is a warning to Taurus: your tremendous power to defend yourself must be without malice. It is Taurus's love of simple pleasures and your peaceful attitude that calm Scorpio's anger and aggression.

In all the zodiac there are no other two signs as stubborn as Taurus and Scorpio. It is almost impossible to change your mind when you are uncomfortable or angry. One of the most challenging things Taurus/Scorpio has to learn is how to be more flexible in order to adjust to life's constant challenges. A tall building must have sway designed into its structure or it will topple in earthquakes or heavy winds.

Scorpio's soul power of transformation and Taurus's soul power of manifestation work together to heal the self-gratifying traits of both signs. Being compulsively focused on the outcome doesn't produce the desired effect. The present is where all the work is done and where all the pleasure lies.

As Scorpios, you need Taurus's richness of feeling and extrasensory perception to understand the emotional needs of others or to simply enjoy your life. Scorpio, the healer with the soul power of transformation, must give up your ego blockage of domination and compassionately do psychic surgery on Taurus's deep-seated fears of abandonment and lack of love. Worn-out longings, attitudes, and desires must be cut away and released to create a receptive and enthusiastic expectancy.

Beauty is God's gift. It is not really necessary for functional reasons, but as a reassuring clue of universal concern for human delight, it gives Taurus and Scorpio the hope of *transformed values*.

Gemini and Sagittarius

Inspired Visions

Gemini and Sagittarius rule versatility and movement; they are signs of duality.

Gemini is the sign of facts and opinions, of preferences and aversions, while Sagittarius is a long-visioned sign of great truths and spiritual concepts. Both of these signs rule communication.

Geminis are constantly searching for variety. You can scatter your energy by trying to do too many things at the same time. By playing both ends against the middle you leave a lot of people very frustrated. One might think you would come up short, but you seem blessed in your ability to materialize what is needed, even at the last minute. More often than not your inventive minds triumph and you delight all who are blessed to know you—except when your delicate balance is lost. Sometimes your magic works and at times it does not—perhaps when your planetary ruler, Mercury, goes retrograde.

Sagittarians are expressive, acting with fiery determination. You are straight shooters, making decisions based on the long run and you approach your goals from a moral and ethical state of consciousness. Sagittarians can be duplicitous, too, but you tend to hide the truth more than tell an out-and-out lie. Being positive, you always want to paint a good picture, and since you are always looking long-term, you sometimes cannot see the trees for the forest.

Gemini needs Sagittarius's long-term vision in order to transcend the dualities that plague you daily, and Sagittarius needs Gemini's concern with minute details. The little things in life that are so precious can pass Sags by as you race through life looking for greener pastures. Remember Don Quixote, a Sagittarian type who was always tilting at windmills. Gemini's love of conversation and socializing benefits when combined with Sagittarian concern over what is best for the long haul, in spiritual terms, instead of just seeking mental diversion.

Eternally young, Gemini can learn commitment and responsibility from Sagittarius. When Geminis slow down and give a subject the time it really needs, you are very productive. Sagittarian soul power of vision and aspiration is inside the mind, waiting to be released into the consciousness. All Gemini has to do is slow down and look at the big picture, taking your share of responsibility.

When Sagittarius is open to the mental creativity of Gemini, you often become inspired communicators, such as public speakers and published writers. Sometimes Sagittarius's theoretical mind is too far into the future and needs Gemini's close attention to what's happening right now.

Gemini's ego blockage of being easily swayed and scattered is remedied through Sagittarius's soul power of aspiration—you must seek a spiritual commitment. Sagittarius's ego blockage of extravagance and wishful thinking can be pulled into harmony by Gemini's soul power of inspiration. The here and now is where things really happen. The hands-on capability of Gemini complements Sagittarian theories and concepts.

Gemini and Sagittarius are signs of movement and advancement. Your *inspired visions* contribute to an interesting and exciting lifestyle that influences everyone you come in contact with.

Cancer and Capricorn

Nurturing Guidance

Cancer's compassion and Capricorn's discipline, when balanced, lead to a path of wisdom.

These are the signs of nesting, of the deep-seated desire to form a familial unit and have a safe place to nurture your young.

Capricorn is the father and Cancer is the mother, the parents of the zodiac and in your old-fashioned way, conservative and reliable. The polarity from Cancer to Capricorn combines nurturing with discipline, from personal satisfaction to satisfying others. The primary gift you have to offer your subjects is the ability to provide structure. Cancer and Capricorn both honor the past and create your lifestyles around tradition.

Cancer works on the psychic, instinctual, and unconscious feeling level; your feelings and emotions are much stronger than logic. You invest a lot of emotional energy in everything you do and expect a return on your investment.

Capricorn feels a great responsibility to family, and to society at large. You feel it is your duty to go out into the world to support your home. You are very conscious of your obligations to your family of origin as well as to the community.

Cancer is the Great Goddess and Capricorn is Father Time. Although you are polar opposites, you are not as far apart as some of the other signs. When Cancer marries Capricorn you are very compatible, like bread and butter. Capricorn needs the gentleness and warmth of Cancer. Capricorn needs Cancer's free-flowing feelings to relate to love and affection. Cancer always puts family first, whereas Capricorn feels pulled into societal commitments.

Being ruled by the Moon, Cancerians are very affected by lunar cycles, and being intuitors, you flow with nature. You are very much in tune with the basic self that is the animal instinct in your personality. The Moon rules the unconscious, making Cancers highly sensitive to environments.

Saturn is the planet that rules Capricorn and has a sobering influence on the decisions you make daily. Saturn is a planet of reasoning and makes sure that the facts are on the table. His rulership forces Capricorn to face limitations, causing you to be chronic worriers. His true service is to promote what's real and to bring your consciousness out of the darkness of maya.

I always say that Saturn turns on the overhead lights, to be sure everything is perceived in sharp relief. Capricorns are prone to perfectionism, and this draining trait seems to bounce over into Cancer, causing you a lot of grief. On the other hand, Capricorn rigidity is softened by Cancer's love of gentleness and ability to provide comfort, whether it is good, wholesome food or a comfortable environment to rest in. The Moon soulfully combined with Saturn creates a firm foundation based on real needs.

When Capricorn's soul power of contribution joins with Cancer's soul power of nurturing, this synergy creates a wonderful ability to be sensitive to others and come up with a practical and comfortable plan. The self-possession of *nurturing guidance* with deep compassion for all humankind provides a serene environment at home or in the office.

Leo and Aquarius

Innovative Giving

There is a lot of electricity and excitement in the Leo/Aquarius connection.

You are signs of freedom and unity. Leo desires the freedom to govern your own domain, while Aquarius wants unity for all.

Leo is the sign that rules the ego. That is why you are often so overly sensitive to what people think of you and long for the supreme power of ancient kings. We all have Leo in our chart somewhere and have the divine right to be who we are. Until we face who we are (our Sun sign), how can we expect to become the person we want to be? How can we find our soul? Before we can surrender the ego to the soul, we must first have an ego to surrender. This is Leo's contribution.

Aquarius has a mental approach to life. You are interested in people, and your altruism is one of your best traits. Aquarius is a sign of groups, of community, and of organizations that aid humanity, such as governments and institutions. Aquarius is not egoless at all. You have strong minds and think in terms of the whole, not separately.

Leo, with all the expression and drama of that Sun sign, has the latent traits of Aquarius waiting to be used. In the same way Aquarius, with all its objectivity and analytical ability, has a Leo inside wanting to play games and have some fun. Aquarius is an abstract thinker and wants to look at everything from a scientific point of view. Leo, you could use some of this analytical thinking to help plan your goals more logically.

Generosity of spirit, the soul power of Leo, and originality, the soul power of Aquarius, create the ideas and expressions that can produce the sensational when they are combined. Leos are the stars of the zodiac.

Leo's ego blockage of excessive optimism can be aggravated by Aquarian rebelliousness, giving an egocentric sense of self-importance, of "I can do no wrong." Here we have the rebel without a cause, the revolutionary without the support of the public. Blocked Leo/Aquarius enhances the ego's fear of personal failure, of criticism, of not being loved. This fear sets up a defensive and rebellious attitude against any authority figure you can find, real or imagined. The animal nature of Leo must be transformed into the humanitarian Aquarius to be perfected, to become soulful or divine, which is the refinement of the two.

The Leo/Aquarius attraction to power is abused when you lose sight of your higher purpose and ignore your soul powers. By watching your emotional and defensive reactions to the conflict of opposing views, arguments, or even war, you can find your weak points. Self-doubt thrives on division; however, without opposition there would be stagnation. We need the stimulation of opposites. As you refine your concepts of power with what's best for all concerned, a new level of consciousness is opened.

With a balanced Leo/Aquarius polarity a sense of natural authority is expressed and the fears of failure disappear. If Leo/Aquarius will stop and observe reactive and defensive behavior, your soul's intention for growth in this lifetime can be seen. Leo/Aquarius's desire to rule and serve is manifested with humility and sensitivity. This balance brings *innovative giving*.

Virgo and Pisces

Selfless Service

Virgo/Pisces approaches the soul with love and the desire to serve.

Productive Virgo, a sign of purification, combined with imaginative Pisces aesthetically transforms anything you touch into a higher form. Many great musicians, artists, and writers are Virgo/Pisces. These are signs of skill and artfulness, and what is art without technique?

Pisces is a sign of the creative process, and the Virgo polarity is very necessary to add style and presentation. Pisces can have a wonderful idea and let it float away unclaimed into the ether. Virgos, with your rational mind and meticulous attention to detail, you are masters of methodically creating a procedure to come up with the best product possible. However, without Pisces' talents of creation, the visual presentation is poor, not aesthetically pleasing. It's interesting to note that the word *art*, which is synonymous with creativity, a Virgo/Pisces power, sounds very much like *heart*, and *art*, as in "thou art," is the second-person singular of the verb *to be*. The gift of art is divinely inspired. We have to get our egos out of the way to be master craftworkers. Then art, creativity, and love all relate to our soul power.

Humility is an attribute of both of these signs. Your ideology is faith, grace, and redemption. Virgo/Pisces has a tendency to merge into the vibration of others. This is all well and good, but boundaries have to be set by both signs or you will become victims of high ideals and have no defenses. Virgo's soul power of discrimination helps to define the proper action, and Pisces' soul power of empathy gives a spirit of kindness, mercy, and the benefit of the doubt. Mother Teresa, a Virgo, was a perfect example of the combination of the two signs. Her selfless service nurtured many people, and she continues to be an inspiration to us all.

Thoth/Hermes and the magician Merlin are Virgo types. These great beings of mythology were of the purest level of integrity. They taught gods and kings how to be more conscious—to know that all forms of matter and all living beings are patterns of divine consciousness. Thoth taught Isis, a female Virgo type, how to heal with sound, when her child Horus was stung by a scorpion. Later Isis gave this information to the people so they would not have to lose their children to the dreaded sting. Merlin was King Arthur's teacher and mentor. Yet he lost his powers for a while when he allowed Morgan le Fay, a sorceress, to seduce him. Virgos can be very naive at times. It's a downward spiral if you allow the Piscean ego blockage of escapism to delude you.

Many Pisces and Virgos have addictions to drugs and alcohol. Love can be just as addictive as any substance. When Virgo is balanced with Pisces, you have facts and feelings at your highest level, and Virgo's soul power of discrimination gives the commitment necessary to be clean and sober on all accounts.

It is a highly skilled Virgo/Pisces who learns how to let go of logic and follow their intuition. You are mutable signs and must learn by your mistakes. Virgo/Pisces have to overcome the tendency to self-negate. You must surrender to your souls with the highest ideals or you can do much damage to yourself and to your loved ones. Gurumayi Chidvilasananda, a Siddha master, said, "We know that God is in our heart; the next step of understanding is, We are in God's heart." Virgo/Pisces are transcendent signs; you open the door to new dimensions and to other planes of consciousness. You must act in harmony with your highest principles. Humility sets the stage for healing, and *selfless service* is the key.

Bibliography

Adams, Evangeline. *Astrology: Your Place in the Sun.* New York: Dodd, Mead & Company, 1927.

Baigent, Michael. *From the Omens of Babylon: Astrology and Ancient Mesopotamia.* London, England: Arkana/Penguin Books, 1994.

ben Shimon Halevi, Z'ev. *The Anatomy of Fate: Kabbalistic Astrology.* York Beach, Maine: Samuel Weiser, 1978.

Bills, Rex E. *The Rulership Book.* Richmond, Va.: Macoy Publishing & Masonic Supply Co., 1976.

Blum, Ralph. *The Book of Runes.* New York: St. Martin's Press, 1982.

Bogart, Gregory C. *Astrology and Spiritual Awakening.* Berkeley, Calif.: Dawn Mountain Press, 1994.

Bucke, Richard M. *Cosmic Consciousness.* Secaucus, N.J.: University Books, 1961.

Burt, Kathleen. *Archetypes of the Zodiac.* St. Paul, Minn.: Llewellyn Publications, 1988.

Campbell, Joseph. *The Hero with a Thousand Faces.* Bollingen Series. Princeton, N.J.: Princeton University Press, 1968.

Capt, E. Raymond. *The Glory of Astrology.* Thousand Oaks, Calif.: Artisan Sales, 1976.

Chapple, Christopher. *Karma and Creativity.* Albany, N.Y.: State University of New York Press, 1986.

Chidvilisananda, Swami. *Inner Treasures.* South Fallsburg, N.Y.: SYDA Foundation, 1995.

Cornelius, Geoffrey, Maggie Hyde, and Chris Webster. *Introducing Astrology.* New York: Totem Books, 1995.

Davidson, Ronald C. *Astrology: Complete Instructions for Casting Your Own Horoscope.* New York: Arco, 1975.

Elwell, Dennis. *Cosmic Loom.* London, England: Unwin Hyman, 1987.

Erlewine, Stephen. *The Circle Book of Charts.* Ann Arbor, Mich.: Circle Books, 1972.

Fillmore, Charles. *The Twelve Powers of Man.* Unity Village, Mo.: Unity Books, 1989.

Fontana, David. *The Secret Language of Symbols.* San Francisco: Chronicle Books, 1994.

George, Llewellyn. *A to Z Horoscope Maker and Delineator.* St. Paul, Minn.: Llewellyn Publications, 1910.

Green, Jeff. *Pluto: The Evolutionary Journey of the Soul.* St. Paul, Minn.: Llewellyn Publications, 1987.

Greene, Liz. *The Astrology of Fate.* York Beach, Maine: Samuel Weiser, 1984.

Grof, Stanislav, ed. *Ancient Wisdom, Modern Science.* Albany, N.Y.: State University of New York Press, 1984.

Guttman, Ariel, and Kenneth Johnson. *Mythic Astrology.* St. Paul, Minn.: Llewellyn Publications, 1993.

Hall, Manly P. *The Secret Teachings of All Ages.* Los Angeles: Philosophical Research Society, 1978.

———. *Astrological Keywords*, 7th ed. Los Angeles: Philosophical Research Society, 1973.

Hastings, Arthur. *With the Tongues of Men and Angels.* Fort Worth, Tex.: Holt, Rinehart & Winston, 1991.

Judith, Anodea. *Wheels of Life.* St. Paul, Minn.: Llewellyn Publications, 1988.

Jung, Carl. *Memories, Dreams, Reflections.* New York: Vintage, 1963.

Lubicz, Isha Schwaller. *The Opening of the Way.* Rochester, Vt.: Inner Traditions International, 1981.

MacNaughton, Robin. *Power Astrology: Make the Most of Your Sun Sign.* New York: Pocket Books, 1990.

Mambert, W. A., and B. Frank Foster. *A Trip into Your Unconscious.* Washington, D.C.: Acropolis Books, 1973.

Mann, A. T. *The Round Art.* New York: Mayflower Books, 1979.

Meditations on the Tarot: A Journey into Christian Hermeticism. Rockport, Maine: Element, 1993.

Mitchell, Eric A. *Power: The Power to Create Your Future.* St. Paul, Minn.: Llewellyn Publications, 1990.

Muktananda, Swami. *Play of Consciousness.* South Fallsburg, N.Y.: SYDA Foundation, 1978.

Pagan, Isabelle M. *The Signs of the Zodiac Analysed.* London, England: Theosophical Publishing House, 1911.

Price, John Randolph. *The Super Beings.* Austin, Tex.: Quartus, 1981.

———. *The Planetary Commission.* Austin, Tex.: Quartus, 1984.

Sakoian, Frances, and Louis S. Acker. *The Astrologer's Handbook.* New York: Harper & Row, 1973.

Sedgwick, Phillip. *The Sun at the Center.* St. Paul, Minn.: Llewellyn Publications, 1990.

Sitchin, Zecharia. *Divine Encounters.* New York: Avon, 1996.

Smith, Huston. *Forgotten Truth.* New York: HarperCollins, 1992.

Steiger, Brad. *American Indian Magic.* New Brunswick, N.J.: Inner Light Publications, 1986.

Steiner, Rudolf. *Knowledge of the Higher Worlds: How It Is Achieved.* London, England: Rudolf Steiner Press, 1969.

Szanto, Gregory. *The Marriage of Heaven and Earth.* London, England: Arkana, 1985.

Thompson, Richard L. *Alien Identities.* Alachua, Fla.: Govardhan Hill Publishing, 1995.

Trevelyan, George. *A Vision of the Aquarian Age.* Walpole, N.H.: Stillpoint Publishing, 1984.

Waterman, Robert D. *Self-Forgiveness: An Act of Life.* Santa Fe, N.M.: Southwestern College of Life Sciences, 1976.

Watts, Alan. *The Wisdom of Insecurity.* New York: Vintage, 1951.

Wegner, Fritz. *Heaven on Earth.* Boston: Little, Brown, 1992.

West, John Anthony. *The Case for Astrology.* London, England: Arkana, 1991.

Wilber, Ken. *The Spectrum of Consciousness*, 2d ed. Wheaten, Ill.: Quest Books, 1977.

Yogananda, Paramahansa. *Autobiography of a Yogi.* Los Angeles: Self-Realization Fellowship, 1973.